THE SHAPING OF AMERICA

Works by John Warwick Montgomery

Published by Bethany Fellowship:

Christianity for the Tough-minded
Crisis in Lutheran Theology (two volumes), 2nd ed.
Damned Through the Church
Demon Possession*
God's Inerrant Word*
How Do We Know There Is a God?
The Law Above the Law
Myth, Allegory, and Gospel*
Principalities and Powers: The World of the Occult, 2nd ed.
The Quest for Noah's Ark, 2nd ed.
The Shape of the Past: A Christian Response to Secular
     Philosophies of History, 2nd ed.
Situation Ethics: True or False? (with Joseph Fletcher)
The Suicide of Christian Theology
Where Is History Going?

Published by Editorial Betania:

¿Como sabemos que hay un Dios? (in Spanish)

Available from Other Publishers:

The Altizer-Montgomery Dialogue (with Thomas J. J. Altizer)
Chytraeus on Sacrifice: A Reformation Treatise in Biblical
     Theology
Computers, Cultural Change, and the Christ (trilingual: English,
     French, German)
Cross and Crucible (two volumes)
Ecumenicity, Evangelicals, and Rome
¿Es confiable el Cristianismo? (in Spanish)
History and Christianity
In Defense of Martin Luther
International Scholars Directory *
The 'Is God Dead?' Controversy
Jurisprudence: A Book of Readings *
La Mort de Dieu (in French)
A Seventeenth Century View of European Libraries *
A Union List of Serial Publications in Chicago-Area Protestant
     Theological Libraries *
Verdammt durch die Kirche? (in German)
The Writing of Research Papers in Theology

*Works edited by Dr. Montgomery

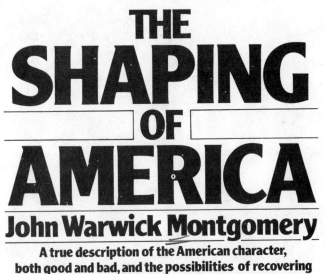

THE
SHAPING
OF
AMERICA

John Warwick Montgomery

A true description of the American character,
both good and bad, and the possibilities of recovering
a national vision before the people perish.

BETHANY FELLOWSHIP, INC.
Minneapolis, Minnesota

Copyright © 1976
Bethany Fellowship, Inc.
All rights reserved

Published by Bethany Fellowship, Inc.
6820 Auto Club Road, Minneapolis, Minnesota 55438

Printed in the United States of America

Library of Congress Cataloging in Publication Data:

Montgomery, John Warwick.
  The shaping of America.

  Bibliography: p.
  1. United States—Religion. 2. United States—Moral conditions.
I. Title.
BR515. M57   200'.973   76-15682
ISBN 0-87123-227-8

In memoriam

THE REV. P. ARTHUR JUERGENSEN
Pastor of Redeemer Lutheran Church
Hyattsville, Maryland
(†February 5, 1976)

Dear Friend:
You missed the Bicentennial observance
by accepting a new and better citizenship

Veni Domine Iesu

Acknowledgments

A tankard of 18th-century ale to (1) the authors and publishers of copyrighted materials quoted herein, (2) the long-suffering professional staff at the Library of Congress, who helped in the verification of esoteric bibliographical citations and very occasionally supplied books from their minute collection which were missing from my grandiose personal library, (3) the vast number of greedy, grubby antiquarian bookdealers in the European and American cities where I have carried out my bibliomaniacal passion and spent my substance acquiring most of the materials employed in the writing of this book, (4) Mrs. Pam Barcalow of Grabill, Indiana, whose typing ability is the closest thing to the El Dorado the explorers were searching for, and (5) my wife Joyce who (praise be!) has not fallen for women's liberation and can still therefore maintain a tranquil household in which a fairly complicated book may be written.

Contents

Illustrations

Preface

Not *Another* Bicentennial Book!

If you send $35 to Apex Plumbing Supply, Rhode Island Avenue, Mt. Ranier, Maryland, you can obtain a fake pewter toilet seat and cover, embossed with the mottoes, "E Pluribus Unum" and "Spirit of '76," and sculpted with the three Revolutionary War figures carrying flag, fife, and drum. Presumably, there is a moral here somewhere, and it may just be that too many people are trying to make hay while the Bicentennial sun shines. So why not a moratorium on Bicentennial books? What earthly reason for doing another one?

Perhaps no earthly reason, but possibly a heavenly one. American history cries out for serious theological interpretation. Declared Bob Maslow—spokesman against the "Buy-Centennial sellebration" and leader of the Peoples Bicentennial Commission, a grassroots alternative to what its members regard as the corporation-dominated, official Bicentennial Administration: "I think the gist of what America is about is ideas. It's not products. I'd like to see more explanation of those ideas."

Whether we like it or not, "those ideas" are fundamentally theological, as well as being theologically fundamental. Religious treatments of America other than the present work will appear in 1976, to be sure, but if they run true to form (e.g., Richard John Neuhaus' *Time Toward Home: The American Experiment as*

Revelation), their biblical perspective will reflect, not so much the historic, Reformation religion that the earliest settlers brought to our shores, but a weakened and emasculated modern variant of it. A critique more in the spirit of classical biblical theology is called for in a time of serious national reflection.

* * * * *

But surely not a book on America written by an obnoxious, self-confessed Francophile—by one who flies eastbound across the ocean at every opportunity (always by Air France) and who considers the cuisine of his own nation to be but a step removed from grubbing for roots? Such criticism is admittedly not far from the mark. Indeed, in a recent trip to the U.S. Virgin Islands, I found people eating *goat*; one trembles to think what the French on nearby Guadeloupe or Martinique would think of *that*. My wife darkly suggested that for me to do a book on America might parallel a history of the Jews written by Eichmann. This, however, is an outrageous exaggeration, characteristic of wives (who invariably exaggerate).

The argument can in fact be turned around—as my wife readily admits after a dinner at Lucas Carton, place de la Madeleine, Paris. What many writers on our nation lack is precisely the perspective to see the country from outside it. One should never forget that the author of "absolutely the first book of reasoned politics on democratic government in America" was the young French traveller Count Alexis de Tocqueville, whose perception into the nascent American character was in large measure the result of the stereoscopic vision his European commitments gave him.

As for the present author, the perspective he brings to bear on the Bicentennial theme stems from a variety of experiences which may be worth recounting at the outset (if only to provide critics with the painless opportunity to refute him *ad hominem*).

First, Canadian residence. From 1960 to 1964, the Montgomerys were "resident aliens" (*immigrants reçus*) in Canada. My youngest daughter was born in Kitchener, and can therefore claim Canadian citizenship. I served as Chairman of the History Department at what was then Waterloo Lutheran University and is now, by the hardly atypical secularization process, Wilfred Laurier

University. I found myself in the unenviable position of teaching United States History to Canadians at the time of the Bay of Pigs incident—a time when our foreign policy was not exactly lauded beyond our borders. Class discussion of the War of 1812 was always a delight, since the Canadian and American school textbooks appear to be describing two entirely different wars when they discuss it. Hopefully I gave students a good historical education; I certainly received one. I well remember my eloquent attempt to delineate the opposing ideologies of the major political parties in our bi-party system, only to have to admit, finally, because of the overwhelming pressure of the evidence my students presented, that in reality both parties did substantially the same things once they came to power, regardless of pre-election pronouncements. A few years after leaving Canada, I returned to McMaster University to debate the late Bishop James Pike at a University Teach-In; my greatest difficulty was to get him to face theological issues, since he preferred to play to the audience by condemning U.S. policy in Vietnam. Finally I quieted the enthusiastic audience by reminding them of the restrictive (indeed, racist) Canadian immigration policies—on the principle that one should remove beams from one's own eye before extracting material from the eyes of others. All in all, Canada helped me to learn something about national sins, both those of my country and those prevalent elsewhere. I found that Romans 3:23 applies as well to nations as to individuals.

Then came the French experience. In 1964 I took my theological doctorate at the University of Strasbourg. During the ensuing decade, the family was in France two full years and roughly half of each other year. We are property owners in Strasbourg (or will be if the mortgage ever gets paid); two of my children count their French friends as their closest friends; and we intend to make France a continuing and permanent aspect of our lives. It was in France that we learned of the assassination of Kennedy. We were there at the height (or depth, depending on one's viewpoint) of Gaullist anti-Americanism, when even the NATO troops were thrown out of France. We lived through the appalling Days of May, 1968, when an abortive miniature revolution nearly crippled the economy and virtually brought the entire nation to a grinding halt. Well do I remember an anarchist in the Latin

Quarter trying to sell me an underground newspaper for a franc; I took it, refused to pay him, and informed him that I was giving him his first lesson in the true nature of Anarchy. With all its political chaos, I have come to love France with a passion, and I am not ashamed to say that I prefer its life-style to that available anywhere in America today. But I have never seriously considered giving up American citizenship. My own nation's values mean too much to me for that. The very tension between these values and the French way of life has provided the strongest incentive to identify and delineate the nature of our own reason-for-existence.

If France forced me to take a hard look at our country's ideological patterns, the same can certainly be said for my regular contacts over the past twelve years with East Germany (the German Democratic Republic). I have made a dozen trips behind the Iron Curtain to the hardest line Marxist country of the Eastern bloc and have close Christian friends there. One of the common aphorisms in the GDR compares the Poles and the East Germans: The Poles have freedom and no bread; East Germans have bread and no freedom. Having observed life in East Germany at firsthand and in depth, I have little patience with the rosy pictures of Marxist social equality painted by spokesmen of American liberal religion—and I note that if these spokesmen have been behind the Iron Curtain at all (which is by no means certain), they have seen only what they wanted to see. But, at the same time, contact with the GDR has reinforced my Lutheran conviction that valid government is not limited to a single political type: all governmental structure, however misconceived, is ordained of God, and the Gospel can and does perform its regenerating work under political conditions that are far from ideal. Such a sobering truth makes one less likely to believe that his own nation is the only conceivable instrument of divine purpose.

During the last stages of the Vietnam War I taught at the Trinity Evangelical Divinity School, in the Chicago suburb of Deerfield. Not long before I came to Trinity, Deerfield gained dubious national prominence because of largely unsuccessful efforts to increase de facto integration in the community. The People's Christian Coalition was formed by Trinity students during the years I was there; Jim Wallis was one of my students and James

Moore served as my teaching assistant. These men came within a hairsbreadth of being expelled from the institution for their activism—which was hopelessly radical from the standpoint of the Evangelical Free Church constituency supporting the institution. My own political views (as this present volume will amply demonstrate) are by no means those of the Coalition or its paper, *The Post-American*, but its efforts must at least be regarded as a healthy counteractive to the naïve identification of Evangelicalism with the political and social Right.

From Chicago we moved to Washington—in time for the Watergate deluge and the demise of Nixon. This was soon followed by another demise, far less newsworthy but more immediately dispiriting personally. I left Trinity to fill the chair of Jurisprudence at the newly founded International School of Law, an institution which was, in the dream of its dean and founder, John W. Brabner-Smith, to restore the biblical foundations of the law as presented in Blackstone and legal instruction during colonial times. I felt that this high purpose should engage my best efforts at a time when the country needed biblically orientated attorneys and statesmen as never before. But in little more than three years, the pietistic trustees ousted the dean and abolished all Jurisprudence from the curriculum, on the assumption that Christianity does not require the integration of theology with legal knowledge, but only "warm hearts" and "moral integrity." Fortunately, the Christian Legal Society holds no such naïve illusions, and my jurisprudential labors continue under its aegis. But the experience of observing Christians despiritualizing an institution that could have been of key importance in national spiritual recovery forced me to reevaluate the evangelical approach to our country's needs. The answer to post-Watergate dilemmas does indeed lie with the beliefs at the center of evangelical religion, but that viewpoint requires radical surgery before it can become healthy enough to deal effectively with the country's ills. The evangelical physician, as we will be at pains to show as this book draws to a close, needs to heal himself—or rather be healed by the Scripture he professes—in order to speak to the country's deepest crises of conscience.

If the foregoing adult experiences give the reader the uncomfortable feeling that he is embarking on a journey with a transplanted, cerebral American who readily sits in criticism on his own origins and even his religious commitment, well, the reader is at least partly right, and hopefully the resultant constructive criticism will be a positive tonic to the body politic. But, to round out the picture, imagine the same critical, cerebral author as an eight-year-old boy sitting on top of a green mailbox (yes, they once *were* painted green) in the sleepy little town of Warsaw, New York, watching enthralled as the Fourth-of-July parade passed by—and then following it to the cemetery, where the American Legion fired salutes to our honored dead in the presence of wizened Civil War veterans who had themselves seen Abraham Lincoln. In high school that same boy was a Barbershopper —more properly, a member in good standing of the S.P.E.B.S.Q.S.A. (Society for the Preservation and Encouragement of Barbershop Quartet Singing in America) —and aside from the Negro Spiritual or New Orleans Dixieland there isn't a more native music in existence than Close Harmony. My childhood could have fitted perfectly into the framework of Meredith Willson's *Music Man*, and I've taken my own children to Disneyland (both the California and the Florida varieties) to give them the flavor of it. One of my greatest thrills was a family pilgrimage to Williamsburg: indeed, it might even be considered the precipitating cause of this volume. (Remarkably, while poking about the Wren Building of the College of William and Mary, I came across a plaque commemorating the visit of World War I hero Maréchal Pétain to the college on October 18, 1931—the day of my birth—to honor French dead who served on the American side during the Revolution. One doesn't often encounter a word of personal prophetic import!)

* * * * *

In sum, the present author is an American by birth and by deep emotional attachment, yet he brings to an analysis of this nation's character and needs a potentially illuminating international perspective. Moreover, he insists on seeing the central ideological issues for what they are, namely *theological* issues. And the theological evaluation he offers is neither an obscurantist rightism which identifies our nation as God's country—"my country right or wrong"—nor an iconoclastic leftism which declares our political, social, and economic structures to be essentially immoral.

So, if the reader is up to a critical yet constructive evaluation of a great national heritage, and is not offended by the introduction of theology into discussions where those who first settled our nation insisted on its centrality, he may find the present work of more than passing interest.

JOHN WARWICK MONTGOMERY

Washington, D.C.
New Year's Day, in the Year of Salvation 1976

"Don't forget, Tim, that we [Irish] are an ancient race. An Englishman is a recent novelty, compared with the Gael— even if he has outstripped him. When the Americans have finally taken over the British Empire, the English will probably begin to feel a bit elderly too, like us."

"Are you telling me that you are more grown-up than we are?"

"What do you think?"

—T. H. White,
The Godstone and The Blackymor

Orientation

Youthful Melancholia on One's 200th Birthday

Two hundred years ago our ragged and half-trained soldiery, aided by foreign troops, won independence from a leading world power. Perhaps our strength was as the strength of ten because our hearts were pure, but a more realistic analysis would suggest that we won largely because the Mother Country finally concluded that to keep us wasn't worth the frustration or the effort. Now, a short two centuries later, we celebrate a major birthday as the richest and most powerful nation on the globe. England, now the economic sick man of Europe, devoid of empire, looks at us with undisguised envy, while attempting to fend off creditors and suppress Scottish nationalism in anticipation of the arrival of North Sea oil, like a deus ex machina in a bad play, to restore financial sanity. Meanwhile the United States, with 5½% of the world's population, continues to use 33% of the world's energy, and her most trivial foreign policy decisions affect virtually every other nation on the face of the earth.

But the English can take perverse satisfaction in the fact that though we are rich, we certainly aren't happy. During the Vietnam War, the longest armed struggle in our history, we managed (1) to learn nothing from the French, repeating their Indochina fiasco on a far more extensive and expensive scale, and (2) *both* to lose militarily *and* to alienate most of world public opinion (no mean feat, since the two achievements seemed incompatible). Then the Watergate catastrophe brought home to roost the moral laxity and situational ethic which had become endemic in our bureaucratic political machinery. Perhaps unethical CIA activities are to be expected (after all, espionage is espionage?), but even the late J. Edgar Hoover, boyhood hero of a generation—the white knight who was supposed to have cleaned up organized crime—is now known to have used his FBI to spy and harass in defiance of constitutional protections and unabashedly to have allowed the end to justify the means. And John F. Kennedy, consistently compared with Lincoln in the popular mythology of the day, turns out to have had at least one doubtful personal relationship and consequent feet of clay. Self-doubt assails us, as the spectre of Russia and China loom ever larger on the horizon of a conveniently undefined détente.

* * * * *

Reinhold Niebuhr, in his classic, *The Irony of American History,* analyzed the paradox in these terms: "Our own nation, always a vivid symbol of the most characteristic attitudes of a bourgeois culture, is less potent to do what it wants in the hour of its greatest strength than it was in the days of its infancy. The infant is more secure in his world than the mature man is in his wider world." The irony of 18th century strength-in-weakness and 20th century weakness-in-strength is profoundly true, but what of the characterization of the early American as a "child" and today's American as a "mature man"?

One of the most penetrating interpretations of the European High Renaissance concludes with a study of Dürer's engraving, *Melancholia,* completed just three years before Luther's posting of the Ninety-Five Theses shook the foundations of the medieval world. Writes Harvard historian Myron P. Gilmore at the close of his *World of Humanism, 1453-1517*:

If a single document were to be selected from all the richness of this period as most profoundly characteristic of this intellectual and spiritual attitude in Renaissance Europe the choice of Dürer's *Melancolia* might be defended.

This celebrated engraving was done in 1514. It represents a personification of melancholy as a heavy despon-

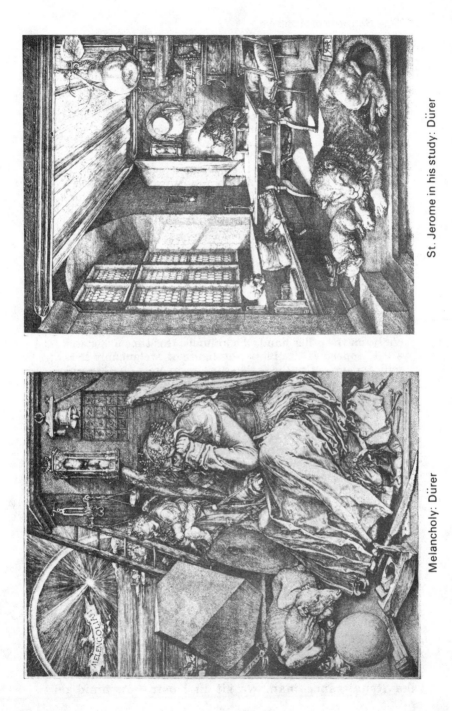

St. Jerome in his study: Dürer

Melancholy: Dürer

dent female figure. She sits surrounded by a collection of
instruments, which include various geometrical figures,
hourglass, magic square, balance, compass and rule, all
strewn about in confusion. On a grindstone a child scrawls
on a slate. Professor Panofsky has pointed out that Dürer
has here combined the popular tradition which represented
the melancholic temperament as a lazy housewife with the
personification of geometry among the seven liberal arts.
Behind this merger lay the influence of Renaissance Platonism, which had developed a new conception of melancholy. In the works of Ficino in particular appeared an
identification of the artistic genius and melancholy. Dürer's picture is accordingly to be interpreted as an analysis
of the frustration of the creative impulse and it implies a
contrast with those conditions in which productive activity
can be realized. This contrast is presented by the engraving of St. Jerome in his study, which belongs to the same
year and is in many ways a companion piece. In the study
of St. Jerome every object is in its ordered place and the
saint is engaged in the happiest contemplative and creative work. Even the animals, the lion and the little dog,
are sleeping with expressions of content. In the *Melancholy*, on the other hand, the animals, this time a dog and
a cat, appear as dismal as the figure of Melancholy herself, and everything is calculated to express the general
chaos of the scene. The little boy is perched on top of
a stone scribbling away without direction and without result. . . .

   . . . The engraving may be taken as a symbol of the
hopes and fears of a generation. Knowledge of the conditions of disharmony, awareness of the inner tensions in
the European intellectual inheritance implied also the belief that these conflicts could be surmounted and harmo-
nized to produce the golden age of achievement of which
Erasmus dreamed. The promise of creativity was more
than fulfilled, but underneath there persisted the danger of
impotence, sterility, despair. It is as if a genius of the
greatest insight had stood on the borderline between
two worlds and prefigured the triumphant course of
European civilization as it moved on toward the conquest
of the world, while at the same time recognizing the
delicacy of the balance between creation and destruction
and the possibility that in the end the outcome might
belie all the greatest hopes of his generation.

One cannot contemplate Dürer's *Melancholia* or reflect on the preceding analysis of it without recognizing
its analogous appropriateness to the American mind-set.
Like Renaissance man, we sit in frustration amid our

tools and our accomplishments. We long to be at peace like St. Jerome, but our existence is terrorized by the dangers of impotence, sterility, and despair; we are immobilized by the disharmony and inner tensions of our inheritance.

It is important to note that this problem is particularly a Renaissance phenomenon: a phenomenon which occurs in periods of innovation and newness, when originality outruns the integration of what is new into the existing scheme of things, or when the old bottles are incapable of containing new wine without bursting.

Consider these historical parallels:

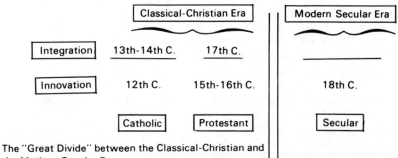

The "Great Divide" between the Classical-Christian and the Modern Secular Eras

As I have argued in extenso in my *Shape of the Past* and "Libraries of France at the Ascendancy of Mazarin," one sees remarkable similarities between what Charles Homer Haskins has called "the renaissance of the 12th century," on the one hand, and Burckhardt's "civilization of the Renaissance in Italy" and the Protestant Reformation on the other: both eras of newness were followed by periods of systematization—the gathering up, organizing, and assimilating of new knowledge by way of late medieval Catholic Scholasticism or through Protestant Orthodoxy (the former accompanied by Feudalism, Gothic architecture, and the Guilds; the latter accompanied by the summing up of the classical musical tradition in Bach and the classical artistic tradition in the Baroque). The 17th-century Protestant syntheses by the great Lutheran, Calvinist, and Anglican dogmaticians ended an age; then came that hiatus in Western thought which C. S. Lewis characterized as "the Great Divide" separating a Christian view of the world from the modern secular orientation. (For Lewis, the Divide is to be placed somewhat later, but few would disagree that by the American and French Revolutions at the end of the 18th century the gulf is clearly visible.)

We shall maintain in the present work that the American spiritual heritage substantially derives both from the Christian tradition, as exemplified in its classical 17th-century Protestant formulation, and from that innovative early expression of modern secularism represented by the so-called "Enlightenment" of the 18th century. Much of our national melancholia results from the fundamental tension between these two superficially similar, but essentially incompatible world-views; and we shall be at pains to assist the reader to make the proper choice between them—a choice which such current events as the School Prayer and Abortion decisions of the Supreme Court have forced upon us in a manner unknown to previous generations of Americans.

The diagram just presented suggests a related consideration pertinent to our national melancholia. Earlier periods of innovation in Western history were resolved into times of integration, when new insights and discoveries were brought into synthesis with already existing values. But suppose modern secularism, which first appeared as a philosophy of life in the century of our nation's independence, is inherently incapable of integration with past truth and is indeed so inherently incompatible with the real nature of things that it cannot become an integrated world-view; what then? Since the 17th-century western man has not experienced a time of genuine synthesis; 18th century secular innovation has not produced an era of integrated experience. Indeed, fragmentation rather than integration seems the defining mark of our modern world, and the America of today has drunk that cup almost to the dregs. Hopefully, our analysis will offer a way out of this contemporary slough of despond.

*   *   *   *   *

But melancholy is a complex business—as Burton so well demonstrated in his 17th-century classic, *The Anatomy of Melancholy* (long before the far less literary psychoanalysts and social historians went to work on the subject). The source of our national melancholia is not

limited to the tension between Orthodoxy and Enlightenment or to the built-in inadequacies of the Enlightenment
perspective. It is due also to our youthfulness. Observe
again Dürer's angelic figure: how young she is! And note
the central position of the boy who, in Gilmore's words,
"scribbles away without direction and without result."
It is as if a youthful Madonna and Child somehow became
separated from the Gospel story and lost their way. The
artist thereby reminds us of a great danger in every
renaissance: the Promethean danger of humanistic self-
confidence, of attempting, like Leonardo da Vinci, to do
everything, with the result that one accomplishes far less
than would be possible through the Christian self-awareness of a Michelangelo. Renaissances are especially prone
to superficiality and to the evils of exuberant adolescence.

In our own national history, this predilection for youthful superficiality was compounded by the Frontier phenomenon, about which we shall have much to say.
Through most of our country's history, the possibility of
"movin' on" to new frontiers permitted the American
to live in the illusion of perpetual adolescence—to believe
that he had actually drunk of Ponce de León's Fountain
of Youth. Only in very recent years have we come regretfully to the point of having to face political and economic limitations, those harsh realities of an adult world.
Had we become "mature men" in Niebuhr's sense—or,
better, in the biblical sense of "growing up into Christ,"
we would be capable of facing the ironies and agonies
of a fallen existence. But, to a very great degree, we
still remain children, blown about by every wind of mo-
dernity; and the icy winds of 20th-century secularism
are enough to chill the soul of any nation.

One might well ask where the Church has been in
these difficulties. Has not religion served as a natural
corrective to the problems just described? Is ours not
a "Christian nation," and therefore must not any portrait of American melancholia be grossly overdrawn?
Such sentiments are characteristic of not a few glad-
tidings religious publications, such as Benjamin Weiss's
God in American History (foreword by Congressman
Walter H. Judd), whose author declares: "Our nation
has become the outstanding validation of the soundness
of Western Christian culture and civilization," and who
commences to illustrate his theme with our country's official motto, "In God We Trust," which by Congressional

Act of July 11, 1955, must now appear on all our currency and coins.

Quite frankly, I am not much impressed by such arguments. The American melancholia exists, whether we are willing to face it or not; and the country is not de facto Christian, whatever it may be de jure. Some years ago I obtained in England a Roman coin from the time of the Emperor Marcus Aurelius; on the obverse side it carries the figure of the god Hilaritas, standing with palm and cornucopia. I wanted this particular coin because it illustrated a key passage in Ethelbert Stauffer's *Christ and the Caesars*:

> Theatres and games and festivals were organized in unprecedented number, grain and wine and money were distributed, and coins were struck with such words of guidance as FELICITAS and HILARITAS. But meanwhile the Germanic tribes were breaking through the frontiers, and the old order was tottering to its end. One contemporary account compares the sick gaiety with the effect of the "Sardonian root," a poisonous plant which forces a convulsive smile across the face of the dying.

Coinage sometimes has a more profound message than is at first apparent.

We shall have more than a little to say about the relation of religion and the American melancholia, and much of it will be critical. The confusion of generalized "civil religion" with historic Christianity has greatly weakened the impact of the Gospel on the American scene, denaturing the best remedy for our ideological sickness. And the churches have all too often prostituted their calling either through modernistic compromise of the historic Christian message or through childish evangelicalism that partakes of the adolescent superficiality to which it should be ministering. Melancholia does indeed require a religious treatment; but the religion must be God's religion, not a human nostrum attractively packaged to look like it.

* * * * *

What has been said so far presupposes the possibility of delineating "the American character" as a basis for understanding and speaking to current national ills. Is such a delineation realistic? Many are inclined to the viewpoint expressed in the title of Hamilton Fyfe's work, *The Illusion of National Character*; he endeavors to illustrate his theme with chapters on "Many Kinds of Frenchmen" and "All Sorts of Americans."

To be sure, the concept of a uniform national character can be overdone, particularly in the case of a nation such as ours that has prided itself on welcoming immigrants of the most diverse backgrounds from the four corners of the earth. However, the excesses in some interpretations of national character (well critiqued by Fyfe) do not destroy the validity of the concept as such. As in the case of the fundamental philosophical problem of the One and the Many, two equal and corresponding errors are possible: the insistence that there is only unity (to the destruction of all genuine diversity) and a fascination with multiplicity which completely loses sight of underlying oneness.

NOTE FREY'S WORK

Only the most obtuse student of human nature can read such volumes as V. S. Naravane's *Modern Indian Thought* or Hajime Nakamura's *Ways of Thinking of Eastern Peoples* without concluding that, in spite of the unavoidable employment of deductive and inductive inference by all thinking men, the Eastern peoples do in fact move in an ideological climate which differs profoundly from that of the West. For example, Nakamura isolates such identifiers of Indian thought as the following: preference for the negative, minimizing individuality and specific particulars, subjective comprehension of personality, subservience to universals, alienation from the objective natural world, and a focus on introspection. Similarly, readers of Lafcadio Hearn's *Japan: An Interpretation* or such classical treatments of the Japanese Tea Ceremony as those by Okakura Kakuzo and Julia Nakamura will agree that the Japanese world-view embraces in a peculiar way elements of formalism, paradox, becoming as opposed to being, incompleteness—in a word, the profound conviction that there is "no reality except that which concerns the working of our own minds." How often has the preaching of the Gospel to other peoples been impeded by a lack of recognition of such vital cultural differences!

Moving to the West, we might suppose that national differences would be obliterated by the common denominator of Western civilization. However, these differences are clearly visible and are of great practical importance.

Salvador de Madariaga, formerly Professor of Spanish
Studies at Oxford, provided an especially astute example
of European national character analysis in his trilingual
book, *Englishmen, Frenchmen, Spaniards*: he found the
key to English character in the notion of "fair play,"
the understanding of the French mind in the concept of
"le droit" (right, law), and the secret of the Spanish
personality in *"el honor,"* thereby effectively classifying
these peoples on the basis of their central preoccupations
with, respectively, action, thought, and passion. Luigi
Barzini's *The Italians* is another illustration of the validity
of studies of the national character of particular Western
nations; he puts under his microscope "the Italian way
of life which makes all laws and institutions function
defectively," and shows how that life-style is "the illusion
of a solution, lotus-eating, the resigned acceptance of the
very evils man has tried to defeat, the art of decorating,
ennobling them, calling them by different names and living with them." When we compare these peoples with
ourselves, we are struck with differences such as that
emphasized by Professor B. Carl in an Association of
American Law Schools Clinic in Transnational Legal Communication (July 20, 1973): "U.S. attorneys tend to use
inductive reasoning and search for pragmatic solutions.
Frenchmen more often favor deductive reasoning and
look for a neat, orderly structure of legal norms. As a
consequence of these different approaches, the competent
foreign lawyer may ruthlessly follow the strict dictates
or logic, while his American counterpart is more interested in how the proposed rule will work if applied to
a particular set of facts."

If the existence of identifiable national character is
granted, at least in principle, how can the complex American character be discovered? Assuming that in some
real sense the stream of explorers, colonists, and immigrants to our shores have entered a "melting pot,"
how is the temperature of that brew to be taken?

In the chapter to follow we shall build up a portrait
of the archetypal American on the basis of successive
layers of historical experience. Today's American is the
product of at least four ideological epochs, each of which
has left a permanent imprint on the national soul.* Only

---

*It is not an oversight that we place no special emphasis on the
particular experiences of individual immigrant groups. To be sure, these

by appreciating this complexity in the formation of the American character can we hope to understand or treat our current melancholia; and only by an analysis of this kind can a sensible answer be given to the deceptively simple question as to whether we are a "Christian nation."

One can schematize the American experience as a four-level structure:

```
┌──────────────────────────────────────────────────────┐
│        20th C.: THE DIALECTIC OF DESPAIR              │
│        (World Wars & the Age of Extermination)        │
├──────────────────────────────────────────────────────┤
│  19th C.: PROGRESSIVISTIC MIRAGE(Triumph of Technology)│
├──────────────────────────────────────────────────────┤
│   18th C.: THE ENLIGHTENMENT SPIRIT (Founding Fathers) │
├──────────────────────────────────────────────────────┤
│ 15th-17th C.: THE QUEST FOR A NEW EDEN (Explorers & Pilgrims) │
└──────────────────────────────────────────────────────┘
```

The advantage of such a model is that it properly aligns the historical epochs relative to each other and reminds us that it is the past which grounds the present, not the other way around. In the sage words of La Rochefoucauld: "Those who refuse to learn from history are forced to repeat its mistakes."

However, the same scheme can be presented in a less static, more dynamic way by conceiving of a stone thrown into water, producing a series of concentric rings that move outward from the center and from each other.

---

groups reach our shores at different stages of the historical process and might therefore be thought to lack the earlier formative influences already present on the American scene at their arrival. But as they enter the "melting pot" the pressures to become fully and genuinely American bring about an assimilation of existing American values. The ghetto cannot survive this pressure, and the immigrant sooner or later becomes "Americanized"; indeed (to employ William James' useful distinction), the immigrant, like most "twice-born" converts, generally becomes a more enthusiastic believer than the older, more settled, "once-born" American. Even the American Indian or the American Black, whose experiences in this land have been tragically saddened by oppression at the hands of dominant social groups, display the same assimilation of values; the assimilation process in these cases is much slowed by persecution, but it inexorably goes on.

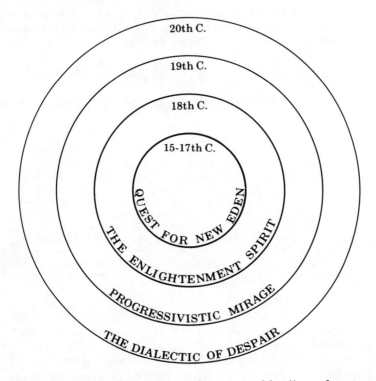

Think of "Columbus sailing the ocean blue" as the stone thrown into the stream of history (or, if you are anti-Italian, pro-Scandinavian, think of your favorite Viking). The waves of historical experience spread out—and behold, the Concentric American appears. If Whyte's *Organization Man* and Riesman's *Lonely Crowd* are correct, today's American, whether conformist "Fat-cat" or conformist "nonconformist," is anything but *ec*centric; but do not be surprised to find him *con*centric in the chapters to follow. As this book draws to a close we shall try to help our Concentric American overcome melancholy by overcoming his youthful predilection to run in circles.

PART ONE

The Concentric American

Here independent power shall hold sway
And public virtue warm the patriot's
    breast.
No traces shall remain of tyranny
And laws and patterns for the world beside
Be here enacted first.
A new Jerusalem sent down from heaven
Shall grace our happy earth.

— Philip Morin Freneau (1752-1832)

1

Questing for a New Eden

The term "bicentennial" has its deceptive side, for it can give the impression that one need go back only two hundred years to discover American origins. But in fact the dial on the time machine must be set for double that number of years in order to comprehend the American character. Long before the Enlightenment—that secular period of innovation when our official beginning as a nation took place—the first layer of our national character was being formed through essentially Christian influences: Renaissance exploration and Protestant colonization.

The Age of Exploration

The Italian Renaissance, whose beginnings can be clearly seen in the work of Petrarch and Giotto at the beginning of the 14th century, and which reached its greatness in Florence after the fall of Constantinople to the Ottoman Turks in 1453, was peculiarly a utopian movement. Renaissance scholars, artists, and philosophers sought to discover the ideal as reflected in man and in nature and thereby to open up new vistas for the human spirit. The dominant philosophical viewpoint of the Renaissance was a revived Platonism—or, to be more precise, a repristination of the views of Neo-Platonists such as Plotinus, who had intensified the mystical side of Plato's teachings. For the Platonic idealist, the idea or the ideal is never fully represented in the objects of our experience, so satisfaction with what we have can never be complete. The incompleteness of things in Platonic thought had finally brought a searching Augustine in the 4th century from Neo-Platonism to Christianity; as he wrote in those wondrous lines at the beginning of his *Confessions*: "Thou hast made us for Thyself, O God, and our hearts are restless until they find their rest in Thee." The same sense of incompleteness drove Renaissance man to seek for new ideas, new visual experiences, and new lands.

Characteristically, it is Plato who gives Western man his first glimpse of utopia. In the *Timaens* and in the *Critias* he presents a detailed picture of an idyllic kingdom which once existed in the western ocean, beyond the Pillars of Hercules. A few lines from his account of Atlantis in the *Critias* will convey the flavor of this hypnotic legend:

> The gods ... divided the whole earth amongst themselves in portions differing in extent, and made for themselves temples and sacrifices. And Poseidon, receiving for his lot the island of Atlantis, begat children by a mortal woman, and settled them in a part of the island which I will proceed to describe. On the side toward the sea, and in the center of the whole island, there was a plain which is said to have been the fairest of all plains, and very fertile. ... Here, too, was Poseidon's own temple, of a stadium in length and half a stadium in width, and of a proportionate height, having a sort of barbaric splendor. All the outside of the temple, with the exception of the pinnacles, they covered with silver, and the pinnacles with gold. In the interior of the temple the roof was of ivory, adorned everywhere with gold and silver. ... Such was the vast power which the god settled in the lost island of Atlantis.

During the High Renaissance, Ficino's Platonic Academy at Florence bent every effort to substitute the authority of the "Divine Plato" for that of Aristotle, whose philosophical influence had dominated medieval thought. Thus did the Atlantis myth become part of the mental furniture of an age.

The locus of the Atlantic for Plato's utopian myth is of more than passing significance. Throughout the history of the West the very notion of westernness has been infused with a positive value, and the converse direction, the East, has been viewed negatively. In the deep myths of the West we find that the Fairies, as human depravity increases on the earth, travel farther and farther west, until finally they leave Europe entirely, departing from Ireland in ships to resettle in the "Western isles." Since the early invasions of Persians, Goths, Huns, and Mongols, the westerner has been terrified of "Eastern barbarians" and the "yellow peril." At the Imperial Diet at Augsburg in 1530, when Protestants first offered a united Confession to Emperor Charles V, they found it impossible to persuade him to take their theological position seriously: all he could think of was the danger to Europe presented by the Turkish armies at the gates of Vienna—the armies that had already made an end to Christian civilization in Constantinople. Regularly and consistently, Western man has turned his fearful eyes from the East and gazed with hope and longing on unknown possibilities to the West.

Prescott, in his *History of Ferdinand and Isabella,* drew attention to lines by a Florentine Renaissance poet that illustrate well the all-pervasiveness of the western dream at that critical period of history. Wrote Pulci (1431-1487) in his *Morgante Maggiore:*

> Men shall descry another hemisphere,
> Since to one common center all things tend;
> So earth, by curious mystery divine
> Well balanced, hangs amid the starry spheres.
> At our Antipodes are cities, states,
> And thronged empires, ne'er divined of yore.
> But see, the sun speeds on his western path
> To glad the nations with expected light.

The very word "utopia" entered the English language during the Renaissance. Sir Thomas More—that "man for all seasons"—coined the word as the title for his delightful story of European discoverers who chance upon an island whose inhabitants do not suffer from the political ills that beset the England of More's day, and whose self-awareness has created in them a longing for the Christian Gospel. More's *Utopia* can without exaggeration be regarded as the literary equivalent of—if not a charter for—the age of Renaissance exploration.

Geoffrey Ashe provides a balanced summary of the case for utopian motivation in the Renaissance discovery of America when he writes in the concluding chapter of his superlative work, *The Quest for America:*

> To speak of America as the goal of a Quest may sound misleading. So far as we can tell, a trans-Atlantic con-

tinent was never deliberately searched for by anyone.
Explorers in other regions have had more precise ob-
jectives. The Polos searched for Cathay, and found it.
Hudson searched for the North-West Passage, and failed
to find it. Tasman searched for a southern continent,
and found, not exactly that, but Australia and New Zea-
land. By contrast, those who were borne towards the
New World, in mind or body, seem to have made the
voyage in comparative vagueness and even delusion.
Columbus himself never tried to find it. In a sense he
tried not to.

However, a quest is more profound than a search. It
is a spiritual adventure. It need not imply any exact
idea of what one is looking for. Rather, it is rooted in
a persistent unrest or yearning, a reaching out. The
familiar life is unsatisfying; the familiar world is not
all; somewhere *out there* is a mystery. There are those,
like the speaker in Housman's poem, who feel the mystery
but fear it, and turn away. There are others, the ques-
ters, who go forward to probe it.

For people in the Old World before Columbus, 'that-
which-lies-across-the-Ocean' was a mystery which
slowly acquired a character. The impulse to prove—
even in imagination—never affected more than a few
at any time; but it came and went and then came
again, in different forms and with a variety of motives. Whether or not Plato and Plutarch drew on traditions of actual voyaging, their myths were the specu-
lative flights of bold minds, unwilling to be enclosed
in the Oecumene. The same dialogue of Plutarch that
portrays his 'America' also discusses whether the Moon
is inhabited. At the opposite extreme, the practical
Norsemen were restless because of the scarcity of good
land, the rigours of an arctic climate, the feeling that
beyond Greenland there must be something better. Between those extremes we must place Columbus's weird
mixture of religion, fantasy, greed and genius; and the
Celtic imagination that carried real and fictitious cur-
raghs into the sunset; and the obscure energies that
drove anonymous seafarers outward from the ancient
Mediterranean and Japan.

Always mystery lay beyond the horizon. The spirit
which tried to pierce it was a questing spirit. And embedded in the mystery, as it turned out, was a continent.

The theological dimension of the Renaissance utopian
dream and its American quest must not be overlooked.
As I have argued in my *Principalities and Powers*: "Ren-

aissance explorers brought back tales of strange wonders and hidden mysteries—from Ponce de León's Ciudad de Oro and Fountain of Youth to the story of the Christian Kingdom of Prester John, an ideal Priest-King whose land of plenty stood impregnable though surrounded by Muslim infidels. These tales, like the Atlantis legend, bespeak the longings of man for a New Age that would restore the lost Eden."

The Edenic parallel is in no way overdrawn. Whether one reads Plato's Atlantis myth or the explorers' dreams of cities of gold and fountains of youth in the New World, one is struck by remarkable similarities to the Genesis description of the Garden of Eden and the apocalyptic portions of Holy Scripture such as the concluding chapters of the book of Revelation where the New Jerusalem is described. Consider, as but one example, the following passage from Columbus' letter of March 14, 1493, recounting to his Sovereigns the details of his first voyage:

> All these islands are very beautiful, and distinguished by a diversity of scenery; they are filled with a great variety of trees of immense height, and which I believe to retain their foliage in all seasons; for when I saw them they were as verdant and luxuriant as they usually are in Spain in the month of May,—some of them were blossoming, some bearing fruit, and all flourishing in the greatest perfection, according to their respective stages of growth, and the nature and quality of each: yet the islands are not so thickly wooded as to be impassable. The nightingale and various birds were singing in countless numbers, and that in November, the month in which I arrived there. There are besides in the same island of Juana seven or eight kinds of palm trees, which, like all the other trees, herbs, and fruits, considerably surpass ours in height and beauty. The pines also are very handsome, and there are very extensive fields and meadows, a variety of birds, different kinds of honey, and many sorts of metals, but no iron.
>
> In that island also which I have before said we named Española, there are mountains of very great size and beauty, vast plains, groves, and very fruitful fields, admirably adapted for tillage, pasture, and habitation. The convenience and excellence of the harbours in this island, and the abundance of the rivers, so indispensable to the health of man, surpass anything that would be believed by one who had not seen it.

In another letter to his royal patrons he expressly declares: "I think that the water I have described may proceed from the earthly paradise, though it be far off, and that stopping at the place which I have just left, it forms this lake. There are great indications of this being the terrestrial paradise, for its site coincides with the opinion of the holy and wise theologians whom I have mentioned."

The explorers who discovered and mapped the New World in the 15th and 16th centuries were professing Christians who consciously related their activity to their Christian belief. After due account has been taken of the disparity that sometimes existed between their faith and their practice, and after admitting to the mixed motives of wealth, national interest, and sheer adventure that Hakluyt in 1584 sets forth along with missionary zeal as justification for "western planting," we must still recognize that the context of belief into which the explorers placed their endeavors and their lives was that of historic Christianity. What other conclusion is possible when we read throughout Columbus' journal, which begins "In the Name of Our Lord Jesus Christ," such entries as the following: "As the sea was calm and smooth, the people murmured, saying that, as there was there no great sea, it would never blow so as to carry them back to Spain. But afterwards the sea, without wind, rose greatly, and this amazed them ... because such a thing had not been seen save in the time of the Jews, when those of Egypt came out against Moses who was leading them out of captivity" (entry for September 23, 1492). Samuel Eliot Morison notes that each day on board Columbus' vessels began with the chant, "Blessed be the light of day/And the Holy Cross, we say," and that every half hour similar chanteys were sung "whatever the weather." The first map to show the New World, drawn in 1500 by Juan de la Cosa, who had shipped with Columbus in 1492 and 1493, displays a huge cartouche of St. Christopher (note the intentional play on the Admiral's name), bearing Christ across "that river without a bridge which can only be crossed at great peril of drowning." The monumental statue of Columbus in the heart of Old San Juan, Puerto Rico, properly represents him with a cross in his upraised hand.

The discoverers and explorers of the American continent during the period of the High Renaissance were not running from their Christian heritage. Quite the opposite: they were looking for a fuller expression of it. In that quest, they were true children of the Renaissance, which was at root an effort to rediscover a dimension of Christian faith almost lost sight of in medieval times. John Addington Symonds' words, though reflective of his 19th-century Romanticism, nonetheless ring true:

> During the Middle Ages man had lived enveloped in a cowl. He had not seen the beauty of the world, or had seen it only to cross himself, and turn aside and tell his beads and pray. Like St. Bernard travelling along the shores of the Lake Leman, and noticing neither the azure of the waters, nor the luxuriance of the vines, nor the radiance of the mountains with their robe of sun and snow, but bending a thought-burdened forehead over the neck of his mule; even like this monk, humanity had passed, a careful pilgrim, along the highways of the world, and had scarcely known that they were sightworthy or that life is a blessing.

Michelet's famous description of the Renaissance as "the discovery of the world and of man" is entirely accurate—if we remember that this discovery took place *sub specie aeternitatis.* The deepest chord of the Renaissance was struck, not by the critic Valla, the sensuist Botticelli, the rationalist Pomponazzi, or even by the Promethean Leonardo da Vinci, but by the Moses and David of Michelangelo and the printed Greek New Testament of Erasmus. As "Erasmus laid the egg that Luther hatched" (in the popular aphorism of the time), so the Renaissance laid the egg the Reformation hatched. And the quest for a new Eden which motivated the explorers of the 17th and 16th centuries was handed on as a legacy to the Protestant settlers who came to the American shores in the 17th century. Both the wonder and the danger of that dream were transmitted by the earliest explorers to those who followed them.

The Puritan Heritage

The invasion of Florence by King Charles VIII of France in 1494 heralded the impact of the Renaissance spirit on northern Europe. France experienced her Renaissance in the 16th century, as did the German territories, where cultural rebirth became indistinguishable from religious Reformation. Moving steadily northward, Renaissance ideals came to full flowering in England as late as the Elizabethan period, though, as in Germany,

they were already blending with the Reformation perspective a century earlier. With the Renaissance came
the utopian dream of a western paradise. The French
traders in the New World were imbued by it. Wrote
H. S. Bellamy in *The Atlantis Myth*: "In 1689 the French
cartographer Sanson boldly published a map of America
showing how the continent had been parcelled out among
the sons of Poseidon. Since then it has been the endeavour
of many to seek Atlantis in America." How very true,
and in a far deeper sense than Bellamy realized!

The English, who won the struggle for control of the
North American continent, were no less affected by
the utopian ideal. Shakespeare's Gonzalo well expresses
this dream in *The Tempest*:

Gonzalo: Had I plantation of this isle, my lord,—
Antonio: He'd sow't with nettle-seed.
Sebastian: or docks, or mallows
Gonzalo: And were the king on't, what would I do?
Sebastian: Scape being drunk, for want of wine.
Gonzalo: I' the commonwealth I would by contraries
Execute all things; for no kind of traffic
Would I admit; no name of magistrate;
Letters should not be known; riches, poverty,
And use of service, none; contract, succession,
Bourn, bound of land, tilth, vineyard, none;
No use of metal, corn, or wine, or oil;
No occupation; all men idle, all;
And women too, but innocent and pure;
No sovereignty;—
Sebastian: Yet he would be king on't.
Antonio: The latter end of his commonwealth forgets
    the beginning.
Gonzalo: All things in common nature should produce
Without sweat or endeavour; treason, felony,
Sword, pike, knife, gun, or need of any engine,
Would I not have; but nature should bring forth,
Of its own kind, all foison, all abundance,
To feed my innocent people.
Sebastian: No marrying 'mong his subjects?
Antonio: None, man; all idle; whores and knaves.
Gonzalo: I would with such perfection govern, sir,
To excel the golden age.
Sebastian: Save his majesty!
Antonio: Long live Gonzalo!

Worth noting in this passage is the Bard's recognition
of the fundamental problem in all "new Edens": Those

who create them would eliminate all injustice ("no sovereignty"); yet they themselves "would be king on't." We shall see later that Shakespeare was precisely correct in observing how often "the latter end" of the utopian's commonwealth "forgets the beginning."

Daniel Boorstin, in *The Americans: The Colonial Experience* identifies four fundamental types of colonial dream that English settlers endeavored to realize in America. The Virginia colonists held the dream of the transplanter; the Georgia settlers, the dream of the philanthropist; the Pennsylvania Quakers, the dream of the perfectionist; and the New England Puritans, the grand vision of a new Zion. All but the Puritan dream had built-in limitations which kept them from becoming dominant. Thus

> The leadership of Virginians in Federal life continued only so long as the national government was an aristocratic camaraderie like that of Virginia. When the United States ceased to be a greater Virginia, Virginians ceased to govern the United States. The virtues of 18th-century Virginia, when writ large, would seem to be vices. Localism would become sectionalism; the special interests of where a man lived would come to seem petty and disruptive.

As for the philanthropic vision of Oglethorpe in Georgia,

> However intractable were the London poor to the schemes of the Trustees, the silkworms proved even more so. The fiat of London philanthropists made not the slightest impression on them.... Their [the Trustees'] essential weakness was a frame of mind which stifled the spontaneity and experimental spirit which were the real spiritual wealth of America.

The failings of the Quakers are worth a more extended quotation, since their pietistic, anti-intellectual, subjective spirituality has uncomfortable parallels with a large segment of today's Evangelicalism:

> Their self-righteousness and their rigidity are symbolized by an anecdote which John Churchman relates. During his ministerial wanderings in the 1750's he came to know a thoughtful and studious barber whose shop he patronized. On one occasion the barber proudly showed his visitor a difficult work in algebra which he had been studying on his own. "I said it might be useful to some," Churchman answered sanctimoniously, "but that I could take up grubbing, or follow the

plough, without studying algebra; as he might also shave a man, &c. without it. Besides I found it a more profitable and delightful study, to be quietly employed in learning the law of the Lord written in mine own heart, so that I might walk before him acceptably".... The Quaker was preoccupied with his rites of self-purification. With the obstinacy of the mystic he refused to admit the existence of the enemy's cudgel, even though his own or another's head be broken by it.... Finally, the Quakers made a dogma of the absence of dogma.... This deprived the Quaker of that theological security which had enabled the Puritan gradually to adapt Calvinism to American life. The Quaker was haunted by fear that every compromise was a defeat, that to modify anything might be to lose everything. Because his doctrine was suffused with the haze of mystical enthusiasm, he could not discern clearly which were the foundations and buttresses of his cathedral and which the ornamental gargoyles.

The Puritan-Pilgrim dream, however, lined out with utmost precision "the foundations and buttresses of its cathedral"; and it became the determinative element in the formation of the American character in the colonial period. Let us therefore examine the vital constituent elements of the Puritan world-view.*

First and foremost, the Puritans were biblical Christians of the Reformation tradition. This hardly requires emphasizing, since it is a matter of common knowledge that the motivation which led both Pilgrims and Puritans

---

* We shall not endeavor to distinguish between the separatist Pilgrims who arrived at Plymouth in 1620 and the (originally) non-separatist Puritans of Massachusetts Bay. William Warren Sweet, dean of American church historians, gives the following succinct statement of their differences: "The Plymouth Pilgrims repudiated the Church of England in all its parts and would have nothing to do with it; the Puritans of the Massachusetts Bay colony, following the lead of William Bradshaw and William Ames, the leading Puritan casuists, while accepting the Congregational form of church government as Scriptural, at the same time avowed their loyalty to the Church of England"; for more detail, see Perry Miller's *Orthodoxy in Massachusetts.* Except in this matter of official separation from the English Church, the doctrinal perspective of Pilgrims and Puritans was virtually identical. Doubtless, however, this difference will assume considerable importance in the minds of readers in evangelical traditions where one must not even "fellowship" with those who agree with one's group in all respects except in their refusal to separate from still other groups!

to our shores was their all-consuming desire to worship in accord with what they conceived to be scriptural principle. But less widely appreciated is the fact that the Puritans, living a century after the first generation Reformers, represent that period of strict systematic theology which has been called the era of "Classical Protestant Orthodoxy." As pointed out earlier, in our introductory Orientation, the 17th century for Protestantism corresponded to the Roman Catholic 13th and 14th centuries: a time of assimilating, integrating, and organizing into a coherent whole the insights of the preceding period of innovation and newness. The 17th century systematized the insights of the Reformation and endeavored to apply them consistently to all areas of experience. The Puritans were thus active participants in the last great epoch of integrated Christian thought prior to the onset of the modern secular era; and it was this developed Protestant world-view that formed the first articulate layer of the American character.

The era of Classical Protestant Orthodoxy has been consistently maligned by secular historians as well as by most church historians and theologians since the Enlightenment. A. C. McGiffert, for example, in his influential *Protestant Thought before Kant*, pontificates, *inter alia*: "Compared with that of the Middle Ages, Protestant scholasticism was much more barren, and at the same time narrower and more oppressive.... The period, even from a theological point of view, was barren and dreary to the last degree. Of dogmatics there was plenty,... but it was a dogmatic of the narrowest type, without relation to the thought of the world at large, and without effect upon the religious and moral life of Christian people." I have devoted two works to refutations in depth of such scurrilous and unfounded attacks: both my *Chytraeus on Sacrifice* and my *Cross and Crucible* show by example how the theology of the epoch was an encyclopedic fulfillment of the Reformation —a veritable ideological equivalent of Bach's contemporaneous synthesis of the classical musical tradition— and had the most far-reaching and positive scientific, artistic, and social consequences. What is it that really bothers the critics of 17th-century theology? McGiffert speaks for most of them when he asserts that "the most original part of the theology of the day was the doctrine of the Bible"; by "original" he means "deviant," for he cannot cease but castigate the 17th-century theologians for their belief in verbally inspired, inerrant Scripture.

Our Puritan forebears did indeed hold to an entirely trustworthy Bible; but this was no innovation. It was, as the essays in my *God's Inerrant Word* plainly demonstrate, the very position of Luther and Calvin, and thus the belief the first-century Reformers held in common with the entire classical Christian tradition. No one can read the prolific theological works of the Puritan divines without finding in them consistent reiteration of the two cardinal principles of Reformation Orthodoxy: the "formal" principle, that *sola Scriptura*—Scripture alone —is to be the source of Christian doctrine, and the "material" principle, that *solus Christus*—Christ alone— is by His Gospel of free grace and the forgiveness of sins the way to eternal life. Belief in these cardinal truths is a weakness only if God's Word is a weakness!

Because of their biblical orthodoxy, the Puritan fathers had an uncompromising anthropology: they held, as the Bible does, to man's total depravity. For them man was utterly incapable of saving himself; in the words of Scripture, "every imagination of the thoughts of his heart was only evil continually." The inevitable consequence of such an anthropology was limited government under law. No sinful man, however honorable and upright he might appear to be, could be trusted to hold the reins of government in his unrestrained hands: constitutional limitations and legal checks and balances were an absolute necessity for survival. The Puritans had had enough experience with tyranny to see the practical application of the biblical picture of fallen man. John Winthrop wrote that "the people had long desired a body of laws, and thought their condition very unsafe, while so much power rested in the discretion of magistrates." Thus their "Body of Liberties" (1641), the first compilation of Massachusetts law, commenced with a paraphrase of the Magna Charta and contained a statement of the limitations applicable to judicial procedure; throughout the document "liberties" are defined in terms of appropriate restraints on the concentration of power. Declared John Cotton:

It is most wholsome for Magistrates and Officers in Church and Common-wealth, never to affect more liberty and authority than will do them good, and the People good; for what ever transcendant power is given, will certainly over-run those that give it, and those that receive it: There is a straine in a mans heart that will sometime or other runne out to excesse, unlesse the Lord restraine it, but it is not good to venture it: It is necessary, therefore, that all power that is on earth be limited.

But there was another, far less attractive, side to Puritan government. Though the need for limited government was recognized and though church polity, in its congregational opposition to episcopacy, had a democratic look to it, Puritan New England was anything but democratic. It was in fact an oligarchy in which the ruling party consisted of only ten percent of the populace. To vote or hold office in the Massachusetts Bay colony, one had to be a "freeman," and to be a freeman one had to be admitted to church membership—and membership required approval by the elders and the whole congregation with reference not only to doctrinal belief but also to conduct and to "the worke of grace upon his soule, or how God hath beene dealing with him about his conversion." The expulsion of dissidents such as Roger Williams is well known; evidently the Puritans (like the Israelis today who limit citizenship to Jews) did not consider the persecutions they suffered at others' hands a sufficient reason for being tolerant themselves. The legislation of morals reached frightening proportions among the Puritans. By 1648 they had extended the list of capital crimes to idolatry (in reference to the First Commandment), blasphemy, the cursing of a parent by a child above the age of sixteen (Ex. 21:17), and the offense of being a "rebellious son" (Deut. 21:20-21).

What was the source of these notions? They proceeded from a theocratic view of government. John Cotton stated the Puritan political philosophy in straightforward terms:

Democracy, I do not conceive that God ever did ordain as a fit government either for church or for commonwealth. If the people be governors, who shall be governed? As for monarchy and aristocracy they are both of them clearly approved and directed in Scripture, yet so as referreth the sovereignty to Himself and setteth up theocracy in both as the best form of government in the commonwealth as well as in the church.

And where did this theocratic viewpoint arise? Not so accidentally, the same fundamental approach to the state and the same moralistic life-style characterized Calvin's efforts in Geneva and Cromwell's Commonwealth in England. The peculiar emphases of Calvinist theology worked in all these situations to produce unfortunate political and social side effects.

Three particular differences in theological approach between the original Reformation position of Luther and the later Calvinist development are noteworthy. Consider them in tabular form:

	LUTHERANISM	CALVINISM
DOGMATICS—Starting point is:	Christ crucified	God's sovereign decrees in eternity
ECCLESIOLOGY—The marks of the true church are:	Gospel and sacraments	Gospel, sacraments, and church discipline
EXEGETICS—The Bible is conceived as:	OT, completed by NT	NT, prepared for by OT

Calvinism begins its theologizing with the sovereign God in eternity, whose divine decrees determine all that occurs; such an approach explains in large part the Puritan preference for an authoritarian, theocratic state. For Luther, this was a *theologia gloriae* (theology of glory) rather than a *theologia crucis* (theology of the cross), and had some of the same potential dangers as Roman Catholicism—in particular the danger of playing God here on earth. In its understanding of the church, Calvinism went beyond the definition in the Augsburg Confession, Art. VII ("The Church is the assembly of believers in which the Gospel is rightly taught and the Sacraments rightly administered"), to include an additional mark or identifying characteristic: church discipline. In some Calvinist churches (such as Presbyterian) this meant an obligatory form of church government; in others, such as the Puritan congregations, it meant an observation of conduct, morals, and attitudes that could easily reach the level of spiritual tyranny. Legislation of morals was also encouraged by Calvin's preference for the so-called Third Use of the Law (the Law as a sanctifying power in the life of the believer) over the Law's function "as a schoolmaster to bring us to Christ" (Luther's preferred use). But the most influential factor in creating a legalistic tone in Puritanism was doubtless the Calvinist stress on a single covenant in Scripture (contrast the Lutheran emphasis on the New Covenant as compared with the Old), which elevated the Old Testament to a position of great prominence in Puritan theology. Old Testament laws were indiscriminately applied to New Testament situations (cf. Earle's detailed work, *The Sabbath in Puritan New England*), and the Puritan at his worst seemed to display the characteristics of a Pharisee redivivus. In Luther's terms, there was neglect of "the proper distinction between Law and Gospel": Gospel was often obscured by Old Testament legalism.

Puritan-Calvinist preoccupation with the history of salvation in the Old Testament gave a special cast to the New England colonists' western dream. Like the 16th-century explorers that preceded them to the New World, to be sure, they saw the Western Hemisphere as a region of Edenic and Apocalyptic hope. Samuel Sewall (1652-1730), that distinguished Chief Justice of the Massachusetts Supreme Court whose public recantation of the part he played in the New England witch trials I have commented upon in an essay in my *Law above the Law*, wrote a work appropriately titled, *Phaenomena quaedam Apocalyptica ad aspectum Novi Orbis configurata; or, Some few Lines towards a description of the New Heaven as it makes to those who stand upon the New Earth;* there he gives common expression to the western dream: "May it not with more or equal strength be argued New Jerusalem is not the same with Jerusalem: but as Jerusalem was to the westward of Babylon, so New Jerusalem must be to the westward of Rome, to avoid disturbance in the order of mysteries."

However, the Puritans did not stop with the notion of a New Eden or even a New Jerusalem; consistent with their Old Testament interests, they went on to identify themselves with Israel, reading their own history as the story of a new Chosen People. Wrote Cotton Mather in his *Wonders of the Invisible World* (1693):

> The first Planters of these Colonies were a Chosen Generation of men, who were first so Pure, as to disrelish many things which they thought wanted Reformation elsewhere; and yet withal so peaceable, that they Embraced a Voluntary Exile in a Squalid, horrid, American Desart, rather than to Live in Contentions with their Brethren.... The New-Englanders are a People of God settled in

those, which were once the Devil's Territories; and
it may easily be supposed that the Devil was Exceedingly disturbed, when he perceived such a people here
accomplishing the Promise of old made unto our Blessed
Jesus, That He should have the Utmost parts of the Earth
for His possession. . . . The Devil thus Irritated, immediately try'd all sorts of Methods to overturn this poor
Plantation and so much of the Church, as was Fled
into this Wilderness.

Mather here employs the metaphor of an "enclosed
garden in the wilderness" which the Puritans so often
used to picture the situation of their New Israel: they
were like the conquerors of the Promised Land surrounded
by hostile Canaanites. As George H. Williams so well
pointed out in his treatment of *Wilderness and Paradise
in Christian Thought,* this theme connects the Puritan
dream with the motif of the Frontier which has had such
continuous influence in the formation of the American
character. The Puritans believed that God had raised
them up as a New Israel to clear a wilderness and trans-
form a frontier into the New Jerusalem.

Roland Bainton describes the Puritan vision in the
most attractive terms:

> They came cherishing a magnificent dream. Here
> unimpeded by bishops and archbishops they could erect
> a holy commonwealth, a divine society under "God as
> governor" and living in accord with His ordinances as
> delivered in His Holy Word. The great purpose of God
> once partially achieved in ancient Israel should at last
> reach consummation through a people chosen with no
> reference to blood or soil but solely because their hearts
> had been warmed and their lives refashioned by the grace
> of God in Christ.

On the deepest level, this was a genuinely Christian dream
—inherited from the Reformers' recovery of the scriptural
Gospel. But dangerous additives had already entered into
the substance of that dream and would eventually work
against the very Gospel ideals so cherished by the Puritan
fathers. The idea of a New Israel was capable of suggest-
ing New Revelation—a particularly lethal commodity as
the dawn of the modern secular age was breaking.

2

The Enlightenment Spirit

The primal layer of the American character was fully formed prior to the century of the "founding fathers." The explorers of the 15th and 16th centuries had applied the Renaissance dream of utopia to the Western world, and the 17th-century Puritan settlers had infused that dream with even more explicit biblical and theological content. The result was a scripturally informed concept of limited government, in recognition of man's sin and consequent need for Christ's saving Word. Well before the obtuseness of George III drove the colonies to independence, the American spirit had developed along lines established by biblical principle and Reformation theology. It cannot be too strongly emphasized that the colonial history of our nation took place during the last years of the "Classical-Christian era"—during the century of systematization and integration which brought that era to a close. With Revolutionary times we move into a very different atmosphere, for by the 1700's the onset of modern secularism is clearly in evidence.

From Theism to Deism

Eighteenth-century man was, like Renaissance man, conscious that he was living in an era of innovation and newness. Men of the 15th century had self-consciously coined the term "Middle Ages" to refer to what they regarded as a benighted interval separating their own time from the classical world; in 1784 the philosopher Kant wrote an essay significantly titled, "Beantwortung der Frage: Was Ist Aufklärung?" (In Answer to the Question: What Is the Enlightenment?). To this question one of the foremost modern students of the epoch, Peter Gay, succinctly replies: "The Enlightenment was a volatile mixture of classicism, impiety, and science; the philosophes, in a phrase, were modern pagans." It was this spirit of modern paganism which suffused the thought world of the century of American Independence.

To be sure, as in every historical period, there was diversity of viewpoint and diversity of life-style. Boorstin is correct, on one level, to depreciate the uniformitarian "logical construct" of the Enlightenment; in his *America and the Image of Europe,* he presents "the 18th-century mind as a miscellany and a museum vs. the logical construct of historians," arguing: "We somehow expect from 18th-century thinking a coherence which would have been possible only if the world had been created anew in the year 1700." Yet what we emphasized in our Orientation chapter concerning the possibility of identifying distinctive national characteristics applies equally well here: to recognize diversity is not to disprove underlying unity. In point of fact, a specific and identifiable philosophical viewpoint characterized the 18th century. In Peter Gay's felicitous phrase, the Enlightenment was "a single army with a single banner, with a large central corps, a right and left wing, daring scouts and lame stragglers."

That single banner was Deism: a philosophical religion setting itself against the Theistic belief of classical Christianity that God had intervened in His own created universe by giving a "special revelation" through the inspired Scriptures and in the latter days through His own Son. For the Deist, the "light of Nature" was enough to reveal the permanent standards of moral conduct; man was no fallen sinner in need of special divine guidance, much less a blood Redemption: he had outgrown such primitivism and was on the threshold of a new day of enlightened morality, freedom, and progress. Let us accompany Stromberg as he analyzes *Religious Liberalism in 18th-Century England* by "essaying a brief imaginative tour into the mind of a typical deist."

He had been impressed by Newton's discoveries—too impressed. This vast universe controlled by immutable laws, this wonderfully constructed machine, undoubtedly had a Maker. The deist was not an atheist. But would such a Being as headed this marvellous world-machine condescend to reveal himself to Moses, an obscure man of a benighted race on a petty planet? The

deist could not see the majesty of this, always hereto-
fore regarded as the greatest wonder; it was unworthy
of God. We meet here an aesthetic quarrel possibly at
the root of the whole matter: what had once seemed
infinitely pleasing and wonderful and inspiring now (to
some) began to seem infinitely ridiculous and de-
grading. The deist could not reconcile Newton's master
physicist with the Jehovah who had wrestled with Jacob—
and it must be admitted he had a point. This last, he
assumed, was all a tale made up by ignorant barbarians
and then imposed upon mankind by priests, known to
be a deceitful and mercenary class. This inference of a
conspiracy was perhaps not necessary, but it was plaus-
ible and indeed very nearly inevitable at a time when the
historical sense of a development in human affairs was
notably lacking. Perhaps the Judaic sort of religion was
necessary for the literal-minded mob, but no "philosopher" could believe it. God revealed himself to man,
no doubt—but was not Nature enough of a revelation?
Eagerly the physico-theologians had proved the existence
of God by pointing to his masterly works; the deists now
inquired why it was then necessary to go any farther.

Jesus, the alleged Messiah and self-styled Son of
God, seemed to the deist an excellent moralist, but not
a super-human agent. That he was the Son of God was
only another Hebraic myth. The excellent moral code
taught by Jesus was not a divine revelation, but could
be found in Nature, surely, if one searched. Just how
and where, the deist was never able to state clearly, but
he believed strongly in the idea nevertheless. The moral
rules, everywhere alike, could perhaps be found in universal reason, or perhaps in the heart of man, a divinely
implanted instinct. In any event they were discernible
independently of any special revelation. The proof of
this was that all men had arrived at a similar code of
morals, though theologies differed; and Europe was now
aware of the existence of other religions apparently
similar to but quite independent of Christianity. Christianity, had it not been corrupted by priests and metaphy-
sicians, would have agreed perfectly with this "natural
religion."

The Deistic philosophy seems almost impossible to
state in a persuasive way today; one finds any "imaginative tour into a typical Deist's mind" an exercise
in suspended disbelief more challenging than perhaps
the miraculous appeared to skeptic Hume. Twentieth-
century man is appalled by the anti-Semitic, racial over-
tones of the Deistic criticism of Old Testament Revelation
(cf. Arthur Hertzberg's *The French Enlightenment and*

the Jews), and the general naïveté of Deistic belief makes us wonder why the philosophes found little problems such as the Incarnation an affront to credulity! Today the only institutional remnant of Deism is Free Masonry, if we put aside some few Unitarian-Universalists who might wish to classify themselves in this camp.

To be sure, we have the inestimable benefit of hindsight—the global catastrophies of our century have given us a far more realistic insight into man's nature than Deism offered at its best—but we may still wonder why such a viewpoint captured stage center in the history of ideas for a century. Stromberg is quite correct in asserting that Deistic ideas were "taken up and exploited by a very few men, who succeeded in making a noise out of all proportion to their numbers and even their talents. It seems evident that this was more because of Christianity's weakness than because of deism's strength." What weakness? In particular, I would suggest, the tendency of the church in the Old World to identify with caste and privilege instead of actively striving for the amelioration of the lot of the downtrodden. The identification of the church with the nobility in France during the closing years of the Old Régime was clearly responsible for much of the success Deism achieved through its alignment with the Revolution of 1789.

The success of Deism was due neither to profundity (which it lacked) nor to effective intellectual criticism of historic Christianity (contemporary refutations of Paine, Voltaire, Hume, *et al.* were far more trenchant than these skeptical views required). Deistic success was essentially nonrational, a victory by default. The Age of Reason came to dominance irrationally—but its success should teach Christian believers the all-important lesson that the truth of the Gospel will be ignored and the most specious arguments against it will be accepted if Christianity does not live up to its profession.

Deism and the Founding Fathers

In certain circles at the far right of the religious spectrum it is customary to wax eloquent on the "Bible religion of our Founding Fathers." We are implored to "return to the simple Gospel that made our Founding Fathers great," etc. Unhappily, though we might fervently wish that these sentiments were accurate, the fact is that they express a pure mythology. The idea of believing Christian Founding Fathers is very largely a pious myth, and if we want to arrive at a balanced and mature understanding of the relation between scriptural religion and our national heritage, we must rigorously carry out a process of de-mythologization at this point. To that end, we shall take a brief but hard look at the religious convictions of Tom Paine, Thomas Jefferson, George Washington, and Ben Franklin.

Historian John Anthony Scott expresses a near-universal judgment when he calls Thomas Paine "one of the most brilliant among many fine American revolutionary propagandists." Though not an original thinker, Paine was such an incisive publicist that his pamphlet *Common Sense,* which appeared in early January, 1776, can be regarded as the *literary* musket shot heard round the world. In *Common Sense* and in the booklets that followed it (*The American Crisis* series), he introduced such watchwords of the Revolution as " 'Tis time to part," "The sun never shined on a cause of greater worth," "These are the times that try men's souls"; his proclamation of the Western utopian dream is evidenced by his oft-quoted lines: "Europe regards [Freedom] like a stranger, and England hath given her warning to depart. O! receive the fugitive, and prepare in time an asylum for mankind." At the same time, he was, as Thomas A. Bailey reminds us, "dirty, slothful, boorish, opinionated, and unduly addicted to alcohol."

Tom Paine's theology (more precisely, "deology," for he was a thoroughgoing Deist) is set forth in his influential *Age of Reason,* the entire second part of which consists of an attempt to demonstrate the existence of errors, contradictions, immoralities, and absurdities in the Bible. For Paine, "special revelation" (Scripture) is a pretense; the Book of Nature replaces the Book of Scripture in giving us a true picture of God and our religio-moral duties. He writes:

> Soon after I had published the pamphlet *Common Sense,* in America, I saw the exceeding probability that a revolution in the system of government would be followed by a revolution in the system of religion. The adulterous connection of church and state, wherever it had taken place, whether Jewish, Christian, or Turkish, had so effectually prohibited by pains and penalties, every discussion upon established creeds, and upon

first principles of religion, that until the system of government should be changed, those subjects could not be brought fairly and openly before the world; but that whenever this should be done, a revolution in the system of religion would follow. Human inventions and priestcraft would be detected; and man would return to the pure, unmixed and unadulterated belief of one God, and no more.

Every national church or religion has established itself by pretending some special mission from God, communicated to certain individuals. The Jews have their Moses; the Christians their Jesus Christ, their apostles and saints; and the Turks their Mahomet, as if the way to God was not open to every man alike.

. . . .

Having now extended the subject to a greater length than I first intended, I shall bring it to a close by abstracting a summary from the whole.

First—That the idea or belief of a word of God existing in print, or in writing, or in speech, is inconsistent in itself for reasons already assigned. These reasons, among many others, are the want of a universal language; the mutability of language; the errors to which translations are subject; the possibility of totally suppressing such a word; the probability of altering it, or of fabricating the whole, and imposing it upon the world.

Secondly—That the Creation we behold is the real and ever-existing word of God, in which we cannot be deceived. It proclaims his power, it demonstrates his wisdom, it manifests his goodness and beneficence.

Thirdly—That the moral duty of man consists in imitating the moral goodness and beneficence of God, manifested in the creation toward all his creatures. That seeing, as we daily do, the goodness of God to all men, it is an example calling upon all men to practise the same toward each other; and, consequently, that everything of persecution and revenge between man and man, and everything of cruelty to animals, is a violation of moral duty.

I trouble not myself about the manner of future existence. I content myself with believing, even to positive conviction, that the Power that gave me existence is able to continue it, in any form and manner he pleases, either with or without this body; and it appears more probable to me that I shall continue to exist hereafter, than that I should have had existence, as I now have, before that existence began.

It is certain that, in one point, all the nations of the

earth and all religions agree—all believe in a God; the things in which they disagree, are the redundancies annexed to that belief; and, therefore, if ever a universal religion should prevail, it will not be by believing anything new, but in getting rid of redundancies, and believing as man believed at first. Adam, if ever there were such a man, was created a Deist; but in the meantime, let every man follow, as he has a right to do, the religion and the worship he prefers.

Though he held American citizenship, Paine preferred to reside abroad, so his status among the Founding Fathers has been denied by some who find his religious beliefs offensive. But Thomas Jefferson, the author of our Declaration of Independence and our third President, held to a Deism virtually indistinguishable from Paine's. The chief difference lay in Jefferson's high regard for Jesus—but this did not extend beyond an appreciation for Jesus as an ideal man and the fountainhead of moral wisdom. Thus Jefferson produced his famous *Jefferson Bible,* consisting of a pastiche of the Master's ethical teachings and a rigid exclusion of everything miraculous. Commenting on the book, he wrote to Adams in 1813: "I have performed this operation for my own use, by cutting verse by verse out of the printed book [the Bible], and arranging the matter which is evidently his [Jesus'] and which is as easily distinguished as diamonds in a dunghill." Jefferson had all the confidence of a 20th-century demythologizer of the Bible—a confidence which presumptively kept him from seeing who Jesus really was. Just as Bultmann's Jesus is created in the mirror-image of Heideggerian Existentialism, so Jefferson's Jesus turns out to be the reflection of Enlightenment Deism.

In his later years Jefferson had much contact with the newly formed Unitarians, whose beliefs ranged from Priestley's Socinian anti-Trinitarianism to the more radical forms of Deism; in a letter to Dr. Benjamin Waterhouse in 1822 he wrote: "I trust that there is not a young man now living in the United States who will not die an Unitarian." The general secularity of Jefferson's life is evident from such sketches as Julian Boyd's *Spirit of Christmas at Monticello;* it hardly seems feasible that but a generation separates the humanistic Jeffersonian Christmas from the Christocentric Noëls of Bach's *Christmas Oratorio.* The tragedy of Jefferson's self-confident anthropocentrism—so characteristic of the modern secular era and a harbinger of greater agonies to come—has been detailed in Sheehan's *Seeds of Extinction: Jeffersonian Philanthropy and the American Indian:* by manipulating the Indians' environment, the Jeffersonians confidently expected to turn the Indians into yeoman farmers (again: mirror-images of themselves); the result was failure for the white man and misery for the Indian. Law professor John T. Noonan has recently shown how Jefferson and his legal mentor George Wythe aided in perpetuating a forensic vocabulary that classed blacks as transferable property, thereby permitting whites to carry on slavery while "democratically" supporting human freedom and dignity in the founding documents of the nation. Secular depreciation of biblical revelation leads inevitably to man's confident imposition of non-revelational values on his weaker brethren.*

George Washington did not espouse the radical views of many of his contemporaries, and his formal membership in the Episcopal Church is well known. However, the Anglican tradition, unlike Lutheranism and Calvinism, has never placed much stress on *quia* subscription to its confessions (the confessions are to be accepted *because* they conform to the Word of God); the policy of "comprehension," extending back at least to the Elizabethan settlement, has encouraged diversity among Anglicans on the basis of *quatenus* doctrinal subscription (confessions are held to *insofar as* they reflect revelational truth). Thus 20th-century Anglicanism can display both a C. S. Lewis and a Bishop Robinson, and 18th-century American Episcopalians were hardly orthodox Christians by virtue of their church membership.

Washington's own convictions are revealed by his enthusiastic connection with the Freemasons—a connection to which the architecturally monstrous, but appropriately Babel-like George Washington Masonic National Memorial in Alexandria, Virginia, bears witness. There one can see the chair in which Washington presided as Master of the Alexandria Lodge in 1788 and 1789, and also a portrait of our first President in Masonic regalia, commissioned by the Lodge six years before his death. Freemasonry, originating not in the mysteries of Solomon's Temple but in the rationalism of early modern times,

---

*See Appendix A: "From Enlightenment to Extermination."

George Washington in Masonic Regalia

(William Williams' 1793 Portrait from life; original in the George Washington Masonic National Memorial, Alexandria, Virginia)

is at root Deistic; indeed, the movement may be regarded as a liturgical Deism. It holds to a unitary Supreme Being, the so-called Great Architect of the Universe, denies Christ's unique saviorship and atonement, and reduces religion to a moralistic observance of allegedly common ethical principles. In my *Principalities and Powers: The World of the Occult,* I have quoted a statement of faith by one of Masonry's classic spokesmen:

> Freemasonry ... transcends the bounds of Christian and Western civilization; it includes the Moslem, the Hindoo, the Buddhist, and the Jew. Without waiting for their respective faiths to come together in a visible federation or unity, they can all meet together in their own and in each other's Lodges throughout the world and pray and worship together to the same one-and-only indivisible God whom all religions acknowledge and venerate.

Interestingly enough, Tom Paine wrote an essay on the "Origin of Freemasonry" (1805; first published in 1818) in which he argued that the Masonry derived from the sun-worship of the ancient Druids and that its secrecy is the result of (to be sure!) Christian persecution and priestcraft. Paine's foray into Druidical studies is no more impressive than Jefferson's effort at New Testament form-criticism, but it does make plain that our Founding Fathers were aware of Masonry's unorthodox system of belief.

Benjamin Franklin entertained strong Deistic convictions as a young man and—as far as we know—in spite of the later influence of evangelist George Whitefield on him, never embraced orthodox Christianity. On the basis of Franklin's autobiography Stromberg observes that "he came to think that his youthful deism, 'tho' it might be true, was not very useful,' and thereafter he encouraged a Christianity he clearly felt to be very useful though it might not be true." Here we see a characteristic of the Concentric American that will become much more pronounced in the century to follow—the 19th century—the century of "Progress": a pragmatic concern for what "works," regardless of issues of ultimate truth. Franklin's Deistic creed is worth transcribing, since its omissions betray the glaring lacunae in that viewpoint (no mention whatever of sin, redemption, or Christ):

That there is one God, who made all things. That he

governs the world by his providence. That he ought to be worshipped by adoration, prayer, and thanksgiving. But that the most acceptable service of God is doing good to man.

Whitefield clearly saw that Franklin's beliefs fell short of biblical Christianity at the central point of the Gospel. In one of his letters to Franklin he made the following exemplary witness:

> I find that you grow more and more famous in the learned world. As you have made a pretty considerable progress in the mysteries of electricity, I would now humbly recommend to your diligent unprejudiced pursuit and study the mystery of the new birth. It is a most important, interesting study, and when mastered, will richly answer and repay you for all your pains. One hath solemnly declared that without it "we cannot enter the kingdom of heaven." You will excuse the freedom. I must have something of Christ in all my letters. I am a yet willing pilgrim for His Great Name's sake, and I trust a blessing attends my poor feeble labours.

The contrast between this letter and the beliefs and lifestyle of the Founding Fathers we have discussed could not be more pronounced. Only extreme naïveté or invincible ignorance can claim that the chief midwives at our nation's official birth were representatives of the classical Christian tradition.

The American Revolution: Christian in Spite of Itself

The single most paradoxical aspect of American history is that though the country's Founding Fathers were Deists and not Christians, the nation got off to a Christian start nonetheless. Both the American Revolution and the founding Documents arising from it turned out to be—often in spite of the motives of their creators—fully compatible with historic Christian faith. In this sense our national origins might be said to exemplify the fundamental principle of divine economy that men are saved by God's free grace and not by their own works—"lest any man should boast"!

True enough, as Staughton Lynd (*Intellectual Origins of American Radicalism*) and others with radical axes to grind maintain, the Deists were the ones who in particular strove for revolution, having confidence in their own ability to define the eternal moral law and lacking

any restraint from biblical revelation. Moreover, studies
of the Loyalists by Mary Beth Norton and other special-
ists have emphasized the extent to which the Christians
among them relied upon Romans 13: the believer's duty
to be subject to the governmental powers under which
he lives. Indeed, in the Federalist reaction that occurred
some years after the Revolution, President Timothy
Dwight of Yale—one of the great names in evangelical
Christianity during Revolutionary times—could say that
the Revolution had "unhinged the principles, the morality,
and the religion of the country more than could have
been done by a peace of forty years."

But the support of orthodox Christians for separation
from the Mother Country was at least as powerful as
opposition to it. One thinks at once of Revolutionary general John Peter Muhlenberg (eldest son of pastor Henry
Melchior Muhlenberg, the "patriarch of the Lutheran
church in America"), who saved the American forces
from annihilation at the Brandywine; or of John Witherspoon, distinguished Presbyterian clergyman and signer
of the Declaration of Independence. Particularly among
Calvinists, who looked back with approval on the behead-
ing of Charles I and the era of the Commonwealth, revolution was justified when a sovereign so exceeded his legitimate powers that he could be said to have abrogated
his proper sovereignty; being no longer sovereign except
in name, he could be toppled from his throne without
violating Romans 13. This viewpoint harks back at least
to Thomas Aquinas' definition of human law in the
Summa: law is "nothing else than an ordinance of reason
for the common good, made by him who has care of
the community, and promulgated"; by such a definition,
laws that are not reasonable or for the common good
can be regarded as no laws at all and disregarded or
opposed by revolutionary action without falling into sin.

But such an approach oversimplifies the issues and
is highly dangerous theologically. Who is to determine
what laws are *really* for the common good or are *truly*
reasonable, or whether a sovereign has exceeded his
powers to such a degree that he can be opposed by revolution without violating the Apostolic command to sub-
jection? In a sinful world where untainted laws, princes,
and governments never put in an appearance, such a
political philosophy theoretically allows Romans 13 to be
deemed inapplicable in any given case—and thus saps
it of all meaning!

The proper theological answer to this dilemma of maintaining authority yet opposing tyranny comes with recognition of the lesser-of-evils principle in Christian ethics. Over against Aquinas (whose casuistic, hierarchial ethic is at opposite poles to central Reformation teaching), Romans 13 applies universally, for it is an unqualified assertion: it is always wrong to oppose constituted authority, for God himself has established the ordered structures of life to prevent us as sinful men from anarchically destroying ourselves. Even the worst laws and rulers are better than none, and they too fall within the purview of Romans 13. However, another fundamental scriptural teaching has to be taken into account: the absolute necessity of freedom of choice in order for genuine acceptance of Christ to occur (John 7:17). Curtailment of freedom of choice may destroy effective Gospel preachment, and this may become a greater evil than the (admitted) evil of revolution against constituted authority. The agonies of such a situation for believers are tremendous, and not every Christian will weigh the pros and the cons identically: some will agonizingly opt for authority, while recognizing that they sin by aiding and abetting tyranny of conscience; others will opt for revolution, aware that they are perhaps unleashing the demons of anarchy on an already sin-impregnated earth. Werner Elert, in his *Christian Ethos*, has well described the *Angst* experienced by German Christians who faced this choice in the early years of the Hitler régime.

Our Christian forebears in the Revolutionary era had this same agony of decision before them. Some—the Loyalists—believed that the limitations of freedom imposed first by George III and later by the English Parliament were not sufficient to warrant revolution. But, as Norton has emphasized, even they generally admitted (thereby incidentally showing themselves to be better Whigs than Tories!) that "an oppressive use of political power gave the injured populace a right to seek redress of its grievances." For the Loyalists, the Mother Country had not yet so oppressively abridged colonial freedoms that revolution was the lesser of evils; but in principle such a point could be reached. Christian believers on the side of independence were convinced that the point of tyrannous oppression of conscience had already arrived and that to revolt was therefore less blameworthy than to permit the continuing abridgment of freedom. They viewed their action, in any case, not as an innovative overthrow of the shackles of the past or a departure from established values, but as a conservative restoration of the true liberties of Englishmen guaranteed by the Magna Charta and grounded in Holy Writ; as Edmund Burke asserted, theirs was "a Revolution not made, but prevented," in the sense that their action preserved historic freedoms which were in danger of being lost in the Mother Country.

Were the Revolutionaries correct and the Loyalists wrong? To the casual observer, it may appear very doubtful that in an age of increasing Parliamentarianism George III really offered a serious threat to English liberties, and taxation without representation seems a considerable distance from that abridgment of free decision-making which would imperil the Gospel. Likewise, the belief of many colonial pastors that the potential establishment of the bishopric in America would unify church and state so as to eliminate free expression religiously and politically (cf. Carl Bridenbaugh's *Mitre and Sceptre*) perhaps appears to be little more than a typical example of escalation-theory among the clergy. However, we of the 20th century have—or should have—a perspective on totalitarianism which the 18th century itself lacked, and we can now see how fragile a flower liberty is and how readily its abridgment in one respect can lead to its destruction in general. The fact that England did retain her liberties and came eventually to provide her Empire with home rule is no proof that the American Revolution was unnecessary or scripturally indefensible: a better case can be made for the proposition that it was the very loss of her American colonies that helped to bring the Mother Country to her senses. Professor Charles Andrews' judgment is a balanced one:

> The American Revolution, like nearly all revolutions in history, was an uprising not against a king and his ministers, but against a system and a state of mind. Nor was the system the work of George III, Hillsborough, Townshend, or Lord North, for they were its products not its creators. . . . They did not see that just as an original stock transplanted to a new soil perpetuates the best qualities of the old but develops faster than the mother plant, so the colonies in America were far more advanced, politically, socially, and morally, than the mother country and could not longer be held in leading strings. Having diagnosed the case wrongly, they ap-

plied the wrong remedy, that of coercion, which not only did not cement more closely the colonial relationship but destroyed it altogether. The problem was not one of mercantile subordination or of imperial authority, but concerned the very constitution of the British empire; and such constitutional concessions as would have satisfied the demands of the colonists, these British statesmen could not make, because they were barred by the mental limitations of their own time and class. Only the threatened collapse of the entire colonial system in the thirties of the next century, the rise of a group of young enthusiasts who refused to believe that matured dependencies were necessarily foreordained to revolt, and a ten years' war with the stubborn bureaucracy of Downing Street finally convinced the British official mind that colonies might be entrusted with responsible self-government and still be retained as parts of the empire.

In rebelling against a "system and a state of mind," the American revolutionists, whatever the theoretical justification they personally offered for their action and however unbiblical the beliefs of some of them were, did in fact choose to preserve the scriptural ideal of liberty and became the chief torchbearers of that ideal in the modern world. As is so often the case in a fallen creation, to opt for one teaching of Scripture is to run afoul of another, and our revolutionary forefathers can well be faulted for the ease with which they glossed over the obligations of Romans 13 in choosing the "liberty wherewith Christ hath made us free." But their dilemma is the dilemma of every man in a fallen world, and—looking back on their decision from a 200-year vantage point—it is difficult to believe that they erred in creating a nation dedicated to the principle of individual freedom, where "decisions for Christ" could occur without fear or favor.

The Founding Documents:
Scriptural in Spite of Themselves

We have already emphasized the hold that Deism exercised over the minds of leading Founding Fathers, Jefferson being a particularly unfortunate example. Does it not follow that such founding documents of our nation as the Declaration of Independence—our very birth certificate—will therefore express an essentially non-Christian ideology?

Such a judgment is set out in particularly bald terms

by strict Calvinist C. Gregg Singer in his *Theological Interpretation of American History*. Singer defends the Puritan theocracy, contrasting it with the 18th-century democracy of the Founding Fathers which he regards as utterly unscriptural. In his view, democracy and the social contract theory of the 18th century are but reflections of the autonomous view of man which becomes dominant with the rise of secularism and leads mankind down the road to hell—a path clearly marked in our day by the welfare state and the United Nations! A sampling from Singer's book is perhaps in order, to indicate that our summary of his viewpoint is no exaggeration:

> The whole conception of government that would later be proclaimed by John Locke and others, which placed the sovereignty in the hands of the people and which found the origin of government in a human compact was utterly unknown to the Puritans. They did not believe in a government by the people, but they did believe in government for the people.... American history is characterized, in its political aspects, by a continuing conflict between the Puritan political philosophy on the one hand, and the rise of a democratic conception of the state and human liberty which has emanated from non-biblical sources. The insistence that God is truly sovereign and that his sovereignty must be recognized in the political affairs of mankind is an anathema to those modern schools of thought which seek to enthrone man as a sovereign in his own right.
>
> . . . .
>
> The Scriptures clearly teach that human government is of divine ordination and does not have its origin in any social compact or contract, as Hobbes and Locke taught, nor was it created by man himself to meet the needs of his society. Rather does Christian theism insist that government was ordained of God for man and that its just powers come from him and not from man. Government is not ordained primarily to defend human liberty, but to insure that kind of society necessary for man to carry out those duties which he owes to God alone. Thus, government has clearly defined powers and operates in a clearly defined sphere. The basic error of liberalism at this point has been its insistence that human government is a social institution, responsible to those men who created it and is primarily concerned with the preservation of human rights as they were defined by Jefferson and others of that day. This error is very popular among Christian people as well as the nation at large and it has

been productive of great error for it has allowed the forces of political liberalism to extend the operations of government into those spheres where it has no right to be. . . . When human government enters into the field of labor relations, education, mental and physical health, agriculture, housing, and those many other areas of legislation so characteristic of the federal government today, it leaves its proper functions.

Singer's position is really the political application of the Calvinist presuppositionalism maintained by theologian Cornelius Van Til and philosopher Gordon Clark—positions which I have criticized in detail in my contributions to the Festschriften for them issued by Presbyterian and Reformed Publishing House. For all of these thinkers, the Calvinist preoccupation with sovereignty leads to a general condemnation of human freewill and autonomy, and thus to a denial of genuine apologetic common ground on which the believer can demonstrate to the unbeliever the veracity and existential pertinence of the Christian message. Thus in turning to the political sphere Singer can hardly be sympathetic to the struggle for freedom of decision which was at the very heart of the American revolutionary ideal. Such a striving for liberty can only be interpreted as autonomous man shaking his Promethean fist at heaven's sovereign absolutes. Singer is entirely unappreciative of the apologetic common ground which the founding documents offer to Christians who would help the secular American to understand the true nature of his national heritage.

The trouble with Calvinist theocracy—as with presuppositionalism, for that matter—is that it leaves unanswered the question as to who makes the decisions. By definition, the presuppositionalist will not prove his starting-point; he can only prevail if he can shout louder than the man with an alternative presuppositional point-of-departure. Likewise with theocracy—for the problem is to decide on *whose* theocracy. "The Bible's, to be sure," comes the answer; but as Puritan New England so well demonstrated, this answer begs the question, for disputes arose almost immediately as to which interpreters should have the right to determine the application of biblical teaching to community organization. The Bible contains innumerable moral laws; which are to be legislated in the human community? Capital punishment for blasphemy and for being a "rebellious son"? Moreover, in a sinful world the state will necessarily consist not only of "sanctified" Christian believers but also of the unregenerate and backsliders. Even assuming that the true believers can be identified with political accuracy, will those in the out-group tolerate a Puritan oligarchy in which 10% of the populace imposes its standards on them? Government which is *for* the people but not *by* the people always requires some caste to declare what is "truly" for the people (whether they like it or not)—and the arguments of the Puritans in this regard, as well as the practical effects of their illiberal policies, have the most uncomfortable parallels with modern autocracy in general, up to and not excluding George Orwell's projections in *1984*. Plato had no success locating satisfactory philosopher-kings in Syracuse or among 4th-century B.C. Athenians; they are equally hard to find among Christians. Only presumptiveness or naïveté leads to the conclusion that "our" Christian position is somehow immune from the sin or error that corrupts other aristocracies.

We thus begin to see that in spite of the Deistic flavor of terminology in our founding documents, these documents actually convey a view of government which gives expression to some of the most basic biblical principles. When Jefferson wrote, "We hold these Truths to be self-evident, that all Men are created equal, that they are endowed by their Creator with certain unalienable Rights," he was thinking of the supposed natural goodness of man, with Deistic obliviousness to man's wretched fallen state; but the guarantee of equality before the law voiced by the Declaration is precisely what sinful men need for political survival in a world which even atheistic social-contract theorist Hobbes recognized to be "nasty and brutish." As Carl Becker has so thoroughly demonstrated in his classic work on the Declaration, the social-compact philosophy which most influenced Jefferson was neither that of Hobbes nor even that of Enlightenment social-theorist Rousseau, but was rather the political theory of Christian philosopher John Locke—whose empirical defense of Christian faith (*The Reasonableness of Christianity*) remains an apologetic classic. (Is Locke's evidential approach to the defense of the faith another reason why presuppositionalist Singer wants to be rid of him?)

Government by agreement or compact is hardly unbiblical, particularly when vital biblically based rights are thereby held inalienable. The specification of inalienable rights prevents a Hobbesian relegation of one's freedoms to a sovereign power who, in exchange for protecting the citizens, can subject them to totalitarian control. Singer commits the presbyterian error of finding a single ideal form of government (presbytery in the church, theocracy in the state) taught in the Bible; but though Scripture declares Government (i.e., Order) to be God-given, it does not baptize any single form of it. Even democracy is valuable not because Scripture elevates it above other forms of the state but because it maximizes the biblical ideal of freedom, so essential for Gospel decision-making. Singer, in other words, confuses government in general (which is indeed created by God alone as one of the *Schöpfungsordnungen*—one of the Orders of Creation—necessary to human survival in a sinful world) with particular governmental types (which certainly can be chosen by compact, as long as scripturally established fundamental human rights are not thereby alienated).

As a matter of fact—and Singer himself must admit it—17th-century Christian principles of limited government were directly incorporated into our Constitution, providing appropriate checks and balances on human sinfulness. Indeed, the eminent constitutional scholar Edward Corwin has documented the solid impact of the concept of "higher" or revelational law, as embodied in Christianity from its earliest history, on the making of the American Constitution (*The "Higher Law" Background of American Constitutional Law*).

How could a government incorporating fundamental Christian insights have arisen in the ideological milieu of Deism? Do we have an application of Joseph's words to his brothers: "Ye thought evil against me, but God meant it unto good"? Doubtless, for, as Luther stressed, the divine Dramatist is always working behind the scenes of history. But a concrete factor, already suggested, must be taken into account, namely, the continuing presence of orthodox Christians whose ideas influenced the general climate of opinion even after the rise of the modern secular era. The century of American national origins was not only the time of Jefferson and Franklin but also the epoch of Bible-believers Patrick Henry, Alexander Hamilton, Jonathan Edwards, and Noah Webster—to say nothing of Muhlenberg, Witherspoon, Whitefield, and Dwight. An examination of the surviving book collection of influential colonial clergyman Wilhelm Christoph Berkenmeyer (1686-1751), for which I first provided full bibliographic description, offers the most specific proof that the orthodox theology of the classical Christian era was still being proclaimed in depth on the American scene in the years when our nation was moving toward independence.*

Even de Tocqueville, whose own views placed him squarely in the stream of the philosophes, observed as late as 1831 that "American morals are, I think, the most chaste that exist in any nation" and attributed this in large part to the fact that "religion still holds great sway over their souls. They have even retained some of the traditions of the strictest religious sects." † A striking illustration of the accuracy of de Tocqueville's observation is provided by the school texts of the period: Clifton Johnson's study of early American school books shows how thoroughly biblical they were, not only in Puritan times but well into the 19th century. Hazen, in his examination of *Contemporary American Opinion of the French Revolution,* effectively demonstrated that one of the major factors in growing American opposition to the French Revolution—even on the part of those who had been leading supporters of American independence—was revulsion at the unorthodox religious views of the French revolutionaries. Patrick Henry, for example, in viewing the French Revolution, spoke of Deism as "but another name for vice and depravity" and John Adams wrote in 1790 that he knew not "what to make of a republic of thirty million atheists." The sentiments are a bit strong, but their very vehemence shows that powerful and influential voices for orthodox Christianity could still be heard in America in the Revolutionary years.

Moreover—and it is a point of such consequence that

---

*See Appendix C.

† The morals of the Deists and those sympathetic to them were a different matter entirely. School texts in American history courses carefully omit any mention of Benjamin Franklin's scatological and erotic writings (such as his essay on the merits of seducing older women). There is factual basis for the waggish comment that George Washington was father of our country in more ways than one.

it deserves detailed treatment later—Deism served unwittingly as a vehicle to carry biblical truth into our founding documents. Not full biblical truth, to be sure, and not even the Gospel. But the moral ideals of Deism, such as man's endowment by his Creator with certain unalienable rights, derived from biblical revelation itself. The Deist convinced himself that he had succeeded in discovering these ideals by "reading the Book of Nature," and that the Book of Scripture was an erroneous collection of primitive beliefs foisted on mankind by priestcraft; but in fact, had there been no Bible, the Deist would never have been able to set forth his morality with anything approaching confidence or clarity. The American Deist lived precariously on inherited capital; but he thereby passed on biblical morality and a scriptural awareness of man's limitations to subsequent generations of his countrymen.

This is hardly to say, however, that mainline 18th-century thought recognized its dependence on historic Christianity. A new era had dawned—the era of Enlightenment—and men believed that human potentiality could now be realized to the fullest. The American dream of utopia was divested of its biblical framework—no longer could Eden or Israel or the New Earth be taken literally —and the ideal was recast in anthropocentric terms. Thus Freneau, a Jeffersonian poet who rejected biblical orthodoxy, metaphorically employed scriptural conceits to predict that in America "no traces shall remain of tyranny / And laws and patterns for the world beside / Be here enacted first." Jefferson himself wrote in 1824 that the American government was "destined to be the primitive and precious model of what is to change the condition of man over the globe." When both Jefferson and Adams died on July 4, 1826—exactly fifty years to the day after their signing of the Declaration of Independence—this was widely held to be a portent of the divine destiny inherent in the American nation. Thus the utopian dreams of Renaissance explorers and Puritan settlers were not destroyed by the new secularism; they were taken up, transformed, transmuted so as to reflect the humanistic self-confidence of the modern secular era.

It has been argued by H. Shelton Smith and others that of far more practical influence than either Deism or biblical orthodoxy on the formation of the late 18th-century mind was the religious liberalism represented by Jonathan Mayhew, Charles Chauncy, William Emerson (father of Ralph Waldo Emerson) and other Boston clergymen reacting against extreme Calvinism. Mayhew, as pastor of Boston's West Church, delivered a "Discourse" on the 100th anniversary of the execution of Charles I which John Adams termed "the opening gun of the Revolution." These liberals rejected the obvious extremes of Deism (such as its general denial of biblical inspiration), but, like 4th-century heretic Arius, would not affirm the full deity of Christ. By toning down the most unpopular features of Deism, they were able to make its essential humanism more palatable. Like the "moderate" religionists of our own day, they served as conduits through which the essence of more radical views passed into the general climate of opinion. Christ's preeminence was replaced by man's potentiality, and the doors were thrown open for the evolution of a "civil religion": the belief that American values are themselves, by definition, divine values, and that the true God is the God identified with our national destiny. On the eve of the 19th century the Concentric American had succeeded in laminating future-directed self-confidence onto his utopian hopes and biblical expectations; time would tell whether he was building on rock or sand.

3

Progressivistic Mirage

To Western man in general and to the American citizen in particular the 19th century appeared to be the fulfillment of all the promises of the Enlightenment. Science, technology, politics, economics: all pointed to a millennium of human accomplishment. On the American continent the agonies of the Civil War interrupted for less than a lustrum what proved to be an inexorable conquest of the entire vast territory from Atlantic to Pacific. To the utopian dream of America as the New Eden, humanistically reorientated in the 18th century so as to focus attention on man's ability rather than on God's design, was now added the seemingly axiomatic conviction that perfection was just around the corner.

The Train That Laid Its Own Track

In his epochal novel *The Siege of Krishnapur*, J. G. Farrell uses the Great Exhibition of 1851 as the archetypal representation of the 19th-century mind. Only the hideous realities of the Indian Mutiny are capable of convincing the novel's leading characters that Western technological progress, as worshipped at the Exhibition, is by no means an invincible force for good or a self-evident answer to the needs of the world. But Farrell's analysis benefits from a century of hindsight; very few 19th-century thinkers could look critically on the progressive ideal of their time, much less see the irony in its symbols.

The aim of the Great Exhibition, for which the vast Crystal Palace was built in London to house the scientific and cultural triumphs of 19th-century man, was grandiosely stated in the *Edinburgh Review*'s commentary on the Official Catalogue of the Exhibition: "to seize the living scroll of human progress, inscribed with every successive conquest of man's intellect." Prince Albert, who more than any other single person was responsible for bringing the Exhibition to practical realization, made a similar declaration in his Mansion House speech of March 21, 1850:

> Nobody who has paid any attention to the peculiar features of our present era will doubt for a moment that we are living at a period of most wonderful transition, which tends rapidly to accomplish that great end to which indeed all history points—*the realisation of the unity of mankind.* ... The distances which separated the different nations and parts of the globe are rapidly vanishing before the achievements of modern invention, and we can traverse them with incredible ease; the languages of all nations are known, and their acquirements placed within the reach of everybody; thought is communicated with the rapidity, and even by the power, of lightning. On the other hand, the *great principle of division of labour,* which may be called the moving power of civilisation, is being extended to all branches of science, industry, and art. ... Gentlemen, the Exhibition of 1851 is to give us a true test and a living picture of the point of development at which the whole of mankind has arrived in this great task, and a new starting-point from which all nations will be able to direct their further exertions.

As for the specific content of the Exhibition and its influence on those who saw it, one can do no better than to quote Farrell's semi-fictional Collector (Chief Administrator) Hopkins at Krishnapur—prior to the Indian Mutiny that crushed forever his naïve confidence in human progress:

> Every invention, however great, however small, is a humble emulation of the greatest invention of all, the Universe. Let me just quote at random from this catalogue of the Exhibition to which the Padre referred a moment ago, that Exhibition which I beg you to consider as a collective prayer of all the civilized nations. Let me see, Number 382: Instrument to teach the blind to write. Model of an aerial machine and of a navigable balloon. A fire annihilator by R. Weare of Plumstead Common. A domestic telegraph requiring only one bell for any number of rooms. An expanding pianoforte for yachts etc. Artificial teeth carved in hippopotamus ivory

The dispersion of the works of all nations from the Great Exhibition 1851.   Etching by Cruikshank.

by Sinclair and Hockley of Soho. A universal drill for removing decay from teeth. A jaw-lever for keeping animals' mouths open. Improved double truss for hernia, invented by a labouring man. There seems to be no end to the ingenuity of mankind and I could continue indefinitely quoting examples of it. But I ask you only to consider these humble artefacts of man's God-given ability to observe and calculate as minute steps in the progress of mankind towards union with that Supreme Being in whom all knowledge is, and ever shall be.

. . . .

I believe that we are all part of a society which by its communal efforts of faith and reason is gradually raising itself to a higher state. There are rules of morality to be followed if we are to advance, just as there are rules of scientific investigation. Mrs. Lang, we are raising ourselves, however painfully, so that mankind may enjoy in the future a superior life which now we can hardly conceive! The foundations on which the new men will build their lives are Faith, Science, Respectability, Geology, Mechanical Invention, Ventilation and Rotation of Crops!

. . . .

The study was the Collector's favourite room; it was panelled in teak and contained many beloved objects. The most important of these was undoubtedly *The Spirit of Science Conquers Ignorance and Prejudice,* a bas-relief in marble by the window; it was here that the angle of the light gave most life to the brutish expression of Ignorance at the moment of being disembowelled by Truth's sabre, and yet emphasised at the same time how hopelessly Prejudice, on the point of throwing a net over Truth, had become enmeshed in its own toils. . . .

Yet Art did not hold sway alone in the Collector's study for on one corner of the desk in front of him there stood a tribute to scientific invention; he had come across it during those ecstatic summer days, now as remote as a dream, which he had spent in the Crystal Palace. It was the model of a carriage which supplied its own railway, laying it down as it advanced and taking it up again after the wheels had passed over. So ingenious had this invention seemed to the Collector, such was the enthusiasm it had excited at the Exhibition, that he could not fathom why six years should have passed away without one seeing these machines crawling about everywhere.

Of course the Collector "could not fathom" why this train had not been put into use everywhere! The train that laid its own track can be regarded as the archsymbol of the 19th-century mind: the horizontal equivalent of pulling oneself to heaven by one's own bootstraps. For a train to have any advantage over an ordinary conveyance, its tracks must be so firmly anchored—independent of the train—that the train can build up great speed while safely relying on their stability. A train that lays its own track and takes it up again would have no superiority over a vehicle not running on tracks at all, for its tracks would be no more solidly anchored than the train itself. This was the 19th century: trying to lay its own tracks through technological inventiveness, achieving only pseudo-stability, and blind to the crash that will inevitably destroy all individual and societal engineers who refuse to let Christ provide a stable track (*hodos*—John 14:6) for their lives.

But what has the Great Exhibition to do with our Concentric American? A great deal, since he was conspicuously represented there. The Rev. Hampton, before the Indian Mutiny forces him to return to the biblical doctrine of man's sinfulness, is especially impressed by America's contribution to the Exhibition:

> "Mr. Hopkins, as you know, I had the privilege like yourself of attending the Great Exhibition which opened in our homeland six years ago almost to this very day. To wander about in that vast building of glass, so immense that the elms it enclosed looked like Christmas trees, was to walk in a wonderland of beauty and of Man's ingenuity. But of all the many marvels it contained there was one in the American section which made a particular impression on me because it seemed to combine so happily both the spiritual and the practical. I am referring to the Floating Church for Seamen from Philadelphia. This unusual construction floated on the twin hulls of two New York clipper ships and was entirely in the Gothic style, with a tower surmounted by a spire. Inside, it contained a bishop's chair; outside, it was painted to resemble brown stone. As I looked at it I thought of all the churches built by men throughout the ages and said to myself: 'There has surely never been a more consummate embodiment of Faith than this.' "

"A splendid example," agreed the Collector. "A very happy marriage of fact and spirit, of deed and ghost."

Our nation had little difficulty in entering the spirit of the Great Exhibition, for her confidence in the future was, if possible, even greater than that of her former Mother Country. England was at the height of her imperial glory, but America had the entire expanse of the future stretching out before her like John Locke's *tabula rasa.* Her voyage into the future, like the Floating Church for Seamen, was the assured fulfillment of divine purpose. The American section of the Great Exhibition certainly matched England's in bombast, and exceeded it in bad taste.

Moreover, our nation had its own symbolic equivalent of the Exhibition not many years later: the celebration of its first 100th birthday. In preparation for it, emancipationist and radical Reconstructionist Charles Sumner published in 1874 his *Prophetic Voices concerning America,* a work of secular eschatology; in the Preface he wrote: "In the celebration of our hundredth birthday as a nation, now fast approaching, these prophetic voices will be heard, teaching how much of present fame and power was foreseen, also what remains to be accomplished." In 1876, the Centennial Exposition in Philadelphia displayed the machinery of progress as had the Great Exhibition in London. In commenting on President Grant's dramatic firing of a gigantic steam engine at the Exposition, journalists Mathews and Baker (with Bicentennial perspective) refer to our 19th-century "age of optimism and hot air":

It was the grandest ball of the Gilded Age—a birthday celebration that opened with a prophetic blast of steam whistles, a 100-gun salute and the swelling harmonies of a 1,000-voice choir singing Handel's "Hallelujah Chorus." In its day, the great Centennial Exposition of 1876 in Philadelphia stood out as an optimistic tribute in iron, steel, glass—and hot air—to America's unshakable faith in its own future. Now, with the United States lurching toward a rather haphazard celebration of its Bicentennial, the festival in Fairmount Park suddenly looks a good deal more instructive than it did 100 years ago. "A new kind of world was dawning," observed Prof. Henry Graff of Columbia last week. "It was a time of worship for machinery—and a lust for industrial and political power beyond anything anyone had ever known before."

The gala looked like a fantasy of J. Pierpont Morgan with trappings by P. T. Barnum. It cost Congress, the the state of Pennsylvania and the city of Philadelphia $3 million—at a time when the total Federal budget was running a modest $500 million a year. Nearly 10 million visitors plunked down 50 cents each to pass through the turnstiles. Before they staggered out of the 450 acres of buildings and exhibits they saw everything from the latest-model false teeth to such marvels as Alexander Graham Bell's telephone and George H. Corliss's steam engine, a behemoth that towered over 40 feet, generated 2,500 horsepower and ran 8,000 assorted gadgets in Machinery Hall. . . .

President Grant had promised that the Exposition would sport the most modern products of "law, medicine, theology, science, literature, philosophy and the fine arts." In the end, the fair ran long on technology—and short on culture. There were machines for spinning cloth and shredding hemp, folding envelopes, printing newspapers and making shoes. The Burial Casket Building drew duly impressed crowds—as did the forearm and torch of Frederic Bartholdi's still-unfinished Statue of Liberty. The air brake, refrigerator car, self-binding reaper all made their public debuts—along with an ingenious telegraph that could dispatch two cables over one wire. France sent textiles, Britain displayed furniture and Germany sent the arms of Krupp—including a monstrous, 100-ton cannon that led an embarrassed German official to wonder aloud: "Is this the real expression of Germany's mission?"

Americans had cause for a blush or two themselves. "We were not competing successfully with the rest of the world in producing superior objects of fine art," observed Prof. Neil Harris of the University of Chicago last week. The most popular attraction in the art galleries was a scantily clad wax statue of Cleopatra. One American artist contributed a classical head of Iolanthe— sculpted in butter. Another worked up a Liberty Bell— made of tobacco plugs. . . .

If Americans were innocents a hundred years ago, they were also imbued with an overweening—and ultimately disastrous—confidence in a destiny that turned out to be considerably less manifest than anyone expected.

Of more than routine interest is the sobering fact that the "Centennial March" was supplied by Richard Wagner —the composer par excellence of 19th-century pagan romanticism, whose works would be much appreciated sixty years later as the musical accompaniment for National Socialism.

The Specifics of Progress

Optimistic confidence in man and future-directed assurance of inevitable progress thus constituted the very air that the 19th century breathed. But what were the particular elements that simultaneously reflected and contributed to this mythology? I have outlined them in my *Shape of the Past,* and they need only be touched on here. Philosophically, the 19th century was the age of modern Idealism—not the transcendent Idealism of Plato or of the Italian Renaissance but the immanent Idealism of a Hegel who saw the human race as a reflection of the World Spirit of Reason, conveying history dialectically to its ultimate fulfillment. As Kierkegaard so well observed, this viewpoint was in fact a presumptive deification of man; and it provided the "ideal" ideological underpinnings for a century committed to narcissistic auto-idolatry. Lines from one of Auden's last poems ("Address to the Beasts") comes inevitably to mind:

> If you cannot engender
> a genius like Mozart,
> neither can you
> plague the earth
> with brilliant sillies like Hegel

Politically, the year of revolutions, 1848, reinforced the conviction of many that the end of oppression and unjust societal class structures was just around the corner. Marx's *Das Kapital* employed Hegel's dialectic in even more characteristically 19th-century fashion—materialistically—to argue for the inevitable arrival of the classless society. Deeply, though unconsciously, influenced by the eschatological drama of Old Testament history, Marx secularized the biblical plan of salvation: Divine Providence was reduced to the dialectic process; the saints to proletarians; sinners to capitalists; the battle of Armageddon to class-war; and the millennium to the classless society. As Bertrand Russell has well said of Marxist doctrine: "It is man's destiny, willy-nilly, to work out the behests of a strange Hegelian-Hebraic Deity." But this deity was not so strange in 19th-century context, for confidence in man was replacing confidence in God on all levels.

Scientifically, the theory of evolution seemed to offer 19th-century man the final vindication of his world-view: mankind was indeed on an upward spiral to the stars.

Science and technology had already provided the most concrete and visible evidences of genuine progress (let us not forget the expanding pianoforte for yachts—or the train that lays its own tracks), so the scientific discovery of the evolution of the species could only serve as a capstone to the temple of human fulfillment. And how well it all interlocked! How coherently everything fitted! Wrote Marx to Engels in 1860 concerning Darwin's *Origin of Species:* "Although it is developed in the crude English style, this is the book which contains the basis in natural history for our view"; Marx even wanted to dedicate the English translation of *Das Kapital* to Darwin (mild-mannered, unrevolutionary Darwin refused).

Our concern here, however, is with the American brand of progress-thinking in the 19th century. Three characteristic aspects can be isolated, though they often blended together in various proportions in the thought of the day. We refer to Transcendental Romanticism, Social Darwinianism, and Pragmatism.

Few are unacquainted with the name of Ralph Waldo Emerson; and legions of schoolchildren have been subjected to Thoreau's dubious puttering about at Walden pond. The expression "New England Renaissance" is frequently employed, and some have read Van Wyck Brooks' attractive volume, *The Flowering of New England.* But what exactly did the Transcendentalists espouse? Were they neo-Platonists, opposing the Hegelian immanentism of the time? A strict philosophical reading of the term Transcendentalist might lead to such a conclusion, but the first and perhaps the most basic thing to note about the 19th-century American Transcendentalists was that they did not read anything very strictly. They *felt* more than they thought, and when they read, they read to find support and illustrations for what they felt. Emerson claimed to have taken the concept of Transcendentalism from Kant, referring to Kant's transcendental forms as "intuitions of the mind" and arguing therefore that the new Transcendentalism embraced "whatever belongs to the class of intuitive thought." As philosopher Michael Moran has quite properly observed: "Here, of course, the word 'intuitive' is being employed in its most general sense, quite dissociated from any philosophical use, so that Emerson could immediately go on lamely to characterize the 'Transcendentalist' as one who displays a predominant 'tendency to respect [his] intuitions.' " The subjectivity and lack of intellectual rigor in the movement led its most prominent intellectual historian, Frothingham, to speak of it as "an enthusiasm, a wave of sentiment, a breath of wind that caught up such as were prepared to receive it, elated them, transported them, and passed on—no man knowing whither it went." In a word, the Transcendentalists were par excellence William James' "tender-minded."

But their tender-mindedness had definite characteristics, specifically, anthropocentrism and romanticism. As children of the Enlightenment, they focused on human potentiality. Again to quote Moran, they held to "a vague yet exalting conception of the godlike nature of the human spirit and an insistence on the authority of the individual conscience." Thus Thoreau, after observing that most men lead "lives of quiet desperation," sought a personal solution in self-cultivation and self-exploration. He endeavored to free himself from what he called "greasy familiarity"; fellowship for him was "the virtue of pigs in a litter, which lie close together to keep each other warm." He went on to apply his individualistic, isolationistic approach eschatologically: "Not satisfied with defiling one another in this world, we would all go to heaven together."

Such a humanistic, anthropocentric outlook reminds us that New England Transcendentalism grew from the soil of 18th-century liberal religion. It will be recalled that Ralph Waldo Emerson's father, William Emerson, was one of the prominent liberal clergy of Boston who made Deistic ideas more palatable in the days of the Founding Fathers. Unitarian clergy of the Emerson variety were the connecting link between Deism and Transcendentalism. And it is generally admitted that the growth of humanistic, voluntaristic Unitarianism occurred largely in reaction to the extreme stress of Puritan Calvinism on God's sovereign decrees in eternity—just as "bundling" and other dubious ethical practices arose in reaction to the Puritans' legalistic misapplication of Old Testament morality. Whenever orthodox theology does not maintain a strictly biblical balance, not only in its doctrine but also in its practice, equal and corresponding heresies inevitably rear their heads. Moran rightly observes that

The majority of its [American Transcendentalism's] original adherents, including Channing, Emerson, Parker,

Ripley, and Cranch, were, or had been, Unitarian clergy-men, and from the point of view of cultural history the advent of transcendentalism must be seen as the final liberation of the American religious consciousness from the narrow Calvinism that Unitarianism had already done much to ameliorate. This is not, however, to imply that transcendentalism was primarily a movement within the Christian church. For its outcome, as the works of Emerson and Thoreau, for example, amply testify, was essentially secular and humanist in the widest sense.

The romantic side of Transcendentalism deserves equal emphasis. New England Transcendentalists were powerfully moved by the German *Sturm und Drang* period —the epoch of literary "storm and stress" centering on the work of Goethe and Schiller at Weimar.* I have emphasized in my *Cross and Crucible* that the Weimar littérateurs, though they began as 18th-century classi-cists, soon absorbed a romantic nature-mysticism which can be traced back at least to alchemist Paracelsus' *Naturphilosophie*. As Goethe wandered through Europe, weeping for lost antiquity on castle ruins in the moonlight, so the New England Transcendentalists infused their world with a warm glow of romantic sentimentality. They found evolutionary theory particularly hospitable, for they wished to see the universe not as an impersonal machine but as the product of pulsating, organic life.

Especially attractive to them also was the romanti-cized conception of the American as a "new man"—a view that had been classically set forth in 1782 by the transplanted French nobleman de Crèvecoeur in his *Letters from an American Farmer*—a work, incidentally, which at the time of its publication lured some five hun-dred French families to the wilds of Ohio, where they perished. R. W. B. Lewis (*The American Adam*) has traced through the Transcendentalist and other American literature of the 19th century the theme of the American as a new and secularized Adam—an innocent Adam in a bright new world, in process of dissociating himself from the constraints and evils of the past. Particularly revealing in this connection is the notion of the "Fortu-nate Fall," as set out, for example, in the strange theologi-cal speculations of the elder Henry James (the father of psychologist William James and novelist Henry

---

*Cf. Appendix A: "From Enlightenment to Extermination."

James), and subsequently developed as a literary motif by 19th-century American romantics. James—a Sweden-borgian—wished to get beyond Thoreau's individualism and the "feeble Unitarian sentimentality" of those who naïvely conceived of America as an unspoiled Eden; his means of doing so was to reintroduce the Fall as a symbol of social rebirth—an allegory of everyman's spiritual adventure in coming not merely to self-awareness but also to awareness of others. The Fall was thus positive—"fortunate"—for only thus could a people come to full maturity. Transcendental doctrine was extended and transformed so as to incorporate even the Fall as an element in man's upward climb to perfection. Wrote James:

> In Adam, then, formed from the dust and placed in Eden, we find man's natural evolution distinctly symbolized—his purely instinctual and passional condition—as winning and innocent as infancy no doubt, but also, happily, quite as evanescent. It is his purely genetic and *premoral* state, a state of blissful infantile delight unperturbed as yet by those fierce storms of the intellect which are soon to envelope and sweep it away, but also unvisited by a single glimpse of that Divine and halcyon calm of the heart in which these hideous storms will finally rock themselves to sleep. Nothing can indeed be more remote (except in pure imagery) from distinctively *human* attributes, or from the spontaneous life of man, than this sleek and comely Adamic condition, provided it should turn out an abiding one: because man in that case would prove a mere dimpled nursling of the skies, without ever rising into the slightest Divine communion or fellowship, without ever realising a truly Divine manhood and dignity.

Here is epitomized the Transcendental romantic's hope for America: the realization of "a truly Divine manhood and dignity." The quoted passage is taken from James' *Christianity the Logic of Creation,* which was published in 1857; two years later Darwin's *Origin of Species* appeared, offering innumerable correlative possibilities. For the romantics, even when they fulminated against the cold impersonality of a technological age and found solace in nature and in organic values, the history of their time represented inevitable progress onward and upward no less than it did for the technocrat. Emerson lauds "plain old Adam, the simple genuine self against the whole world" and declares that "ours is a country of beginnings, of projects, of vast designs and expectations. It has no past; all has an onward and prospective look." In America, even a Fall had to be a Fall upward.

American response to the publication of Darwin's theory is most instructive. Theological objections there were, of course, but (and this will give us pause for reflection later on) they came not from the opinion-makers or from the centers of culture and learning, but from the societal periphery—from pulpits and revival tents out of which negativities were accustomed to flow. In general, the learned public approved of the Darwinian thesis, and did so with an alacrity bordering on the neurotic. On March 28, 1860, The *New York Times* reviewer wrote of the *Origin of Species:* "We have no sympathy with those who, to use the admirable language of Baden Powell —'behold the Deity more clearly in the dark than in the light'—in confusion, interruption and catastrophe, more than in order, continuity and progress." As a matter of fact, Darwin's book had had virtually nothing to say in direct terms about the activities of the Deity, and it contains only the briefest allusion to the possibility of human evolution (in the rather effusive final chapter). The book was written by a naturalist whose interests focus on problems of classification, nomenclature, biological variations, and the general principle of uniformitarianism as supposedly aiding in the analysis of scientific questions. But American reviewers immediately transformed Darwin's book into the realm of philosophy and theology of history! Why? because they saw it as the perfect illustration of what they believed already: that American society was evolving—progressing—to higher and higher levels. As Hofstadter has so well demonstrated in his *Social Darwinism in American Thought,* evolutionary theory became a social doctrine almost overnight, for it seemed to say exactly what the 19th-century American wanted to believe: the American Adam was moving upward from grace to grace by his own inherent capabilities.

Darwinian views of natural selection and the "survival of the fittest" became the justification for the activities of Northern carpetbaggers in the South after the Civil War and for the cut-throat ruthlessness of the robber barons during the (allegedly) halcyon days of Big Business prior to the establishment of federal income tax and the passing of the Sherman Anti-Trust Act. Those who lost or those who failed had only themselves to blame:

unbridled economic competition was in line with scientific, evolutionary principle! And here we reach the late 19th-century Horatio Alger ideal—what Wyllie in *The Self-Made Man in America* terms "the myth of rags to riches." The American is capable of success; all he need do is to exert his inherent powers, and wealth, happiness, and all the good things of life will eventually come to him. "The ambition to succeed may be and always ought to be a laudable one," preached Lyman Abbott, clerical spokesman for his age. "It is emphatically an American ambition.... It makes the difference between a people that are a stream and a people that are a pool; between America and China." Russell H. Conwell's famed *Acres of Diamonds* claimed that 98 out of 100 wealthy Americans were more honest than other men and this was one of the secrets of their success; indeed, seeking wealth is man's "Christian and godly duty."

In discussing the relations between the mainline churches and the self-made man ideal, Wyllie significantly observes:

> Virtually all the leading Protestant denominations, with the exception of the Lutheran, produced at least one nationally known clergyman who honored the wealth-through-virtue theme.... A substantial number were Calvinists: the Congregational church produced more prominent self-help publicists than any other denomination.... It was no accident that the Episcopal and Congregational churches, which had led all others in providing spokesmen for the self-help cult before 1890, became the most productive of clergymen of the social gospel after that date.

Following Troeltsch, Wyllie thinks the Lutheran exception was due to a supposed belief on Luther's part that agricultural pursuits were preferable to business. Is it not more likely that the Lutherans, as the Protestants most closely wedded to original Reformation theology, immediately saw the yawning gulf between the 19th-century American ideal of progressivistic, evolutionary self-help and the Gospel message that man is saved by grace alone, through Christ alone, apart from works, and that "all our righteousness is as filthy rags"?

The 19th-century American was imbued not only with a spirit of Transcendental progressivism and social Darwinianism, but also with a strong dose of Pragmatism: the epistemology of C. S. Peirce, William James, and later John Dewey, which redefined truth in terms of utility.* In my *Shape of the Past* I have summarized the numerous objections to this viewpoint, which in essence reduce to the twin propositions that many things that are false do in fact "work," and just as many things that do not have any demonstrable utility are true! But the heady wine of technological and business success had so entered the blood of our 19th-century Concentric American that he was immune to such considerations; for him it was perfectly obvious that all was "working" in America and that therefore America was in a unique sense the purveyor of truth. Eden was in process of being recreated in the Western Hemisphere on the basis of man's self-effort, and if truth had any meaning this was surely it!

Historians of philosophy have regarded Pragmatism as the one original contribution America has made to the history of ideas, and—if this be granted—it says much about our national perspective in modern times. Bertrand Russell's judgment is a sobering one:

> From the highest flights of philosophy to the silliest movie, the distinctive feature of American thought and feeling is a determination to have done with the notion of "fact." We used to think it a good thing if our beliefs were "true," and we imagined that "truth" consisted in correspondence with "fact." If you believe (say) that Edinburgh is north of London, you believe truly, because of a geographical fact which is quite independent of your belief. And so we thought it our duty to recognize "facts," even if they were unpleasant. Not so, says pragmatism, which is the typical American philosophy: there are no "facts" that have to be passively acknowledged, and "truth" is a mistaken concept. Dewey, the leading philosopher of America, replaces "truth" by "warranted assertibility." This is arrived at, not by merely observing the environment, but by an interaction with it which continues until it has been so modified as to become acceptable to us. For passive "truth" he substitutes active "inquiry," which he says, "is concerned with objective transformations of objective subject-matter."
>
> "Inquiry," according to this view, is like extracting a metal from the ore, or turning raw cotton into cloth. The raw material offered to our senses is not assimilable,

---

*"Peirce, James, and Dewey, with native American makeshift wit, tried to reverse the divine current and wag the transcendental Dog with the tail of credulity's practical benefits"—John Updike, *A Month of Sundays.*

and we put it through a process until, like an invalid food, it becomes easy to digest. A belief only has "warranted assertibility" when the consequences of holding the belief are satisfactory. Some governments have not been slow to realize that the police can decide what beliefs shall have "satisfactory" consequences. In old days, a belief might be "true" even if the Government frowned on it; now it cannot have "warranted assertibility" if the police object to it—unless those who hold it are strong enough to promote a successful revolution.

The political consequences of such a philosophy have been worked out with ruthless logic in George Orwell's book, *Nineteen Eighty-Four.* But none of his gloomy forecasts will have "warranted assertibility" if they turn out to be "true," for anyone who adheres to them after they have been realized will be liquidated, and therefore the consequences of adhering to them will not be "satisfactory."

The parallel with Orwell's *1984* may seem at first glance to be impossibly overdrawn—yet the events of our own century remind us how very treacherous a road any nation embarks upon when it ceases to hold to an objective, fact-orientated standard of truth. Is Watergate really very far from *1984*? Noteworthy also, in passing, is the unified opposition of virtually all current mainline theology to a "correspondence view of truth": the interpreter is so locked into the circle of interpretation that he can never assert that the Bible or Christian doctrine makes objective and definable demands that are universally true. So Christian truth is relativized and becomes the plaything of theological speculation or ecumenical "big business." The pragmatic 19th century bestowed upon its offspring, both secular and religious, character weaknesses of a most deleterious sort.

Clouds No Bigger Than a Man's Hand

To be sure, there were warnings, had the 19th-century American been looking for them. De Ferron, in his *Théorie du progrès* (1867) expressed what today is recognized as axiomatic: "Toutes nos merveilleuses inventions sont aussi puissantes pour le mal que pour le bien"— all our marvelous inventions are as capable of evil as of good. Even the German idealist philosopher Lotze wrote in his *Microcosmus* (1864) that thus far the advance of knowledge and growth of business organization had not produced a corresponding increase in the degree of human happiness, the reason being that each step forward technologically brings increased pressure along with it. The Franco-Prussian War of 1870 was a solemn reminder of the effect modern technology could have if turned to military uses, and the success of a formerly decentralized but now unified Germany showed what imperialistic possibilities were open to those who employed progress, disciplined self-help, and organization for nationalistic ends. Perceptive writers such as Melville saw the handwriting on the wall: Captain Ahab is the 19th-century American writ large, totally—monomaniacally—convinced that the universe is his oyster, that Nature (represented by the godlike white whale, Moby Dick, who simultaneously elicits numinous attraction and repulsion—Rudolf Otto's sacral *numen*) must bend to his will, and who is finally destroyed by his self-confidence and egomania.

But just as the European Hegelian would not listen to Kierkegaard, so the self-made American would not give ear to Melville. "Hearing ye shall hear and shall not understand; and seeing ye shall see and shall not perceive: for this people's heart is waxed gross, and their ears are dull of hearing, and their eyes they have closed, lest at any time they should see with their eyes, and hear with their ears, and should understand with their heart, and should be converted, and I should heal them." As the century drew to its close, such books flooded the American market as the composite volume by Ellis and others, *The 19th Century: Its History, Progress, and Marvelous Achievements; the Wonderful Story of the World for One Hundred Years.* Here the American Book and Bible House gave the enthralled reader not only a decade by decade account of Progress, 200 portraits of the World's Great Men, and "Tables showing Growth of the Nations from 1800 to 1900 (also latest Census of the United States)," but also stirring essays on "The Scientific Achievements of the Century," "Home Development and Commercial Expansion," and "Coming Wonders of the 20th Century." In the Introduction, accomplishments and prophecy are smoothly blended:

> The peoples of the earth, always climbing with their vision fixed upon the stars, move slowly, perhaps with checks and hesitation, toward the ideals of civilization, enlightenment, and Christianity, which must be attained before the full sunburst of that dawning when the mission of man shall be accomplished and the day of wrong

and evil be relegated to the gloom of the past ages.

The hundred years drawing to a close have been well called the Wonderful Century, for in many of its marvels it has surpassed all that have gone before. . . .

Had any man a hundred years ago sought to win the reputation of a lunatic, he could have taken no surer step than to prophesy that the close of the century would see messages flashed under the ocean from continent to continent in a few seconds; passengers traveling in comfort at the rate of seventy miles an hour; people a thousand miles apart conversing with and recognizing the voices of one another; crossing the Atlantic in less than six days; telegraphing not only with, but without the aid of wires; the transfer of the prodigious power of Niagara Falls to a distance of more than a score of miles; fighting with battleships impregnable against the heaviest artillery; traveling over ordinary highways at the rate of thirty or forty miles an hour; sewing cloth by means of machinery that does the work of hundreds of men and women; being lifted in luxurious comfort to the upper rooms of buildings more than twenty stories in height—and all this and much more in our own country, whose States have grown in number from nineteen to forty-five, and whose population has expanded from five millions to seventy-five millions.

And yet all this has come to pass. It was Patrick Henry who said that the only means of forecasting the future is by recalling the past. Applying this rule, it would seem that the wildest prophecy is warranted, and the hardest task of all is that of deciding what will *not* be invented or discovered. . . . The ocean shall be forced to yield the treasures that have moldered in its caverns miles below the surface for untold ages; diamonds shall be as ready of manufacture as building bricks; wherever gold exists, it shall be located by a child's divining rod; the lost arts shall be rediscovered, the Sphinx shall be made to speak, and all the knowledge of the ancients shall become the heritage of the moderns, and shall be added to a hundred-fold.

If Mars and Venus have inhabitants, shall we ever be able to communicate with them? Why not? It is by no means certain that the Marsians have not been striving for some time to attract our attention by signaling. It will be no difficult task to signal to them in turn, but the insuperable obstacle seems at present to be the impossibility of the inhabitants of either world formulating a code whose meaning can be read by the people on the other planet. And yet some American, by and by, will hit upon the key.

Yes, some American would find the key—to the lost

arts, the treasure of the Sphinx, the secret of the universe. The Concentric American, in the naïveté and overweening self-confidence of his national adolescence, saw no limits to his powers. The utopian dream of his fathers was now thoroughly secularized: with due appreciation to the Reformers' God of Scripture and the Deists' God of Nature for past favors rendered, he now bade them *Adieu*. At century's end, the God-concept was ready to become a convenient symbol for man's own accomplishments, and "in God we trust" a metaphor for the civil religion by which we reverentially meditate on the greatness of our nation and rededicate ourselves to its future possibilities.

4

The Dialectic of Despair

During the first decade and a half of our present century the meteor of Progress continued to rise. In 1904, Hugo Münsterberg, professor of psychology at Harvard and a colleague of William James, wrote a book for Germans to help them to understand the American spirit. Ten years later, in 1914, just before the Great War broke upon the world, he republished it without revision, stating in his preface: "I leave my picture as it is. . . . The Americans have not changed." And the picture? Münsterberg categorized American life under four headings, with a catch-phrase to describe each:

POLITICAL LIFE—The Spirit of Self-Direction
ECONOMIC LIFE—The Spirit of Self-Initiative
INTELLECTUAL LIFE—The Spirit of Self-Perfection
SOCIAL LIFE—The Spirit of Self-Assertion

Self-Self-Self-Self: the sublime confidence of the successful Prometheus.

But already ominous cracks were appearing in the walls of Babel. Artists—whose sensitivity generally permits them to feel the storm coming before others are aware of it—moved away from secure, representative art to what appeared to be bizarre and incomprehensible motifs. Neo-Mannerism, Post-Impressionism, Cubism, Dada: what could they mean? At the 69th Regiment New York Armory Art Show in February, 1913—generally regarded as "the most influential exhibit ever held in the U.S."—the works of such moderns as Matisse, Duchamp, and Kandinsky created a veritable uproar; most of the paintings and art objects were considered meaningless at best, psychotic and lewd at worst. The critics and

The Scream: Edvard Munch (d. 1944)
(Staatsgalerie, Stuttgart)

the general public were incapable of appreciating what Sypher in his *Rococo to Cubism* has termed "Wilhelm Worringer's theory that in periods when man is at home in his world naturalistic art flourishes, and that in periods when man is alarmed by his world non-figurative art appears." The alarm is classically illustrated by Edvard Munch's *The Scream,* drawn as early as 1895 and a precursor of the holocausts to break upon the world in our century. On the back of the lithograph Munch wrote: "I was walking along the road with two friends—the sun set, the heavens became blood-red. . . . I stopped, dead tired. . . . My friends continued on; I remained where I was, trembling with anguish. I seemed to hear the overpowering, infinite scream of all nature." Were Munch's friends the average, color-blind representatives of the Western world, who could not see the blood in the skies and the catastrophe to come?

By the first decade of the 20th century some Americans were already beginning to find a kindred spirit in Dürer's Melancholia. Technology was not solving all problems; indeed, it seemed only to open up an infinite vista of more problems to solve. Prometheus was beginning to discover that it is not enough to steal fire from the gods: you need to be a god to know how to use it properly and, even more important, to be satisfied with it. As perceptive European journalist Robert Jungk has well observed:

> In this newest world, infused by the future, the distinction between day and night, between light and darkness, has lost its validity. The act of the first biblical day of creation is annulled by this latest resurrection of Prometheus. That the modern process of production shall not suffer interruption the artificial suns or electrical projectors burn from sundown to sunrise. In nearly all the big cities of America may be found emporiums and drugstores which announce "We never close." It will be only a short step to the moment when the "northern lights effect" already being developed in a California laboratory will tear the nightdress from heaven forever.
>
> And so it goes with each single act of creation described in holy writ. Man produces artificial matter, he builds his own heavenly bodies and prepares to release them into the firmament. He creates new species of plants and animals, he places his own mechanical beings, robots fitted with superhuman perception, in the world.
>
> There is just one thing he cannot do. It is not given him to cry, in the words of the Bible, "And behold! It

was very good." He may never relax his hands in his lap and say that his creation is completed. Restlessness and discontent remain with him. "For behind each door we open lies a passage with many other doors which again we must unlock, only to find, behind each, others to still others," a chemical research worker—one of the creators of artificial worlds—once remarked to me.

It seems as though the import of all this creation were no more than further creation. Production calls for ever more production, each discovery for further discoveries to serve as a protection against the consequences of the preceding one. Man no longer finds leisure in which to enjoy the world. He consumes himself in fear and worry about it. No sense of joy and no hosanna accompany the new act of creation.

The Age of Extermination

But the unfulfilled promises of technology were nothing to the shock-waves which spread from the assassination of Archduke Francis Ferdinand at Sarajevo. By 1914 Europe was plunged into total war, and by 1917 America had been drawn into the "War to end all wars," confident that her crusade would "make the world safe for Democracy."

Today, with the more immediate backdrop of World War II, we find it difficult to recall just how ghastly the First World War was—or how shockingly it burst the bubble of inevitable evolutionary progress and put the lie to America's facile self-confidence that she had the answer to the world's ills. In proportion to the total number of combatants, more soldiers in World War I were killed or reduced to a vegetative state (particularly as a result of poison gas) than was the case even in World War II; many of these human wrecks still haunt our veterans hospitals. On July 1, 1916, to take a particularly horrifying but by no means atypical example, 110,000 English and Australian troops advanced toward the German barbed wire along the Somme; in a few hours, 60,000 of them were dead or wounded, and it was days before the cries of the abandoned were hushed in no man's land. The Somme offensive went down as the greatest single military slaughter in history. Bits of territory such as the Verdun battlefield were crossed and recrossed by opposing forces, with appalling loss of life, until they looked like moonscape. My son David, in visiting Verdun a few years ago, easily picked up rusting war matériel still remaining from the carnage. On the 50th anniversary of the Armistice, the French weekly, *Paris Match,* found bones with a dog tag at Verdun, identified the soldier, and interviewed several elderly people who had known him.

An important recent work, *The Great War and Modern Memory* by Professor Paul Fussell, successfully argues the thesis that World War I imparted a peculiarly modern consciousness to Western man: it made war a part of his normative thinking, and gave to his literature and cultural expressions the sense of despair, irony, absurdity, and mistrust of constituted authority and existing values that characterize our age. Not Rupert Brooke's Georgian heroics but Edgell Rickword's poetry of decay now pointed to the future:

> His grin got worse and I could see
> he sneered at passion's purity.
> He stank so badly, though we were
>   great chums
> I had to leave him; then rats ate his
>   thumbs.

America recoiled in horror from the Great War, breaking Wilson's heart by refusing to join the League of Nations. But isolationistic foreign policy could not erase the lesson the War had etched on the very soul of the nation: man had not in fact progressed, except perhaps in his tool-making ability, and the tools he had created were now capable of destroying him. The mood of the time was given definitive expression by T. S. Eliot (who, significantly, would find in the acceptance of historic Christianity man's only hope). Wrote Eliot of post-World War I man, unable to forget what he had experienced:

> Webster was much possessed by death
> And saw the skull beneath the skin;
> And breathless creatures under ground
> Leaned backward with a lipless grin.

The First World War was speedily followed by the Great Depression, which was, if possible, harder for America to assimilate than the War itself. The War had directly touched only combatants, their families, and their friends; but the Depression confronted virtually every American—and in the very sphere where the United States was supposed to be impregnable, that of economic success. We had convinced ourselves in the 19th century that the self-made man must always succeed; it followed that a country holding to individual initiative and the work-ethic ought always to proceed from rags to riches. But now the direction was from riches to rags! The great god of science and technology had failed, and his worshippers fell into mocking disillusion. Arthur Guiterman, in *Gaily the Troubadour,* described "The March of Science":

> First, dentistry was painless;
> Then bicycles were chainless
> And carriages were horseless
> And many laws, enforceless.
>
> Next, cookery was fireless,
> Telegraphy was wireless,
> Cigars were nicotineless
> And coffee, caffeinless.
>
> Soon oranges were seedless,
> The putting green was weedless,
> The college boy was hatless,
> The proper diet, fatless.
>
> Now motor roads are dustless,
> The latest steel is rustless,
> Our tennis courts are sodless,
> Our new religions, godless.

Here science is no longer portrayed as a gigantic cornucopia, producing an unending sequence of "more"—more productivity, more success, more happiness—as the 19th century religiously believed it to be—but as a source of progressively diminishing returns, of "less," ending finally in the loss of God himself.

The years 1936 to 1939 marked the Spanish Civil War—and the end of ideology for a generation of young American idealists who still remained convinced that democratic values had to triumph and that Americans would always be able to implement them. Instead of right triumphing, the fascistic insurgents under Generalissimo Franco systematically crushed an admittedly inept Spanish republicanism and exterminated all political opposition.

The same decade brought Hitler to power in Germany and the light of freedom dimmed across the entire European continent. Six million Jews were depersonalized and systematically slaughtered in the Nazi death camps. In line with modern secular man's preoccupation with science, many lost their lives in medical experiments and while forced to work on new and more terrible engines of death. Due largely to America's entrance into the War, the Axis powers were defeated, but—as is so often the case in a sinful and fallen world—our moral victory was severely tainted by the means we thought necessary to employ to attain it. Writes Bruckberger, one of America's greatest European friends and most constructive critics:

> Americans, it is your misfortune as it is the misfortune of the entire West, that you were the first, and until now the only, nation to drop the atom bomb on open cities. It is an added misfortune for you and for the West that you used the atom bomb against a colored race. It does no good to tell us that you were compelled to drop it, and that this terrible act, by shortening the war, saved more lives than it destroyed. The rest of the world remains unconvinced that you were compelled to drop the bomb. But the entire world is absolutely convinced that, even if you were compelled to drop it, you should have gone about it differently. The entire world is absolutely convinced that you should have given some warning, a limited demonstration, and that this act of destruction, the most frightening act ever to have been decided upon in the history of man, was decided in too great haste.

Our rationalizations for this act (shortening the war for the benefit of our own combatants, etc.) pale before the horrors inflicted on the civilian victims—horrors detailed in such careful treatments of the subject as Gigon's *The Bomb*. As if our participation in the growth of modern weaponry were not bad enough (it is estimated that since 1900 the explosive force of military weapons has increased 4 million times), we took on the crushing added burden of an act whose moral quality seems entirely inconsistent with our self-image as the young White Knight of justice and righteousness, tilting against the inhumanities of the old world.

The Great Disenchantment

At least we were the unquestioned victors in World War II; but the years since 1945 have given Americans progressively less confidence in their ability to control the national destiny, much less lead the world. Auden's *Age of Anxiety*, written the year the War ended, pictures us as the perpetual habitués of a Third Avenue bar:

> Self-judged they sit,
> Sad haunters of Perhaps who after years
> To grasp and gaze in have got no further
> Than their first beholding ...

The period of Cold War has witnessed a steady increase in the number of unaligned "Third World" nations which are as unwilling to commit themselves to our leadership as they are hesitant to fall under Marxist hegemony. The Vietnam war was not merely a catastrophe militarily; it was one of the most unfortunate political acts in our entire history, for it alienated our friends and gave our enemies an apparently perfect illustration of our eagerness to inject ourselves into the internal affairs of others for the sake of spreading our national influence. In 1968 I wrote the following judgment on Vietnam for Father Campbell's *Spectrum of Protestant Beliefs*: today I would merely underscore the negativities in it:

> It is a hideous political mess—one of the worst in our nation's history. I spent a day at the 7th Annual Meeting of the American Society of Christian Ethics in January of 1966 listening to a bevy of political scientists speak to this issue in an effort to provide the facts needed so that ethical judgment on the war could be properly made. But the factual considerations are simply too muddy for simplistic ethical analysis. (For example, who is *really* the aggressor? Scripture will not countenance aggressive war, but unless we really know whether the communists got in there first *against the will* of the South Vietnamese—and who on earth knows what the will of the South Vietnamese *is*—how can we say that we, or the communists, are acting immorally?) I wish I could make a pat judgment either for (as the fundamentalists do) or against (as the liberals do), but I wonder if the mark of maturity here is steadfastly to do neither without more data. In the meantime, I must be "subordinate to the higher powers" of my own government (Rom. 13) if I can't show that my country is acting immorally. *But* every day that sees equivocation from the White House (my friends in France call it lying), and confusion and bungling on the field, and men dying in the midst of ambiguities, my positive judgment on the whole business goes down another notch. Wars like this teach us a lesson, however: the lesson that the peoples of this globe are a remarkably stiff-necked lot, and there is not a nation or an individual who (in the

words of the Church father and martyr Cyprian) can "stand upright amid the ruins of the world" apart from the sovereign grace of the Lord Christ.

Not only in international affairs but also on the domestic scene the last thirty years have left us with the vertiginous sensation that things are out of control. This is evidenced wherever we look—but particularly in the realms of technology, urbanization, and ecology. Lewis Mumford, in his two-volume classic, *The Myth of the Machine*, argues that our modern absorption of a mechanical world-picture led to the uncritical acceptance of technical progress as man's highest good, and that this in turn has left us with a Pentagon of interrelated power factors: the tendency toward Political absolutism, pure Power (in the sense of technological energy *per se*), Productivity, pecuniary Profit, and Publicity. These gods feed upon each other, and efforts to control any one of them seem futile because of the strengths of the others.

In our consumer society we make a perpetual and neurotic attempt to convince ourselves that happiness consists of purchasing more and different products of the industrial machine, and these products become less and less durable as the passion increases to manufacture and sell more and more of them. Thus we arrive at what Toffler in *Future Shock* has called the "throw-away society," epitomized by the paper wedding gown. (Personal example: once in Europe I soon learned the difference between enduring automobiles, built there for decades of use, and the three-year chrome junk heap manufactured in Detroit. My 1954 Citroën Traction Avant still sounds as if it just came off the production line.) Edith Lovejoy Pierce expresses the bitter ironies of American consumerism in her "American Prayer":

> I believe in Advertising Almighty,
> And the power and the glory
> Of the ten-engine, streamlined, supersonic
> Method of getting from here to nowhere.
> I believe in the Trinity
> Of Gush, Mush, and Slush.
> Help me to celebrate worthily
> The Holy festival of Dollar Day.
> Clothe me in the form-fitting,
> Peerless, sheer, nonshrink
> Garments of righteousness.
> Anoint my face

With Magic Mirror Cream,
Making every wrinkle
Vanish in a twinkle.
Almighty Advertising,
Give us this day
Our cloud-soft, Puff-quick Biscuits,
And the tangy, bangy goodness
of crustly Crackle-Crunch.
Forgive us the debts on our easy payments,
And that time we wore the wrong hat.
May the incense of our prayer
Rise through a cough-free filter,
And the cool-refreshing dews of Sparkle-juice
Slake our every desire.
In the hour of our death
May we rest on feather-soft,
Mother-soft Marvel Mattress,
And drift into the cosy rosy dozey
Of Rock-a-bye Land. Amen.

Everywhere scientific and technological values—to which our society seems irrevocably committed—entail frightening possibilities or direct consequences which we do not know how to avoid: biological research offers the perverse opportunity for social engineers to engage in the genetic manipulation of the race; our industrialization is progressively augmenting the incidence of birth defects, cancer, and other nightmarish ills. A recent statement by Dr. Umberto Saffiotti of the National Cancer Institute leaves little room for ambiguity: "Cancer in the last quarter of the 20th century can be considered a social disease, a disease whose causation and control are rooted in the technology and economy of our society."

The modern American city is the end product of 19th-century progressivistic industrialism; it was supposed to provide the "advantages" which less advanced rural America lacked. But with the gains in economic efficiency—and in spite of such spurts of culture as the Chicago Renaissance at the end of the last century—general deterioration in the quality of urban life has become more and more painfully apparent. Few American cities have the restful tree-lined boulevards or the lovingly cared for parks that make Paris a delight to visit and a privilege to inhabit; indeed, in most American cities one would take his life in his hands even to venture into a public park after dark—assuming that he could find one worth entering. (In the cities where my family and

I have lived in the U.S.—Chicago and Washington, D.C. —it has never been possible to walk at night; but in our European home city of Strasbourg, France, the children can safely go out alone at night, even in the downtown sections.)

Some will recall Christian littérateur Charles Williams' lyric vision of the City in *All Hallows' Eve,* where he sees superimposed on present-day London all the Londons of the past and the glory of them. Can one seriously regard the contemporary American city in this fashion? Not only does our future-directedness and passion for tearing down historic buildings to build highrises contradict such a vision, but the grime and ugliness of so many urban developments rings the curtain down on metaphysical contemplation. The assertions of Max Picard apply with precision to our urban life: "Noise is manufactured in the city, just as goods are manufactured. The city is the place where noise is kept in stock, completely detached from the object from which it came." And when we observe the near financial bankruptcy of America's largest city, we begin to sense the pressure of the Sorcerer's Apprentice: something has been set into motion which no one any longer seems capable of controlling.

During the summer of 1975 in Paris I took an excellent course in Comparative Environmental Law given by Professor Joseph Sax of the University of Michigan Law School; it was conducted under the joint auspices of the University of San Diego and the Centre Juridique de l'Institut Catholique. One of Professor Sax's particular emphases was the impossibility of applying any single legal technique or remedy to combat all environmental ills. Current environmental problems are simply too complex for any single solution. Sax, who was chiefly responsible for the drafting of the model Michigan Environmental Protection Act, expressed skepticism that any existing federal or state constitutional provision or any proposed constitutional amendments would guarantee the kind of environmental protections we need. Ironically, the attempts at environmental control are themselves now moving in an extremist direction: our aviation industry's work on a supersonic aircraft was killed on very tenuous environmental grounds (would virtually any modern means of transportation have been developed if the criteria of the extreme environmentalists had been

operative?), and there is some doubt that the revolutionary Anglo-French Concorde will be able to land in this
country. Edgar A. Prichard, the genial, polymathic attorney under whom I read law in Virginia, tells the story
of the Lord coming to Noah with good news and bad
news: the good news is that he can be saved from the
forthcoming Flood by building an Ark; the bad news is
that he must first prepare an Environmental Impact
Statement!

So effectively have we boxed ourselves into corners
that Lineberry's *Priorities for Survival* employs the
phrase, "muddling our way to extinction." In his speech
accepting the Nobel Prize for Literature, Faulkner could
declaim: "Man will not only endure—he will prevail"; but
the question is really quite open for argument! Americans
find that one of the most agonizing aspects of their 20th-
century melancholia is their sudden fall from exuberant
youth, where to prevail was taken for granted, to pre-
mature old age, where merely to endure seems often beyond our powers. Consider the energy crisis: once, as
inventors of the automobile, we drove whatever, whenever, and wherever our fancy dictated; now, at our Bicentennial, we who succeeded in putting the first humans
on the Moon by a technological miracle must conserve
every drop of gasoline, in fearful dependence upon Arab
nations the names of which were almost entirely un-
familiar a generation ago. We seem to have fallen into
a strange state where Christ's prophecy to Peter applies
to us as a nation: "When thou wast young, thou girdedst
thyself, and walkedst whither thou wouldest: but when
thou shalt be old, thou shalt stretch forth thy hands,
and another shall gird thee, and carry thee whither thou
wouldest not."

Values in Collapse on the Eve of Century 21

Inevitably, the traumas which we have just discussed
have produced reorientations in American values. One
of the most perceptive examinations of the major shifts
in current values is J. W. Getzels' fourfold typology,
as presented in his study of "The Child in the Changing
Society"; it warrants reproduction *in extenso*:

    1. *From the work-success ethic to sociability.*—In-
stead of the work-success ethic, there is an overriding
value of sociability and frictionless interpersonal relations. The hard-working, self-determined Horatio Alger

hero as a national model is giving way to the affable young man in the gray flannel suit. Let me cite just one relevant study. Two hundred Seniors, both liberal-arts and professional students in twenty colleges and universities, were asked to describe their personal aspirations and life-goals. *Fortune* magazine published the findings under the suggestive title "None of This Ulcer Stuff." Typically, the Seniors talked more about home than about career achievement. They reject the "push" of their fathers and aspire to Suburbia as their goal. As one of their number says quite bluntly, "Dad was a lone wolf, and I wouldn't have the brass." And another adds, "I'm not really interested in one of these big executive jobs. None of this ulcer and breakdown stuff for me—just making money doesn't stack up with keeping your health." One midwesterner sums it all up as follows— and note the emphasis on the "affable" as against the "ambitious" values: "I'm not money-mad by any means, but I'd like enough to buy a house, and have transportation, and of course good clothes for the family. Plus entertainment: I'd like to be able to see all the good plays and movies. And I suppose I'd want a trip every year: visit around in the big urban areas, you know, Berlin, Paris, Rome. I can't set any exact amount I'd like to make, so long as it's enough for the necessities of life."

2. *From future-time orientation to present-time orientation.*—Instead of future-time orientation and consequent self-denial, there is a hedonistic present-time orientation. Our former national slogan, "A penny saved is a penny earned," is giving way to the more modern slogan, "No down payment necessary." As a recent article in *Harper's Bazaar* points out, "The people principally responsible for our twenty-nine billion dollar installment debt on consumer goods are married couples under thirty: two thirds of these young families are in debt. Interest rates are so high that there is often more money to be made in financing merchandise than in retailing it, yet credit men say many young marrieds don't even bother to ask what interest they are paying."

3. *From independence to conformity.*—Instead of independence and the autonomous self, there is compliance and conformity to the group. As Riesman has observed, we are replacing our inner gyroscope with a built-in radar that alerts us to the feelings of others. The goal of behavior is not personal rectitude but group consensus, not originality but adjustment. There are numerous signs of this transformation, and I shall mention only two—one from literature and one from industry—that happened to come my way as I was writing this paper. In literature, for example, a study of "Values in Mass Periodical Fiction,

1921-1940" suggests that "the change [during this peri-od]... represents a shift away from the 'titan' success theme, in which the hero is exalted for his own genius over and above other group values, to the 'little man' success theme, in which the reward symbol is due the hero as the bearer of specific group virtues." In industry, William Whyte points out, there are now master profiles of personal characteristics for various occupational groups, and, the closer one fits the group profile, the better. The three common denominators of these profiles are: extroversion, disinterest in the arts, and a cheerful acceptance of the status quo. If you are being evalu-ated for a job, Whyte suggests you take the following precautions:

(1) When asked for word associations or comments about the world, give the most conventional, run-of-the-mill, pedestrian answer possible.

(2) When in doubt about the most beneficial answer to any question, repeat to yourself:

I loved my mother and my father, but my father a little bit more.

I like things pretty well the way they are.

I never worry much about anything.

I don't care for books or music much.

I love my wife and children.

I don't let them get in the way of company work.

Individual stimulation as a value has given way to group tranquility as a value—the switch on the drug counter has been from benzedrine to "Miltown."

4. *From Puritan morality to moral relativism.—* Finally, instead of Puritan morality or at least moral commitment as a value, there are relativistic moral at-titudes without strong personal commitments. Absolutes in right and wrong are questionable. In a sense, morality has become a statistical rather than an ethical concept: morality is what the group thinks is moral.

The degree to which Getzels' analysis accurately re-flects the current situation could be illustrated by Water-gate alone: the preservation of the political situation, the current party image, at all costs, and the disengagement of the interests of the organizational machine from all ethical standards and concerns. Jonathan Schell, in his superlative treatment of Watergate, *The Time of Illusion*, maintains that the Nixon Administration aimed to "com-pose scenes rather than to solve real problems"—to maintain the illusion of "credibility" both at home and abroad regardless of factual realities or moral imperatives. According to Schell, the Adminstration developed "a new form of rule, in which images were given precedence over substance in every phase of government." Having debated Joseph Fletcher on situation ethics a few years before Watergate, I was most interested to see a laboratory example of what happens in government when moral relativism prevails and the end is confidently employed to justify the means.

A further illustration of Getzels' schema was provided on April 12, 1975, at a symposium on Religion and Family Law sponsored by the Center for Law and Religious Traditions of the Catholic University of America Law School. One of my fellow panelists, Professor Harvey Zuckman, in his paper on "Recent Developments in American Divorce Legislation" pinpointed "self-centrism" as the fundamental source of current marital breakdowns in this country: "The destruction of patriarchy and the loss of religious faith which accompanied it have opened up all sorts of possibilities for self-centered pursuit by men and women and with this pursuit less regard for the family unit. Self development becomes the banner under which we march in the last quarter of the 20th century." He cited Joseph Epstein's seminal work, *Divorced in America:*

> [We] are all possibilists now—unanchored and adrift in the sea of the possible. . . . Switch jobs, change cities, drop a wife and pick up another, give group sex a fling, buggery a try, drugs a go—things have got to get better. Affluence and psychological liberation have made nearly everything possible; not the sky, but only human anatomy is the limit, and yet nothing any longer seems quite good enough.

Luther once described human history as the story of a drunken man reeling from one wall to another. The inability of modern science and technology to fulfill their promises of an American millennium has produced an understandable, if equally immature, reaction to the opposite extreme: feeling and subjectivity have suddenly been elevated to a position of first importance. Thus the current craze for existential values, drug-induced mysticism, Eastern religiosity, the occult, transcendental meditation, etc. When the members of what Roszak calls this "counter culture" are young enough to have no memories of Buchenwald or Hiroshima, they go so far as to claim a saving newness, an Age of Aquarius—or Reich's Consciousness III. Very unlawyerlike law professor Charles Reich proclaims in *The Greening of America* that "beyond the industrial era lies a new age of man. The essence of that age must be the end of the subjugation of man. . . . Surely this new age is not a repudiation of, but a fulfillment of, the American dream." He continues with rhapsodic immaturity:

What Consciousness III represents, in the long range terms of human evolution, is the beginning of the development of new capacities in man—capacities essential to living in the present age. The historical, organic nature of the change is felt by many people. David Crosby, the rock musician, in an interview in *Rolling Stone* (July 23, 1970), described Graham Nash, a friend and co-musician, as "one of the most highly evolved people on the planet. . . ."

The crucial point is that technology has made possible that "change in human nature" which has been sought so long but could not come into existence while scarcity stood in the way. It is just this simple: when there is enough food and shelter for all, man no longer needs to base his society on the assumption that all men are antagonistic to one another. That which we called "human nature" was the work of necessity—the necessity of scarcity and the market system. The new human nature—love and respect—also obeys the law of necessity. It is necessary because only together can we reap the fruits of the technological age. And it is necessary because only love and human solidarity can give us the strength of consciousness to withstand the overwhelming seductions and demands of the machine.

Our present system of government is based on the assumption that "man is a wolf to man" and that "only the law makes us free." It assumes that all men have an unlimited will for power over other men, and therefore it has elaborate constitutional checks and balances to keep power divided and limited. It assumes that all men are primarily motivated by their own material self-interest, and therefore it provides a system of pluralism to balance and compromise these conflicting interests. It assumes that men will infringe each other's rights unless restrained, and therefore it puts the law above all men. It assumes that men care only about themselves, and therefore it establishes as a state religion the worship of the *machinery* of government—the democratic forms—rather than the worship of the *substance* of a good society. Perhaps democracy, law, and constitutional rights will still be wanted in a new society, but they cannot be based or justified any longer on assumptions such as these. . . .

In the summer of 1967, when Consciousness III was just beginning and the forces of repression had not yet moved in to create an atmosphere of tension and hatred, one could see the new community in the streets and shops of Berkeley, near the University of California. For just a few months at the very beginning of Consciousness III, there was a flowering of music, hippie clothes, hand-painted vehicles, and sheer joy to match nature itself. It seemed to be everywhere, but perhaps one could see it best of all in a vast, modern coop supermarket in Berkeley, open late at night, almost a community center with a self-service laundry, a snack bar with sweet fresh doughnuts, a highly intellectual selection of books, and a community bulletin board. It possessed an amazing variety of goods—Polynesian frozen foods, San Francisco sour rye, local underground newpapers and guides to the Sierras, dry Italian sausage, the glories of California vegetable farming, frozen Chinese snow peas—a veritable one world of foods—and genuine, old-fashioned, un-homogenized peanut butter, the very symbol of the world that has enjoyed technology and transcended it. If the foods gave the supermarket its sense of gleaming opulence and richness, the people gave it the sense of community. There were hippies looking like Indians, with headbands and proud, striking features; ordinary middle-class families doing their shopping late at night. Hell's Angels of California, in their black leather jackets; frat men with block letters; very young couples in some stage of transitory housekeeping; threesomes, foursomes, fivesomes, all possible varieties of housekeeping, in fact; people going on camping trips and returning from trips; and the checkout clerks, very much a part of it all, joining with smiles in the general scene. For the atmosphere was one of mutual respect and affection—visibly and, even more, felt in the vibrations that a casual visitor received. Somehow, all these people were together. The checkout lines, with beards, old ladies, mothers with perambulators, and hippies whose purchase was a single carrot or turnip, resembled nothing so much as a peace march where all kinds of people are joined by a common cause. The scene as a whole, though, was not a march but a kingdom—the peacable kingdom of those old American paintings that show all manner of beasts lying down together in harmony and love.

Unredeemed human nature, however, including that of the old-Adamic American, seems remarkably consistent: whether industrial or mystical, it focuses on *self*— if not self-effort, self-consciousness; and always self-made. But in the midst of Consciousness III, college board scores are continually dropping, speech patterns are deteriorating to the level of animal-like grunts ("yeah, man," "yuh know, man"), and what Charles Hall Grandgent thought he saw at the turn of the century may really be occurring in our generation: the onset of a new Dark Age (distinguished from the early medieval period in that those who peopled it at least had a nodding acquaintance with Latin and the Classical-Christian heritage). Sypher's words offer the relativistic 20th-century American a shocking pause for reflection: "The modern artist can believe only in a reality having an infinity of profiles: profiles that appear only by accident and are constantly mobile. And, in Lardera's words, it may be that all these profiles will be 'devoured in space by light'—the light, perhaps, of 20th-century destructions which are brighter than the sun?" Is it perhaps the moment of truth—the Bicentennial moment of truth—for our Concentric American to stop running in circles, distinguish the wheat from the chaff in his national tradition, and arrive at solid values before it is too late?

PART TWO

You *Can* Go Home Again

Columbia, Columbia, to glory arise,
The queen of the world and the child of
the skies!
Thy genius commands thee; with rapture
behold,
While ages on ages thy splendors unfold.

—Timothy Dwight, *Columbia*

1

America East of Eden

During the melancholic post-World War II years, John Steinbeck reminded his fellow citizens that they were not (as so many Americans had believed throughout the history of the nation) residents of Eden, but rather dwellers east of it—children of Cain in a land of Nod, in sight of a Garden that they could not reenter. Just before the War, Thomas Wolfe, in his last novel, had declared that America could not "go home again."

We agree that America's metaphysical coordinates place her—no less than any other country in a fallen world—east of Eden. However, we do believe that a return home is possible—though the way is far different from that marked either on the maps of the modern secularist or in the gazeteers of the Americanist evangelical. To find it, one must be willing to reevaluate the nature of the heritage one has lost and (even more painfully) face up to the national immaturity through which it disappeared.

Is Eden Recoverable?

The preceding chapters have traced the permutations of a remarkable dream. From its earliest days—even in the age of Renaissance exploration—America has been conceived as the locus of actual or potential Utopia. Each great nation, it would seem, requires an ideological thread on which to hang its history and its hopes, a means of giving it self-identity and distinguishing it from all others. France, for example, thinks of herself as a kind of incarnate extension in time of Jeanne d' Arc: the heroic, chivalrous maid who keeps the torch of civilization burning in ages of barbarism. America, since her inception, has seemed to offer an Eden to a tired world. In the familiar words engraved on the base of the Statue of Liberty:

> Give me your tired, your poor,
> Your huddled masses yearning to breathe free,
> The wretched refuse of your teeming shore
> Send these, the homeless, tempest-tost, to me.

We have attempted to show that the American Edenic dream has passed through two main stages, the Christian and the secular, reflecting the rift in Western civilization produced by the 18th-century replacement of Classical-Christian values by modern secularism. During the Classical-Christian era, to the end of the 17th century, the Edenic dream was conceived in terms of biblical motifs (the explorer's search for the lost Garden, the Puritans' attempt to create a New Israel, a New Jerusalem, or a New Earth). The onset of modern secularism did not result in the loss of this dream, but only its transmutation. As in the case of secularism in general, a reverse alchemy occurred: gold was turned into lead. The 18th-century American believed that his utopian dream was "natural"—that it did not require any support from a special divine revelation; by the 19th century, the dream had been thoroughly humanized, and its realization was considered to be inherent in the progressive historical process, requiring only the correlative efforts of self-made American society to bring it to completion.

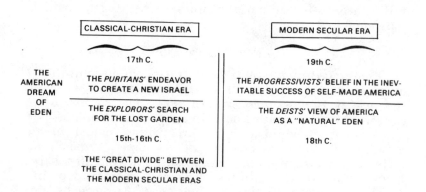

	CLASSICAL-CHRISTIAN ERA	MODERN SECULAR ERA
	17th C.	19th C.
THE AMERICAN DREAM OF EDEN	THE *PURITANS'* ENDEAVOR TO CREATE A NEW ISRAEL	THE *PROGRESSIVISTS'* BELIEF IN THE INEVITABLE SUCCESS OF SELF-MADE AMERICA
	THE *EXPLORORS'* SEARCH FOR THE LOST GARDEN	THE *DEISTS'* VIEW OF AMERICA AS A "NATURAL" EDEN
	15th-16th C.	18th C.
	THE "GREAT DIVIDE" BETWEEN THE CLASSICAL-CHRISTIAN AND THE MODERN SECULAR ERAS	

The international horrors and domestic disenchant-ments of the 20th century have witnessed the crumbling of our national castle-in-air. Except for a limited number of *Greening of America* types (whose excursion into Eastern mysticism has encouraged to climb ropes to nowhere) and overly enthusiastic members of official Bi-centennial committees, most Americans are regretfully willing to admit the country's position east of Eden. Though sad, this state of affairs has its healthy side, for (as Alcoholics Anonymous reminds us) until one is willing to admit just how bad off he is, help is of little consequence. Let us therefore force ourselves to examine critically the American dream in its several stages of development, remembering that one can only go home again when he knows where home really is.

The Age of Exploration. Is it literally possible to re-enter Eden? Some of the Spanish explorers apparently thought so. Certainly the Bible describes Eden as a real place, connected geographically with the "known" world (Gen. 2:10-14). However, the scriptural text makes equally plain that, as a result of the Fall, mankind was ejected from the Garden and no human road leads back into it: "So the Lord God drove out the man; and he placed at the east of the garden of Eden Cherubims, and a flaming sword which turned every way, to keep the way of the tree of life" (Gen. 3:24). The path connecting Eden with the fallen creation has what the French call a "sens unique"—it is a one-way street, going out of and not into Paradise. So those explorers who really expected to find Eden in the Western Hemisphere were doubly mistaken: first, Eden had clear connections, not with the West but with the Near East (its rivers tied it to Assyria, Ethiopia, and the Euphrates system); second, no fallen man literal-ly reenters Eden. *

---

*Where is Eden today? Nothing is said in Scripture as to its "evap-oration" in the course of time, and the Cherubim are apparently to keep perpetual guard at its east gate. Is the Garden perhaps just where it always was—but removed for protection into what science-fiction writers call another "dimension"? (cf. Charles Williams' super-natural novel, *Many Dimensions*). According to Hebrews 12:1 we are "compassed about with so great a cloud of witnesses," but we do not see them: the God of Scripture appears to be in truth a God of many dimensions.

But *metaphorically* can we not speak of reentering Eden? Could the explorers not seek and perhaps find a virgin territory uncorrupted by past evils, and there build a new world in accord with God's revelation? Sad to say, this hope is as chimerical as obtaining real estate in the literal Eden—and for the same reason: *it does not take the Fall seriously enough.* The Fall corrupted mankind in general (the Hebrew word *Adam* means "man in general," just as *Eve* signifies "the mother of all living"). "In Adam's fall, we fell all," as the early American schoolbook so succinctly put it. The people living in the Western Hemisphere when the conquistadores arrived were already sinners (though their sinful specialties were not the same: it took westerners to introduce venereal disease). What Rousseau later called the "noble savage" is romantic nonsense. And even if the explorers had come upon a completely uninhabited area, flowing with (American) milk and honey, (1) they would—like Shakespeare's Gonzalo—"be king on't," corrupting it with their own imported sinfulness, and (2) even the physical environment would already have suffered the effects of sin, since the very ground (Gen. 3:17-19, Rom. 8:22) was cursed because of the Fall. (Monologue at the Fountain of Youth, Ponce de León speaking: "¡Caramba! How did this dead mosquito get in my drinking water?") From the biblical standpoint, there is no "fortunate Fall": the Fall is the absolute barrier to reentering either a literal or a metaphorical Eden from the human side.

The only "reentrance" to Eden—and it is not a physical one until Christ comes the second time to restore all things—occurs when, by personally accepting Christ's work on the Cross, one is restored to fellowship with God and the "handwriting of ordinances that was against us" is thereby blotted out, having been "nailed to His Cross" (Col. 2:14). But this is divinely, not humanly, done; it is a monergism of grace, received by faith—the very antipode of all human effort or discovery (Eph. 2:8-9). And when at the end of time Christ comes in glory, to judge both the quick and the dead, the "new earth" will be the product solely of His creative work, just as the old earth was: it will in no sense be the synergistic product of God's eager cooperation with postmillennialists and activistic social gospelers.

Thus we must regretfully conclude that the dreams of Renaissance explorers for an Edenic new creation were

as doomed to disappointment as the search for the myth-
ical Kingdom of Prester John in Africa. Only when these
dreams are understood as man's longing for salvation,
and drive him to the Cross, do they perform their proper
function. Treated in any other way, they serve only as
a mirage carrying the dreamer farther and farther into
a desert where finally all dreams die.

   The Puritan Heritage. The Puritans added substance
to the Edenic hope of the explorers by recasting it in
terms of the biblical plan of salvation: they would function
as a New Israel and serve as instruments in the establishment of a New Earth. As Froom has shown in his
Prophetic Faith of Our Fathers, virtually all the influential Puritan leaders were premillennialists: John Daven-
port; Samuel, Increase, and Cotton Mather; Samuel Sewall (whose *Phaenomena quaedam Apocalyptica ad
aspectum Novi Orbis configurata,* referred to earlier, attempted to prove that North America, and New England
in particular, would be the seat of the New Jerusalem
when the Messiah returned to set up His millennial kingdom); *et al.* Premillennialism gave the Puritans a
heightened eschatological consciousness (cf. the American Adventist movements of the 19th century): the end
time pressed upon them and they uncritically identified
themselves with Israel in the final apocalyptic period of
her history. In a sense, with their Calvinist passion for
Old Testament legalisms, the Puritans substituted "imitation of Israel" for "imitation of Christ"; they redid Irenaeus' "recapitulation theory" (each Christian life properly
recapitulates Christ's life) to say that the Christian community should recapitulate Israel's history.

   The *imitatio Christi* is dangerous in itself. As I have
argued in my *Chytraeus on Sacrifice,* the Abelardian
atonement theory based on it has consistently led to
depreciation of Christ's substitutionary work on the Cross
for man's salvation. In the form of late medieval Christ-
mysticism, as exemplified in the devotional work attributed to Thomas à Kempis and the Brethren of the Common Life, it fostered doctrinal indifferentism (Erasmus
of Rotterdam was the product of such influences). Charles
M. Sheldon's *In His Steps* and *What Would Jesus Do?*
were precursors of social-gospel liberalism, in which
"following the Master" became a presumptive, sanctimonious substitute for admitting one's lost condition and
receiving Christ's justifying grace. Properly, a life that

"imitates Christ" should come about as a by-product and fruit of a right relationship to the Savior, even as sanctification ought to arise naturally from justification. People who consciously try to "model" their lives on Jesus' earthly life usually end up as cranks. Some of the least attractive characters in church history are those early martyrs who insisted on getting themselves crucified.

If this is true of Christ-imitation (which at least has some biblical warrant: I Pet. 2:21), what can be said in favor of Israel-imitation? Very, very little. Israel constituted a unique people, raised up by direct divine intervention (Gen. 12:1-4), and by the miraculous provision of seed to Abraham (Gen. 17, 18, 21) as a type of Christ's own miraculous birth. When Abraham and Sarai tried to fulfill the Lord's promise by their own (works-righteous) scheming, and Ishmael was born to Hagar, the result was not a chosen people but a thorn in Israel's side from that day to this. Clearly, Israel was formed by God alone as a unique instrument of His saving purposes, to serve as vehicle for the impartation of Old Testament revelation and the womb in which His Son would be given to the world.

Several appalling evils resulted from the Puritans' hermeneutic blunder in identifying themselves with the Israel of scriptural revelation: (1) They came to think of themselves as a "chosen people" and those who disagreed with them or in any way blocked or retarded their aims as Canaanites, Amalekites, Philistines, and the like. In the case of the historic Israel, the people had to be kept untainted from the idolatrous nations round about them so that the vehicle of revelation would not be corrupted, and Scripture records that God commanded Israel more than once to carry out the most devastating attacks on their neighbors in the interests of preserving the deposit of revelation. It cannot be too strongly emphasized that these commands to the historic Israel were unique, and offer no possible precedent to other (necessarily non-revelational) peoples. When the Puritans created an analogy by which not only the Indian tribes who occupied the country before the Mayflower arrived but even Roger Williams' Baptists could be classed as Canaanites, the most horrific possibilities opened up. Certainly this perspective contributed to the depersonalization of the Indian and made it easier through later U.S. history to disenfranchise the red man with little moral compunction.

Moreover, the fallacy that Americans were in a special sense God's "chosen people" permitted subsequent generations to view other people as necessarily inferior, less receptive to divine grace, less within God's plan for the ages—and fair game if they opposed our national interests. From such attitudes to the view that "God is on our side" in all wars and international conflicts is a very small step. Interestingly enough, American evangelical theologians have had little difficulty in recognizing these evils when sects and cults in other countries have identified themselves with the biblical Israel and have expressed themselves chauvinistically or displayed racial prejudice on that basis (one thinks immediately of the Anglo-Israel Movement), but the precisely parallel phenomenon, so inherent in the Puritan version of the American dream, readily passes us by. Removing beams from our own eyes is so laborious, while the removal of motes from the eyes of others offers enjoyable opportunities for theological expertise. . . .

(2) Acceptance of the role of a New Israel, with the attendant possibility of dwelling in a Promised Land not subject to the evils of the Old World, led almost inevitably to spiritual pride and obtuseness to one's actual condition. Thus the Puritans readily labeled as "traditions of men" the Anglican episcopacy and its liturgical trappings, but they sublimely overlooked the extent to which they themselves created legalistic, moralistic social patterns woefully out of harmony with the Pauline "liberty wherewith Christ hath made us free"—the liberty which Luther in the early years of the Reformation described in his revolutionary treatise on *The Freedom of the Christian Man.* Puritan legalisms produced their inexorable reactions, as we have seen: from a hyper-concentration on the sovereignty of God the pendulum of New England thought swung to voluntaristic, Arian Unitarianism, mediating liberalisms, and romantic, humanistic Transcendentalism. Ironically, the Puritans did become much like Israel—but it was the stiff-necked, sanctimonious, Pharisaic Israel of the intertestamental period, which likewise had lost the consciousness of personal sin, human limitations, and the fact that (as Jesus would later remind them) "God is able of these stones to raise up children unto Abraham." Wertenbaker expressed it well in *The Puritan Oligarchy:*

> When the Puritans left England they fled from the things which seemed to them to threaten their souls, from a hostile King, from the bishops, from Church ceremonials,

from lax morals, from disobedience to God's "ordinances"; but they could not flee from human nature, they could not flee from themselves. Upon landing on the shores of Massachusetts Bay they might fall on their knees to ask God to bless their great venture, but it was they themselves who brought the germs of failure.

(3) From a strictly theological standpoint, the Puritans' identification with Israel offered the most perilous temptation of all: the temptation to see their own "Holy Experiment" as a conduit of revelation. But what could be more natural, when it was plain that the Israel of the Old Testament had been called into existence primarily if not exclusively for revelatory purposes? Of considerable significance was the sermon preached by the Rev. John Robinson on July 21, 1620, just before the Pilgrim fathers departed from Leyden on *The Speedwell* for the New World:

> Let us be certain, brethren, that the Lord hath more truth and light yet to break forth out of his holy Word. It cannot be possible that we have so recently come out of such great anti-Christian darkness and already stand in the full light of divine truth. . . . If Luther and Calvin were living, they would be as ready and willing to embrace further light, as that they had received. Search the Scriptures and learn the depth of the covenant God has worked out.

On one level, of course, this stirring message cannot be faulted: it expresses confidence in the "unsearchable riches of Christ" contained in Holy Scripture, and the impossibility that any one generation of Christians should exhaust them. But there is another, and genuinely disquieting level, to Robinson's sermon. A "covenant of further light" is extended into the Puritan community which can potentially give it insights far beyond those of past generations of believers, surpassing even the teachings of the Reformers. From here to modern American religious pluralism is not really a very great step. Europeans are staggered by the number of minute denominations and sects that characterize the American religious landscape. From the (modestly named) Church of Christ to the Two-Seed-in-the-Spirit Predestinarian Baptists to the storefront "Apostolic" churches of every variegated hue, there seems no end to innovation and differentiation. It has been said that in America you shop around for a church like you do for a grocery store (which has the best for the least?) and if you don't find one you like, you start your own!

How has this come about? Not simply as a result of religious freedom, for many countries have no established church and yet denominations have not proliferated there. Perhaps the reason is our early settlers' utterly unfounded self-identification with revelatory Israel, and the consequent expectation of "new light" instead of reliance on "the faith once delivered to the saints." It should give us much pause for reflection that no country in modern times has supplied the world with such a plethora of cults, all claiming "new light" or "new revelation,"* as has the United States: the Mormons, Christian Science, the Jehovah's Witnesses are only the most prominent examples, and it is most instructive to observe that the Latter-Day Saints unabashedly declare by way of the *Book of Mormon* that the American continent was divinely chosen for the completion of God's revelatory work! The Puritans, it would seem, unwittingly laid the groundwork for a depreciation of the very Scriptures they held so high, for any encouragement to regard one's people as a revelatory community opens the gates to sectarian claims that appear, in the eyes of unbelievers, to reduce the Bible to relativism. Whether one judges the Puritan Holy Experiment by secular or by theological criteria, its attempt to establish a New Israel can only be viewed as a great tragedy.

The Enlightenment Spirit. But however valid and powerful the objections to the discovery or establishment of a Western utopia on a theological base, they pale before the irrationalism and impracticality of sustaining such a dream on a secular foundation. Symbolic of the attempt of 18th-century Deists to reinterpret the American quest for Eden in terms of the humanistic creation of a "natural" millennium was de Crèvecoeur's previously mentioned literary idolization of Ohio agriculture—which attracted 500 French families to a wilderness where they perished. Without a realistic view of man and of the world, such catastrophes are inevitable, and the needed realism comes only by listening to the divine judgment on man's condition presented in Holy Scripture. Unhap-

---

*Cf. the quoted passage from pietistic evangelical Watchman Nee in a footnote to our final chapter.

pily, 18th-century man attempted to bring about an epoch of revolutionary newness and innovation apart from God's revealed Word; he would have done well to reflect upon the Renaissance of the 15th and 16th centuries, whose strength was drawn from biblical antiquity, whose greatest artists, philosophers, explorers, and littérateurs were consciously operating with a Classical-Christian worldview, and whose weaknesses and excesses relate directly to the *hubris* and anti-Christian Prometheanism of some of its lesser representatives. Stromberg identifies what he terms "the basic dilemma of deism, on which it fell: if all men can see religious truth so easily and naturally without Revelation, why is it that they do not, and never have? The deist could only answer by referring to a monstrously successful conspiracy of the 'priests' to keep all the world wrapped in ignorance. The answer was hardly credible." Likewise for the Edenic dream of a New Earth: it was but a credulous hope apart from revelational promise.

But how then did the Deistic Founding Fathers sustain their utopian perspective? How did they make their "natural" Eden credible? We have already observed the Jeffersonian poet Freneau to use scriptural motifs and scriptural language to express what for his circle was a dream no longer requiring biblical justification. The fact is that the Deists never ceased to employ scriptural imagery; in actuality, they derived their Edenic hope as well as their alleged "natural" morality from their believing Christian predecessors. In a word, they existed on inherited capital without realizing it. No one has better expressed this than Carl Becker in his *Heavenly City of the 18th-Century Philosophers*:

> If we examine the foundations of their faith, we find that at every turn the *Philosophes* betray their debt to medieval thought without being aware of it. They denounced Christian philosophy, but rather too much, after the manner of those who are but half emancipated from the "superstitions" they scorn. They had put off the fear of God, but maintained a respectful attitude toward the Deity. They ridiculed the idea that the universe had been created in six days, but still believed it to be a beautifully articulated machine designed by the Supreme Being according to a rational plan as an abiding place for mankind. The Garden of Eden was for them a myth, no doubt, but they looked enviously back to the golden age of Roman virtue, or across the waters to the unspoiled

innocence of an Arcadian civilization that flourished in Pennsylvania. They renounced the authority of church and Bible, but exhibited a naïve faith in the authority of nature and reason. They scorned metaphysics, but were proud to be called philosophers. They dismantled heaven, somewhat prematurely it seems, since they retained their faith in the immortality of the soul. They courageously discussed atheism, but not before the servants. They defended toleration valiantly, but could with difficulty tolerate priests. They denied that miracles ever happened, but believed in the perfectibility of the human race. We feel that these Philosophers were at once too credulous and too skeptical. They were the victims of common sense. In spite of their rationalism and their humane sympathies, in spite of their aversion to hocus-pocus and enthusiasm and dim perspectives, in spite of their eager skepticism, their engaging cynicism, their brave youthful blasphemies and talk of hanging the last king in the entrails of the last priest—in spite of all of it, there is more of Christian philosophy in the writings of the *Philosophes* than has yet been dreamt of in our histories.

Had it not been for the biblical account of the Garden of Eden (which they scorned as the mythology of priestcraft) Deistic 18th-century Americans would never have been able to view America in terms of "the unspoiled innocence of an Arcadian civilization." Had the Puritans (whom they despised for their biblicism) not given the Founding Fathers a scriptural view of limited government and inalienable rights, as well as the dream, however ill-conceived, of a "chosen people," they would surely never have arrived at such conclusions. No independent reading of "Nature" would ever have yielded the Arcadian picture of America that the 18th century passed on to 19th-century progressivists. But soon the Edenic dream would float free of all Christian moorings, and a denial of the biblical view of man's sinful limitations would give the newborn secular American the utterly unfounded conviction that, like God himself, he could fashion a New Earth through his own skill and effort.

Progressivistic Mirage. To the naturalistic Eden of 18th-century Deism the 19th century added the motif of inherent evolutionary progress: an immanent historical destiny would carry the self-made American to a secular millennium. What has just been said concerning the impossibility of justifying or sustaining a natural, non-revelational utopia must be even more strongly underscored when the ingredient of Progress is added to secularism's inedible recipe. George P. Grant has shown, in his *Philosophy in the Mass Age,* that "the very spirit of progress takes its form and depends for its origin on the Judaeo-Christian idea of history." As I stress in my *Shape of the Past,* apart from the biblically revealed truth that history moves toward the goal of Last Judgment, the historical drama has been conceived of either as "a tale told by an idiot, signifying nothing" (Hindu-Buddhist thought) or as a perpetual cycle, forever returning to its point of origin (Greek thought). In the absence of revelational perspective, man cannot arrive at any definitive progressive goal for history—and the goal the Bible sets for history is not produced by man but is established by God and realized by Him alone at the end of time. In *Where Is History Going?* I have written:

> Because a man stands in history at a particular place, and cannot see into the future, he cannot possibly demonstrate that his conception of total history will have permanent validity. For the same reason—lack of perspective on the human drama as a whole—he cannot in any absolute sense know what is more or less significant or valuable in the total history of mankind. Moreover, because he is able to acquaint himself personally with only a fraction of all the members of the human race, past, present, and future, his conception of human nature can have only limited value, and is certainly not an adequate basis for historical generalization. Lastly, the secularist's ethical ideals will also reflect his stance in history, and will not be capable of justification in absolute terms.
>
> Now perhaps we see why, to take an especially clear example, Hegel's concept of four "world-historical" epochs (Oriental, Greek, Roman—and Germanic as the goal of the process) appears so ludicrous to us, but was regarded in all seriousness by him. From his early nineteenth-century position in history, the Germanic peoples did seem to be on the side of destiny. From our present historical stance, such a view retains little appeal. The basic problem thus becomes clear: Since no historian or philosopher—or anyone else for that matter—sits "in a house by the side of the road" and watches all of history pass by, no one, from a secular, humanistic viewpoint, can answer the question, "Where is history going?" All of us are—to use Jack Kerouac's phrase—"on the road." Our historical searchlights are incapable of illuminating all of the path we have traversed, and they continually meet a wall of fog ahead of us. In this human

predicament, secular philosophers of history have often, unwittingly, served as blind men leading the blind.

The 19th-century American dream of a progressivistic Eden had no more going for it philosophically or logically than Hegel's chimera, the only difference being that World War II and the subsequent creation of the two Germanies marked the end of German preponderance, while America's star has not yet set that low. But from a secular stance the one "inevitable" progressive goal is no more necessitarian than the other. Eric Voegelin's great work *Order and History* argues that whether secular utopianism is eastern or western, leftist or rightist, Marxist or Capitalist, it is equally unfounded and presumptive. In my *Shape of the Past* Voegelin's position is thus characterized:

> All individuals and societies are subject to the same basic temptation: flight from the reality of existence under God. This evil appears in two forms: Metastasis, "the will to transform reality into something which by essence it is not, . . . the rebellion against the nature of things as ordained by God"; and its modern development, Gnosis, the conviction that "the Christian idea of supernatural perfection through Grace in death [should be] immanentized to become the idea of perfection of mankind in history through individual and collective human action." . . . In the modern national states, Voegelin sees such Gnosis elevated to the position of a "symbolic form of order," and here he thinks especially of Hitlerian fascism which drove him from his homeland, and Soviet communism.

The America of the 19th century was no less contaminated by Metastatic Gnosis, believing religiously (apart from revelational religion and in defiance of it) that it was riding a self-constructed train that laid its own track—and that its last stop would inevitably be the New Earth. The fundamental source of this gross error was of course the elevated view of man which the 19th century inherited from the 18th, and the deceptiveness of the progressivistic mirage would not therefore become clear until the wars and domestic follies of our own time reminded us in unambiguous terms as to who we really were. J. G. Farrell's Padre Hampton benefited from an earlier moment of truth: the carnage and inhumanity of the Indian Mutiny brought home to him in the deepest existential way how he had deceived himself into thinking that the Great Exhibition of 1851 was a proper symbol of the destiny of modern man. As the novel draws to a close, he comes to refer to the Exhibition as "The World's Vanity Fair." Endeavoring at all cost to convert the Collector also, he piles one example upon another: "Think of the American vacuum coffin guaranteed to preserve corpses from decomposing! Was that not against the word of God?" Finally, unable to bring the Collector to precise agreement with his views and half-mad with fatigue and anguish, "a look of despair, of righteous anger came over his face. Suddenly, to the Collector's astonishment, the Padre gripped him by the throat and shouted: 'A matter of opinion! The Crystal Palace was built in the form of a *cathedral*! A cathedral of Beelzebub!' " At this point—the climax of the novel—relief arrives and the siege of Krishnapur is lifted. The Padre, however, is still to be heard ranting: "A cathedral of Baal! A cathedral of Mammon!"

Which, of course, it was. Even that miracle of American ingenuity, the vacuum coffin, could not preserve the secular, progressivistic Eden from decomposition. Founded upon an unhealthy exegesis of Holy Writ by explorers and pilgrims, it was nourished on the contaminated food of modern secularism: the 18th century's misplaced confidence in man and the 19th century's chimerical and credulous belief in the evolution of the cosmos. Such an American Eden is not recoverable, and we should not wish to recover it if we could. It does not represent the true values or the true possibilities of our nation, regardless of how many times during the Bicentennial year misguided and foolish patriots tell us that it does.

But is there an American dream worth recovering? Very definitely, and we will paint its outlines in our concluding chapters. For the moment, let us simply make the essential distinction between the confidence in Scripture maintained by our Renaissance explorers and Puritan forefathers on the one hand, and, on the other, their unfortunate derivation of a New Eden from the biblical text. We can reject their Edenic misapplications of Scripture without losing sight of the Scripture in which they trusted. The valid, essential core of their message was that "except the Lord build the house, they labour in vain that build it: except the Lord keep the city, the watchman waketh but in vain." The Christian heritage upon which our country was founded is not in the final analysis a heritage of utopian speculation, but a conviction that God's scriptural Word is the only proper basis for national hope. And what is Scripture? Scripture, as the Reformers so well observed, is the repository of Law and Gospel; and the foundation we must seek to recover is the foundation of biblical righteousness and Gospel freedom. Edenic, "New Jerusalem" utopianism leads to the reprehensible philosophy of "my country right or wrong"; but commitment to scriptural Law and Gospel impels us to confess our sins and give Christ the lordship of our national life. If God's Kingdom of Law and Gospel (rather than our own chimerical New Eden) is sought first, other things will be added—perhaps even a glimpse of the Promised Land from time to time! With our values straightened out, genuine progress is not an illegitimate hope, for the biblical command still remains to "subdue the earth"; and the conception of our nation as a refuge for the oppressed can be entirely in line with the scriptural admonitions to proclaim liberty to the captives and make available to all the freedom wherewith Christ makes men free. But if the biblical foundations of Law and Gospel are neglected, or relegated to a position of secondary importance, all will be lost, including our freedoms and any possibility of genuine progress: vacuum coffins will indeed become the order of the day.

The Frontier Adolescent

In my *Law above the Law* I have briefly charted the collapse of Western values since the beginning of the modern secular era:

18th C.	Destruction	Bible
19th C.	of:	God
20th C.		Man

We have already observed how the 18th-century Founding Fathers rejected the Bible and then lived off the inherited capital of it, believing that they could retain a God of Nature apart from any special revelation as to His character or attributes. Their endeavor, however, was doomed to failure. Writes Carl Becker in the poignant conclusion to his *Declaration of Independence* (reminding us—though he did not so intend—of the cruciality of retaining Scripture if we would retain our national heritage):

> This faith could not survive the harsh realities of the modern world. Throughout the nineteenth century the trend of action, and the trend of thought which follows

and serves action, gave an appearance of unreality to the favorite ideas of the age of enlightenment. Nationalism and industrialism, easily passing over into an aggressive imperialism, a more trenchant scientific criticism steadily dissolving its own 'universal and eternal laws' into a multiplicity of incomplete and temporary hypotheses— these provided an atmosphere in which faith in Humanity could only gasp for breath. "I have seen Frenchmen, Italians, Russians," said Joseph de Maistre, "but as for Man, I declare I never met him in my life; if he exists, it is without my knowledge." Generally speaking, the nineteenth century doubted the existence of Man. Men it knew, and nations, but not Man. Man in General was not often inquired after. Friends of the Human Race were rarely to be found. Humanity was commonly abandoned to its own devices.

To be precise, it was not until our present century that Western man found his belief in humanity seriously eroded, and the intermediate stage was loss of God. By the second half of the 19th century, those who tried to find God clearly visible in the Book of Nature were no longer able to do so; the pages had become blurred, and the voice of Nietzsche's Zarathustra cried out that God is dead, might makes right, and the Superman (the *Uebermensch*) was justified in transvaluing all values. Actually, the walls of the universe had never contained God's unambiguous script—at least not sixty-six books of it—and that was precisely why God had deigned to provide a special, biblical revelation in the first place. By rejecting it, 18th-century man laid his progeny open to the loss of any meaningful view of God. Thomas Paine was not what Theodore Roosevelt imprecisely branded him, a "filthy little atheist," but his Deism certainly spawned many atheists a century later.*

For early 19th-century man, belief in God had to be sustained, Bible or no, for otherwise there would be no absolute basis for human worth; by the end of the century even that entirely sound proposition had eroded away. David Daiches offers telling illustrations in his lectures on *Some Late Victorian Attitudes:* he contrasts Charles

---

*A consideration that "moderate" theological seminary faculty might reflect upon. First comes loss of confidence in Scripture; then, logically and inevitably, loss of confidence in the Gospel, which is imparted to us only through Scripture.

Kingsley who in 1850 declared that if God were a deceiver "I'd go and blow my brains out and be rid of the whole thing at once," with George Eliot who, on a walk with psychical researcher F. W. H. Myers in 1873, "stirred somewhat beyond her wont, and taking as her text the three words which have been used so often as the inspiring trumpet-calls of men—the words *God, Immortality, Duty*—pronounced, with terrible earnestness, how inconceivable was the *first*, how unbelievable the *second*, and yet how peremptory and absolute the *third.*" Comments Daiches: "One of the reasons why so many Victorians agonized about the existence of God was that all human values seemed to depend on it." Precisely: they did, since without a God, any expression of human value is necessarily relative to the human being expressing it and therefore has no compelling imperative force for others; the only "categorical imperatives" are so tautologically weak that they say nothing morally significant! Thus Eliot's position was untenable, and led inexorably to greater radicalism. "The old-fashioned sceptics may have lost their belief in dogmatic religion, but they never lost their faith in reason or in human nature. The new-fashioned scepticism was more radical." The loss of God meant also the loss of purpose, meaning, and value; "Duty" disappeared along with any absolute valuation of man in general or humanity. The 20th century then opened the way to a practical realization of Nietzsche's philosophy of Will to Power: man is worth only what stronger men say he is, and weaker men are the proper cannon fodder of their betters.

What we have in this sad dysvaluation (not transvaluation!) of all values, characteristic of the modern secular era and as present on one side of the Atlantic as the other, is a repetition of the story of the Prodigal Son. Into the far country goes the secular adolescent, squandering his inheritance, and at Dachau and Buchenwald he ends his days literally eating (if he eats at all) the husks that the swine did eat. Why in particular does the Concentric American take this adolescent path to self-destruction? Why does he leave his Father's house to starve in a far country when the lights at home are still burning for him and the fatted calf is there for the asking?

The answer, in large part, is suggested by the nature of the American frontier experience. Remarked Gertrude Stein: "In the United States there is more room where nobody is than where anybody is. That is what makes America what it is." The most profound contrast between the New World and the Old has been the openness of America as compared with Europe's structured containment. Even when America was first being colonized, the European continent represented centuries of settled existence: there one had to fit into a life that was already patterned geographically and socially, whereas in America the possibilities were as infinite as the undeveloped territory appeared to be.

Moreover, the frontier continued as the predominant defining characteristic of American life to the end of the 19th century—correlating with and coloring the American Edenic dream almost to the end of the era of progressivistic mirage. In 1690 the Massachusetts Bay Colony passed the first measures to regulate the frontier; by the beginning of the 18th century, the Allegheny mountains had been reached; the Missouri Compromise established the Mississippi river as the new frontier boundary in 1820; and though California was settled before the intervening desert lands it was not until 1890—at the height of the progressive epoch of Big Business—that America ceased to have a frontier in the official census definition of the term (only two or three people to the square mile).

Study of the effects of the frontier on the American character began as early as the work of the great historian Francis Parkman, but the thesis that the frontier was the most important formative influence in creating the American spirit was definitively articulated by Frederick Jackson Turner in 1893. Since that time it has been subject to extensive analysis (E. E. Edwards, G. R. Taylor, and, most recently, Bernard Sternsher provide access to this literature), and some powerful critique (especially by Richard Hofstadter). However, the general thrust of the thesis seems undeniable, particularly when one considers the impact of the frontier idea on American thought and letters, as have Roderick Nash (*Wilderness and the American Mind*) and George H. Williams (*Wilderness and Paradise in Christian Thought*). Examples are legion: frontiersman Daniel Boone who, to keep his independence, decided that civilization was too close and that he must move on when he could "see the smoke from a neighborin' cabin"; the persistent struggle at the frontier boundaries between the cattlemen (who tore down fences) and the dirt farmers (who tried to restrict the frontier by putting them up)*; Mark Twain's Huckleberry Finn, whose story concludes with Huck's decision to go off to Indian country to get away from encroaching civilization; the highly publicized collective move of families to Alaska some years ago—consciously in imitation of the wagon trains to California before the frontier officially closed; and the entire ideological success of Kennedy's motif of the "New Frontier."

What were the concrete effects of the frontier experience on the American mentality? Let us hear eminent historian Ray Allen Billington's detailed description of them in his *Westward Movement in the United States:*

> The passing of the frontier did not end its influence on the American people and their institutions. Three centuries of pioneering had endowed them with certain traits and characteristics that were too firmly implanted to be rapidly discarded; these remain today as the principal distinguishing features of the unique civilization of the United States. For the frontier was more than a westward-moving area promising individuals a greater degree of economic and social upward-mobility than they could find elsewhere; frontiering was a process through which artifacts, customs, and institutions imported from the Old World were adapted to suit conditions in the New.

---

*Legal history—ordinarily out of the purview of general historians—offers valuable corroborations of the frontier thesis. Thus the venerable English common law tort rule that an owner, keeper, or agister is liable for the trespass of domestic animals just as if he himself had trespassed was modified in America by the so-called "prairie states doctrine": instead of the owner of cattle being compelled to fence them in at his peril, the burden was placed upon the farmer to fence his crop to protect it from straying animals. In an early Illinois case (*Seely v. Peters,* 5 Gilman 130) the court declared: "However well adapted the rule of the common law may be to a densely populated country like England, it is surely ill adapted to a new country like ours. ... Can it be supposed that when the early settlers of this country located upon the borders of our extensive prairies ... that they designed the millions of fertile acres stretched out before them, to go ungrazed, except as each purchaser from the government was able to enclose his part with a fence?" As the frontier disappeared, the common law rule regained its force. In 1874 the Illinois legislature gave each county the option to choose which of the two rules it preferred; in 1895 the common law rule was reenacted absolutely, since by then the former prairies were settled.

It was, in the words of Frederick Jackson Turner who first expounded the "frontier hypothesis," the area of most rapid "Americanization." . . .

The typical American, as Hector St. John de Creve-coeur remarked in the eighteenth century, was indeed a "new man." He was materialistic in his interests, scornful of esthetic pursuits, and suspicious of "intellec-tuals," just as had been his pioneering forebears. He was more adaptable than the European, always ready to try new tools or techniques, and with little respect for tradi-tion; frontiersmen developed these traits as they daily faced problems for which experience offered no solution. He was unusually mobile both physically and socially; a given place bound him no more firmly than it had his pioneering ancestors while like them he thought in terms of upward mobility where his job or social position were concerned. He was a congenital waster, building his whole economy on the concept of replacement rather than conservation, for he had failed as had the frontiers-men to learn that nature's bounties were exhaustible. Materialism, inventiveness, mobility, and exploitiveness remain characteristics of the American people today, even though they live in a nonexpanding world.

Equally traceable to the pioneering experience are the optimism and individualism so apparent in the United States. Certainly the usual frontiersman was an incurable optimist; he braved the wilderness only because of a com-pelling desire for improvement and firmly believed that continued progress would be his lot. Only this faith allowed backwoodsmen to endure the dangers and back-breaking toil of life in the West; their focus was on the future rather than the past. Nor did they want any interference from government or society as they tapped nature's riches in their unending quest for wealth. Confident that fortune would soon smile, they wanted only to be let alone. Even today Americans are known for their "rugged individual-ism" and their suspicion of "welfare state" concepts that have gained such headway in non-frontier coun-tries. . . .

That the distinctive traits of today's Americans are traceable solely to their pioneering heritage is as un-thinkable as the belief that those characteristics have remained unaltered by industrialization and urbanization. On the other hand, denial that the frontier experience has exerted a continuing influence down to the present is impossible. The American people do display a versatility, a practical ingenuity, an earthy materialism, to a degree uncommon among Europeans. They do squander natural resources with an abandon shocking to others; they are a mobile people both physically and socially. In few other lands is nationalism carried to such extremes of isolationism or international arrogance, or the democratic ideal worshipped with such enthusiasm. Rarely do older societies display such indifference to esthetic creativity or such disrespect for intellectualism; seldom do they cling so tenaciously to the shibboleth of rugged individualism. Nor do Europeans enjoy to the same degree the rosy faith in the future, the heady optimism, the belief in the inevitability of progress, that are part of the national dream. These are pioneer traits, and they have been too firmly implanted to be entirely dislodged by the impact of twentieth-century industrialization.

Noteworthy is the long list of American character traits that relate to the frontier or grow directly from it. To Billington's enumeration may be added: a retrogressive primitivism (not a few early settlers took up the Indian practice of scalping, and today, in contrast to most other nations in the civilized world, there is widespread American opposition to gun controls); pragmatism (the 19th-century development of this exceedingly naïve American philosophy was surely assisted by the frontier conviction that the only truth worth talking about was the truth vindicated by practical workability); anthropocentrism (frontier man created all the civilization there was—he wasn't dependent on the past or on grace for it—"God helps those who help themselves"—even the towns in which he lived didn't "grow up" but were "sectioned out" by the frontiersmen themselves in the unesthetic checkerboard patterns of the "congressional township"); and overweening pride (settlers in the arid Western plains maintained the bizarre theory that their building and tree-planting would actually increase the rainfall).

To be sure, many frontier characteristics were commendable: democratic refusal to be enmeshed and limited by the fusty traditions and social structures of old Europe, and powerful opposition to slavery (settlers in the frontier areas were accustomed to doing their own work, so they did not want to be disadvantaged economically by states with slave economies). But a remarkable number of frontier traits correlate with the most unfortunate aspects of 18th- and 19th-century American secularism: humanistic acceptance of the progress myth, disregard of past values and preference for the immediacy of the present and the future "pot of gold at the end of the rainbow," materialism, cultural colorblindness and the belief that "the bigger, the better," hyper-individualism, cut-throat competition, and exploitiveness.

Particularly instructive is the parallel between frontier values and what psychologists such as Erikson, Gesell, Havighurst, and Seidman have identified as *adolescent* values. Kurt Lewin, in applying his field theory to adolescence, writes: "The basic fact concerning the general situation of the adolescent can be represented as the position of a person during locomotion from one region to another. This includes (1) the widening of the life space (geographically, socially, and in time perspective), and (2) the cognitively unstructured character of the new situation." In a very real sense, the American frontier character is an adolescent character; in the biologist's formula, "ontogeny recapitulates—repeats—phylogeny." Like the adolescent in locomotion from infancy to adulthood, across a cognitively unstructured and ever-widening life space, the secular American has been oblivious of his dependence on prior scriptural values, has sublimely lived on inherited capital until it has run out, has regarded the future as entirely open to his every whim and a potential escape hatch from current responsibility, and has concluded in the egotistic exuberance of youth that he is a demigod who can and must remake the world in his own image and succeed in all his endeavors. Material, pragmatic values fascinate him; he is impatient with culture, learning, art, or related intangibles (think of the average teenager who would not hesitate a moment between a Suzuki motorcycle and a lifetime pass to the Metropolitan Opera).

Perceptive observers of our national history have easily recognized this fundamental characteristic, which has seemed to augment rather than diminish with time. In his *Speech on Conciliation with America,* Edmund Burke described 18th-century Americans as "a people who are still, as it were, but in the gristle, and not yet hardened into the bone of manhood." At the end of the 19th century, Oscar Wilde had one of his characters in *A Woman of No Importance* utter the immortal barb: "The youth of America is their oldest tradition. It has been going on now for three hundred years." And in our own century D. H. Lawrence wrote: "She starts old, old, wrinkled and writhing in an old skin. And there is a gradual sloughing off of the old skin, towards a new youth. It is the myth of America." Ponce de León is generally regarded as a hopeless visionary for believing that the Fountain of Youth could be found over the next hill; but his American successors created a cult in which they actually believed that they were drinking from it.

No better illustration of the correlation between the frontier and the adolescent American personality can be marshalled than the classic American film, particularly the "Western." Think, for example, of *High Noon,* starring Gary Cooper (one of the genuinely high-grade suspense films of this genre). All the nuances, all the grays of mature existence in a sinful, fallen world are excised, resulting in a secular morality play in which Good (represented by the self-made hero) triumphs over superhuman odds and conquers the numerous "Baddies" arrayed against him. A kind of "Christus Victor" motif, to be sure, but the hero isn't a divine Christ: self-made man is elevated to the status of a demigod. In the earlier Westerns (those of my childhood), the producers took no chances that the moral might not get across: the Good Guy (Hopalong Cassidy, *et al.*) always wore a white hat and the Baddies wore black hats; but conspicuous in its absence was any mature realization that the evils of a fallen world can only be conquered by divine grace. Even Bertrand Russell, scientific rationalist that he was, recognized the immaturity of the American celluloid dream factory:

> From pragmatism to the movies is not such a far cry as might be thought. I believe almost every European would agree that the English, the French, the Germans, and the Russians of some twenty years ago, all produced artistically better movies than those emanating from Hollywood. When we see an American film we know beforehand that virtue will be rewarded, that crime will be shown not to pay, and that the heroine, always faultlessly dressed in spite of incredible tribulations, will emerge happily to life-long bliss with the hero. If you object, "But this is a sugary fairy tale only fit for children," producers and American public alike will be simply puzzled, since the object is not to produce something that corresponds to fact, but something that makes you happy by corresponding to daydreams.

To be sure, even the "sugary" movie seems preferable to the films of sex, perversion, raw violence, and catastrophe that constitute the major product of the current American film industry, but the one is no less the product

of adolescent immaturity than the other. Today's mis-
named "realistic" film is just the immature expression
of despair in the face of exploded dreams, while the ideal-
istic "Western" carried adolescent frontier pride to the
screen.

John Updike's character "Rabbit"—the central figure
in his novels *Rabbit, Run* and *Rabbit Redux*—is the finest
literary archetype of the American as perpetual adolescent. He is friendly, enthusiastic, "religious"—and entirely lacking in any real value-system or positive orientation.
His whole existence centers upon his high school years,
when he was a basketball hero, and nothing else seems
to matter much afterward. His life is one of bouncing,
running, dribbling back and forth, with no real object
to it all. He is the victim of a society that stresses sports
and games, and these are distinguished from the real
world by the fact that their rules and prescribed actions
are completely arbitrary (is this perhaps one of the reasons why the Apostle Paul tells us that "bodily exercise profiteth little" and that, unlike secular athletes, he
strives to obtain an incorruptible crown?). Rabbit has
no inner value-system; he is sociologist Riesman's "other-
directed" American, who has no past tradition to sustain
him and who therefore looks to others around him to
provide him with osmotic meaning for his existence. He
cannot commit himself to anything or anyone: neither
to God nor to his wife nor even to his demi-prostitute.
Finally his life of frenetic running grinds to a halt: having
nothing to sustain him he is immobilized. Rabbit reminds
one of Greenwich Village cartoonist Jules Feiffer's as-
tronaut-like character "George" (whom I discuss in *The
Suicide of Christian Theology*): having nothing but himself
to believe in, he begins to worship himself—"and then
he awoke one morning and found that he had forgotten
his name").

Adolescence, we are told by one psychologist, may
be called a "second infancy." What can be done for the
infantile American, caught in the throes of perpetual
adolescence, a victim of frontier-induced arrested development? Is there any way to cure our infantilism
before the complexities of the present day—which require,
above all, a clear-eyed maturity of judgment—immobilize
us and cause us to forget our very name?

Maturity entails a realistic view of who we are and
who God is. As long as we retain the frontier fiction of

godlike, infinite development (which is less and less easy to sustain even on naturalistic grounds as our sphere of national growth and influence reaches undeniable limits), we will continue to make absurd blunders in foreign policy and suffer the melancholia of dashed hopes at home. When an individual or a nation acquires a messianic complex, the sure result is overweening pride when one succeeds and utter despair when one fails. From the wall of pride our Concentric American reeled, drunk with 19th-century frontier self-adulation, to knock himself senseless against the wall of despair in our own time. The only answer is to see ourselves as God sees us, not "as gods, knowing good and evil," but as sinners east of Eden who need above all to recognize our limitations and to rely upon divine grace as we endeavor to hold forth the torch of freedom and human dignity in a fallen world. The only way again to hear the voice of the Lord God walking in the Garden in the cool of the day is to encounter Christ the Living Word, who proclaims both eternal Law and everlasting Gospel in the pages of His scriptural revelation.

2

Tarnished Splendor

With all her Edenic eccentricities and frontier failings, America is still a many-splendored place—still doubtless the greatest land of opportunity on the globe. The danger is that we will lose sight of our genuine values as we agonize over our mistakes, or, conversely, that we will attempt to convince ourselves that our faults are really virtues. Let us therefore try to identify the good and the bad in our national makeup, and then seek to determine how the good can be sustained and the bad counteracted. Finally, we shall face the hard question as to whether the American way ought to be exported beyond our shores, and, if so, how extensively.

Good News . . .

In a recent interview, distinguished British actor Sir John Gielgud waxed oratorical over Disneyland: with the late Vivien Leigh he had spent an entire weekend there, and was ecstatic not only over its cleanliness, the lack of any inebriated patrons, and its attractive staff of young people, but especially because of the sincere and delightful atmosphere of fantasy it conveyed. Disneyland is indeed a "magic kingdom" and its peculiarly American brand of magic rubs off on all those who visit it. My European friends consider it a prime focus of any trip to America— one of the few justifications for making the trip at all (considering the quality of American cuisine—but more about that later). To paraphrase the wretched rationalist who said of Christianity, "any religion that can produce monks who developed Chartreuse liqueur has something going for it": any nation that can produce the mythology of wonder and hope represented by Disneyland has a great deal going for it.

But what, specifically? *Not,* in my judgment, the capitalist system, for that economic philosophy, though frequently and uncritically identified with the essence of the American dream, is at root based upon old Adamic self-centeredness, contributed very largely to the 19th-century progressivistic mirage by encouraging self-made survival of the fittest and the exploitation of the weak, and has necessarily undergone much chastening by the legislatures and the courts (anti-trust laws and unfair competition suits) to make it compatible with American ideals of fair play and justice for all. *Nor,* for that matter, our high standard of living, since we are coming more and more to see in this country that Jesus had our number when He said: "A man's life consisteth not in the abundance of the things which he possesseth." (Moreover, it must be galling for the American-cum-capitalist to note that socialist Scandinavia can boast a higher standard of living than we possess!) I suggest that our great national virtues are not economic, but political, legal, and social.

(1) *The Political Ideal: Constitutional Protection.* Shortly before his death, Robert H. Jackson, Associate Justice of the Supreme Court and Chief Counsel for the United States at the Nuremberg war crimes trials, expressed this ideal eloquently:

> Our foundations were quarried not only from the legal ideas but also from the political, social, philosophical, scientific, and theological learnings of the eighteenth century, "the silver age of the Renaissance." All these were dominated by a belief in "the laws of nature and of nature's God." . . .
> Our judicial, executive, and legislative branches all were grounded in a belief that they were bound by the authority of a clear and universally acceptable natural law, revealed by man's reason and always and everywhere the same. Its fundamentals were proclaimed self-evident truths, as indisputable as the axioms of geometry, which needed only to be declared to be acknowledged as right and just by the opinion of mankind. These truths of natural law to that age stood as the ultimate sanction of liberty and justice, equality and toleration. The whole constitutional philosophy of the time was based on a system of values in which the highest was the freedom of the individual from interference by officialdom—

the rights of man. To supplement this natural order, little man-made government was thought to be needed, and the less the better.

To make certain that these natural rights should have some man-made sanctions, the forefathers added ten Amendments to the original instrument, translating their version of the rights of man into legal limitations on the new government. They did not stop, as the French did, at reciting these in a preamble to the Constitution, where they served as an admonition only to a parliament that was all-powerful because there could be no judicial review of its legislation. On the contrary, the forefathers established a Bill of Rights which conferred as a matter of law, enforceable in court, certain immunities and rights upon citizens which correspondingly limited the power of the majority duly expressed through governmental action.

We have already seen that these immunities—these "inalienable rights"—were derived by the Founding Fathers from scriptural revelation even when they were unaware of it, and that the Puritans, a century before their time, had conveyed this heritage across the Atlantic to the New World.

(2) *The Legal Ideal: Government under Law.* Wrote jurist John F. Dillon, in dependence on Professor Dicey's classic *Lectures on the Law of the Constitution:*

> The glory of the English law, establishing the rights of Englishmen, consists in the following principles: The rule of law excludes the exercise of arbitrary power; "Englishmen are ruled by the law and by the law alone; a man may be punished for a breach of the law, and he can be punished for nothing else." Not only so, but equally, if not more, important is the principle that this breach of the law must be established as to all classes and all persons, official and non-official, in the ordinary courts of law. Arbitrary power and special administrative tribunals such as we find in France and other countries administering what the French call *droit administratif,* do not exist. In England the same law applies to all persons, and it is administered for and against all persons in the great law courts. "The law of England knows nothing of exceptional offences punished by extraordinary tribunals." So also direct personal responsibility for torts—for any invasion of the legal rights of another—exists without limit or exception. No command of an official, not even of the crown, can be pleaded in bar to any wrongful act. . . .

These great and fundamental principles, these distinguishing excellences of the English law, have been adopted in all their scope and vigor in this country. We have gone further, and by constitutional limitations upon legislative power we have placed these primordial rights beyond legislative invasion, thereby giving them a theoretical if not an actual, security greater than they possess in the old country. . . . In these respects I insist that the law of England and America is superior to the Roman law, either as it anciently existed or as it exists in the States of modern Continental Europe.

Why are Anglo-American common law values—those mentioned by Dillon, and the many others discussed in such works as Stein and Shand's *Legal Values in Western Society*—superior to what the Continental civil law has to offer? I have argued in my *Law above the Law* that one primary reason is that whereas the civil law of Continental Europe was necessarily much influenced by pagan Roman law, which the church never succeeded fully in baptizing, the common law grew up as a fresh plant after the Norman conquest, receiving its essential nourishment from Christian sources. John C. H. Wu, Professor of Jurisprudence and former Chief Justice of the Provisional Court of Shanghai—a jurist well acquainted with both the Eastern and the Western legal traditions—had no hesitancy in writing:

Needless to say, no system of human law can be perfect, or even nearly so. But it is no exaggeration to say that Anglo-American jurisprudence—the common law of England before the nineteenth century and the common law of America since the eighteenth century—is permeated with the spirit of Christianity to a greater degree than any other system of law except canon law. You find dark spots here and there; but where the common law is at its best, you feel that Christ Himself would have smiled upon its judgments. It is so because in many cases the judges have not hesitated to draw their inspiration and light from the words of Christ and His Apostles, particularly St. Paul. In American jurisprudence especially, you find traces of the Christian influence wherever you may turn.

Wu provides many specific examples in his fine work from which we just quoted: *Fountain of Justice*. Others are given in H. B. Clark's *Biblical Law* and in materials collected in my *Jurisprudence: A Book of Readings*. An important example not generally cited is the Anglo-American procedural tradition—based on scriptural standards of impartiality in judgment and hatred of undue influence (cf. Col. 3:25)—that separates the triers of fact (the jury) from the judge in the decision-making process. So strong is this tradition that in many American state courts (though not in the federal courts) the judge may not in his instructions to the jury comment on the credibility of the witnesses or the weight of the evidence; and even in those Anglo-American court systems where he may do so, any prejudicial remarks on his part will constitute reversible error.* In France, the judges actually sit with the jury during their deliberations, and as the recent Jean Gabin film, *Le Verdict,* and Sylvain Després' book, ... *Et devant les hommes* painfully show, the result is often the imposition of the judges' personal opinions on a passive and sheeplike jury which should be trying crucial questions of fact in independence of any such influence.**

(3) *The Social Ideal: An Open Society.* Perhaps the greatest positive result of the frontier experience (we should not conclude from its unfortunate aspects that it had no positive consequences!) was the growth of a nation where genuine social mobility exists. True enough, not everyone has been able to benefit equally from it (slaves before the Civil War and many minority groups throughout our history being especially sad examples), and some have turned this ideal into an excuse for Prometheanism and the religion of the self-made man. But

---

*See Appendix D, where Senior Judge Walter E. Hoffman of the U.S. District Court, Norfolk, Va., demonstrates the judicial sensitivity of the American common law even with reference to defendants who plead guilty.

**Writes Britisher Sybille Bedford in her *Faces of Justice:* "The French put up with a degree of regimentation which the heavens be praised would still be unacceptable to us. They have had some form or other of a long, rough compulsory military service for centuries; French people, all of them, must carry identity cards; they cannot get a passport without first obtaining a certificate of *bonne vie et moeurs* from the local police station; and they have always acquiesced in the wide, vague and vested powers of their police.... France—in spite of the Revolution, possibly in a measure because of the Revolution—has never been a "free country" in the sense that the English and the United States and the Dutch and the Scandinavians and the Swiss understand it. The surface of life has been good in the good times for a large number of people of reasonable virtue and of reasonable luck."

after all appropriate qualifications have been made, there has probably never been a society on the face of the earth in all of recorded history that has offered so many opportunities to so many people to reach the level of their actual abilities.

When Maurice Cornforth, Herbert Marcuse and his fellow radicals—and some of the members of the People's Christian Coalition in naïve dependence upon them— declare that our society is really not an open one and requires revolutionary restructuring, they are about as unrealistically wide of the mark as one can possibly be. (Marcuse's very professorship at a state university was the final proof of the nincompoopishness of his views in this respect; in the Marxist societies he espouses, had he uttered one-hundredth of the criticisms he has expressed here, he would have been reduced to a diet of pure salt.) Our society most certainly offers the opportunity for the expression of dissent—and to the widest possible degree short of the destruction of the open society itself. To be sure, we do not permit our citizens to vote away their inalienable rights, nor do we allow government employees to advocate the overthrow of the government by force (activities in the same logical category as cutting off the limb on which one is sitting); but we permit even the open espousal of total revolution, anarchy, solipsism, flat-earthism, polyandry, and cannibalism as long as they do not reach the "clear and present danger" point of calling out "Fire!" in a crowded theatre. Consistent with the preservation of a societal fabric at all, we allow an amazingly wide scope for dissent, even of the most radical sort.

Much as I revel in the high academic standards of the French lycées (philosophy, no less, is taught to high school students!) and the French universities, I must admit that we in America are far wiser to pitch our educational system at the masses (in spite of the fact that it permits accrediting Podunk State Teachers College and Joybells Bible Institute as well as Harvard), so that every person can reach the highest educational level of which he is capable. French education is free and public (even in the university: I paid a franc equivalent of about $50 *in total* for my French doctoral program), but the standards are so high and the entrance requirements so progressively stiff that a vast number of Frenchmen who could certainly have benefited from an American college education get no chance in their country to obtain its equivalent. Thus all over France one meets people working at jobs below their abilities (I have met at least a dozen headwaiters whose linguistic and organizational skills would have made them high-level administrators, at very least, in the United States).

State control encroaches on innumerable areas of life inappropriate to it in other countries: in "westernized" Turkey the government plays archeologist and excludes legitimate attempts to investigate important circumstantial evidence of the Ark's survival on Mount Ararat; in France—one of the freest nations on earth—all university appointments are classed within civil service, so only French citizens can hold tenured university chairs. (This genial idea, which homogenizes French university instruction, arose with Napoleon, who didn't take any chances on being opposed by "intellectuals"—if the profs opposed him, he could retaliate with the final solution: no further salary cheques.) In sum: if as an American you don't think you're living in an open society, you haven't had much experience in living.

... and Bad News

The three great positive merits of our American way of life—constitutional protection, government under law, and the open society—have a common denominator, and it is Freedom. Politically, legally, and socially we really do offer the possibility of a life of freedom, limited only by the equivalent rights of one's fellowmen. And where these freedoms have been or are abridged we offer sufficient checks and balances and opportunities for redress of grievances so that correction can be made without destroying the governmental framework by which our liberties are guaranteed. What will now be said along negatively critical lines must not be allowed to obscure the values just discussed; any country that offers the freedom we enjoy will come up in the black on the balance sheet regardless of the genuine problems to which we now turn our attention. In short, the mature solution to the negativities to follow is not to throw out the national baby with the bathwater, but to try to depollute the water supply.

(1) *Leveling.* The coin of democracy has two sides:

positively, every man has his theoretical say in the open society; but negatively, the tyranny of the majority stifles variety and excellence. Bertrand Russell (who, admittedly, had his own eccentric axe to grind) considered the worst feature of America to be "the tyranny of the herd. Eccentricity is frowned upon, and unusual opinions bring social penalties upon those who hold them." Our public school system, as just emphasized, gives far more opportunities to far more children than is the case almost anywhere else, but it necessarily focuses on the average child—generally with concern for the below-average student as well (to help him reach the level of his peers). But little is done to encourage and promote the interests of the exceptional child, who, ironically, can have an impact on society far out of proportion to that of others. Indeed, education of the exceptional child is often penalized by refusal to allow state aid to private church schools and other religious institutions where his interests are of real concern. In commenting on the 1975 Supreme Court ruling in *Meek v. Pittenger,* forbidding the states to provide special services such as reading therapy to private religious schools, Harold O. J. Brown writes: "It would seem that the Court, consciously or unconsciously, is intent on increasing the cost to individual parents of not submitting to the state-run educational establishment. In other words, the long-range effect of such regulations is to price independent schools out of the market for all but the very wealthy. Thus, without actually closing or forbidding them, the government ultimately will effectively eliminate non-government schools and thus strike a heavy blow against the 'pluralism' and 'freedom of choice' it so greatly extols in other matters."

If the reply is that the Court is not discriminating against private schools per se, but against religious institutions on the ground of the First Amendment, it should be carefully noted that (1) the provision of ordinary services to church schools hardly "establishes a religion" in this country, since any and every religious group can start its own school if it wishes; and (2) the refusal to assist church schools—as has so often been stressed by their advocates—promotes the leveling out of the nation religiously by subjecting all the nation's children to a common school system which, far from representing religious neutrality, actually promotes a secular view of life at best or an idolatrous "civil religion" at worst.

In our open society, there should be every encouragement to educational diversity, as long as minimum standards are maintained.

The same point could be made in almost all other areas of life: a democratic society such as ours must be constantly vigilant to prevent the submerging of excellence in the bathwater of the statistical average. We do not want our nation to take on the character of that archetypal statistician who drowned wading across a river with an average depth of three feet.

(2) *Parochialism.* While conducting a European Graduate Theological Program for the Trinity Seminary, I was showing the glories of Notre Dame cathedral to seminarians and their wives. One wife from Texas remarked: "Wahl, gee, it's ahl right, I guess, but it don't compare with the plains a' Texas." *My* wife averted catastrophe by dragging me away before I could throw the girl into the Seine. Our long standing conviction that we are a "chosen people" and that our country is the Promised Land has given us a naïve—and often arrogant—obtuseness to the values and advantages peculiar to other nations. Having watched American tourists in action for a number of years, I must admit that there is uncomfortable truth in Burdick and Lederer's portrait of *The Ugly American.*

Our linguistic tonedeafness is a particular manifestation of our parochialism: having functioned successfully in our vast land on the basis of a single language, we conclude that English (or rather, American) is the lingua franca of heaven and that we have no good reason to learn any other. Teddy Roosevelt summed up our prevailing linguistic chauvinism when he declared: "We have room but for one Language here and that is the English Language, for we intend to see that the crucible turns our people out as Americans of American nationality and not as dwellers in a polyglot boarding-house." Thus we expect others, as a matter of course, to speak our language, and we feel righteously incensed if they do not. Since language is the golden key to national culture, we thereby deprive ourselves of treasures that could enrich our own national experience. One linguist has even gone so far as to describe the learning of a second language as a "rebirth," since one thereby acquires a new personality pattern reflecting the cultural heritage represented by that language. For almost all Americans that rebirth never occurs, and our nation is correspondingly impoverished by the absence of it.

The term "rebirth" in this connection suggests a theological dimension to the problem: if we took Scripture more seriously, we would realize that our "chosen people" view of ourselves is utterly inconsistent with the Word of God, and that, like Peter, we need to be converted from our chauvinsim to "perceive that God is no respecter of persons: but in every nation he that feareth him, and worketh righteousness, is accepted with him" (Acts 10). We would then come to recognize that in a fallen world no one nation has a corner on virtues, but that there are always gains to be had in identifying with and incorporating the strengths of others, and in listening receptively to the criticism other countries send our way. How many Americans, to take a particularly striking example, would be willing to admit and benefit from the work of the totalitarian German Democratic Republic in the sphere of pollution control, where, as Peter Sand has shown, they have actually developed more advanced industrial anti-pollution contracts than our western free-enterprise system has done? It takes "rebirth," not merely linguistically but theologically, to sit as pupils and learn from our ideological opponents in the very areas of our strength.

(3) *Cultural Colorblindness.* Perhaps we do not inhabit a cultural desert, but the landscape is arid enough to warrant planned reclamation. We have just mentioned the American opaqueness to other languages and cultures—the conviction that all must be melted and melded into our own peculiar alloy. We are correspondingly opaque to the local linguistic scene in which we dwell. Commented Bertrand Russell:

> The lack of aesthetic sense produced by an excessive preoccupation with utility shows also in the matter of speech. Educated people throughout Europe, and peasants on the Continent and in Scotland and Ireland, have a certain beauty of diction: language is not merely a means of communication, but a vehicle for expressing the emotions of joy or sorrow, love or hate, that are the material of poetry. Words, many of them, have beauty; they have a history, and we are, each in our own day, responsible for handing on an unimpaired tradition in diction and enunciation. It is rare to find this feeling among Americans. If you make your meaning clear, what more can be desired? Accordingly their vocabulary

is small, and sounds which should be distinguished are
blurred. . . .

I console myself with the reflection that French,
now such a beautiful language, was in origin the argot
of uneducated Roman soldiers. Perhaps in fifteen hundred years American will become equally admirable.

If Mark Twain was correct when he declared, "There
is no such thing as the Queen's English; the property
has gone into the hands of a joint-stock company, and
we own the bulk of the shares," then everyone should
begin serious worrying, for the market quotation has
been going steadily down. H. L. Mencken thus im-
mortalized the prose of President Warren Gamaliel
Harding:

I have earned most of my livelihood for twenty years
past by translating the bad English of a multitude of
authors into measurably better English. Thus qualified
professionally, I rise to pay my small tribute to Dr.
Harding. Setting aside a college professor or two and
a half dozen dipsomaniacal newspaper reporters, he
takes the first place in my Valhalla of literati. That is
to say, he writes the worst English that I have ever
encountered. It reminds me of a string of wet sponges;
it reminds me of tattered washing on the line; it
reminds me of stale bean-soup, of college yells, of
dogs barking idiotically through endless nights. It is
so bad that a sort of grandeur creeps into it. It drags
itself out of the dark abysm (I was about to write ab-
scess!) of pish, and crawls insanely up the topmost
pinnacle of posh. It is rumble and bumble. It is flap
and doodle. It is balder and dash.

But I grow lyrical. More scientifically, what is the
matter with it? Why does it seem so flabby, so ba-
nal, so confused and childish, so stupidly at war with
sense? If you first read the inaugural address and then
heard it intoned, as I did (at least in part), then you will
perhaps arrive at an answer. That answer is very simple. When Dr. Harding prepares a speech he does
not think it out in terms of an educated reader locked
up in jail, but in terms of a great horde of stoneheads
gathered around a stand. That is to say, the thing is always
a stump speech; it is conceived as a stump speech and
written as a stump speech. More, it is a stump speech addressed primarily to the sort of audience that the speaker has been used to all his life, to wit, an audience of
small town yokels, of low political serfs, or morons
scarcely able to understand a word of more than two
syllables, and wholly unable to pursue a logical idea for
more than two centimeters.

Writers such as Dwight Macdonald, after viewing the rhetorical poverty of the Revised Standard as compared with the King James Version of the Bible, go so far as to speak of "the decline and fall of English"; the critics of today's linguistic scene in Robert Disch's *The Future of Literacy* are no less severe.

That our linguistic stock is close to bankruptcy is nowhere better evidenced than in the hilarious but agonizing best seller, *Strictly Speaking*, by Edwin Newman (possibly, aside from Mencken, the only literate American journalist of the 20th century?). Writes Newman:

Will America be the death of English? I'm glad I asked me that. My well-thought-out mature judgment is that it will. The outlook is dire; it is a later point in time than you think. The evidence is all around us.

In March, 1974, the White House press secretary, Ron Ziegler, explained a request for a four-day extension of a subpoena from the Watergate prosecutor for certain files. The extension was needed, Ziegler said, so that James St.Clair, President Nixon's attorney, could "evaluate and make a judgment in terms of a response."

We are all of us ready to man the barricades for the right to evaluate and make a judgment in terms of a response, but Ziegler could have said that St. Clair wanted more time to think about it. That he didn't is a commentary on the state of language in the United States, and the state of the language is a commentary on the state of our society. It must be obvious that our society, like our language, is in serious trouble when a man who represents the President speaks of evaluating and making a judgment in terms of a response; when the President himself feels no embarrassment (on any score, apparently) in saying, "There must be no white-wash at the White House," describes a possible course of action as taking the hang-out road, and, on asking his legal counsel for a detailed statement, is told, "Let me give you my overall first"; when a vice-president of the United States achieves fame of a sort through alliterative device: "pampered prodigies," "vicars of vacillation," "nattering nabobs of negativism"; when his successor denounces "prophets of negativity" and endorses the administration "policy-wise"; when Mayor John Lindsay of New York, about to step down, says that his youngest child will go to a boys' school because "he needs peer stuff"; when a publisher will put out what purports to be a book of poetry, *Pages,* by Aram Saroyan, in which, occupying an entire page, this constitutes a poem: "Something moving in the garden a cat"; and this: "incomprehensible birds"; and this: "Alice"; and this: "lobstee"; and when nobody takes medicine but rather medication. Indian tribes soon will have medication men. Ours is a time when Secretary of the Treasury William Simon advises Congress, "One cannot ad hoc tax reform." He might have added that there are no bargains at ad hoc shops.

And so on—for 227 excruciating pages. The only experience remotely comparable to reading Newman's book is the perusal of the immortal *Quotations from Mayor Daley,* containing such genuine masterpieces as: "Gentlemen, get the thing straight, once and for all—the policeman isn't there to create disorder, the policeman is there to preserve disorder." If, as the analytical philosopher Wittgenstein maintained, "Anything that can be said can be said clearly," we display an advanced case of National Fuzziness—fuzziness of tongue and fuzziness of mind. (Fuzzy-wuzzy was . . . an American grizzly bear?) I have long maintained that liberal theology is readily swallowed by American seminarians because they have grown up on a diet of nonsequitur TV commercials, have never been taught the rudiments of logic, but have been encouraged to "express themselves" in school and college whether they have anything to say or not. Linguistic sloppiness encourages sloppiness of thought, and vice-versa. We need not only to purge ourselves of linguistic pragmatism and indifferentism, but also to irrigate our cultural desert with the rich literary and intellectual resources of other nations.

Another concrete illustration of our utilitarian backwoodsishness is the area of cuisine (and much of ours is *concrete* in more ways than one). "Only in America," as Harry Golden would put it, could you find a recipe like the following—and it is genuinely typical of the Better Homes and Gardens' *Snacks and Refreshments* book* from which we have shakingly transcribed it:

---

*In this one case, no citation to the quoted publication will be found in the Bibliography at the end of this book. The reader is thereby preserved from the temptation of obtaining other recipes along the same line.

Golden Apricot Roll-ups

1 cup packaged pancake mix
1/2 cup apricot jam
2 slightly beaten eggs
1/2 cup corn-flake crumbs
2 tablespoons butter or margarine

Prepare pancake mix according to package
directions, but using *1 cup milk, 1 egg,* and
1 tablespoon salad oil or melted shortening.
Bake on griddle, as directed on package.
Spread about a tablespoon apricot jam over
each hot cake. Roll up. Dip rolls in egg, then
in corn-flake crumbs. Place, seam side down,
in skillet. Brown in butter over low heat.
Serve hot. Makes 8 roll-ups.

Observe how one enters another world (could one go
so far as to say "another metaphysical plane of existence"?) when listening to Joseph Wechsberg's description of his lunch at the Pyramide restaurant in Vienne,
near Lyons (now run by Mme Fernand Point, but visited
by Wechsberg before the death of her husband):

A waiter placed one of the ivory-colored plates in
front of me, and another waiter served me the first
hors-d'oeuvre, an excellent *pâté campagne en croûte.*
French cooks are generally expert at baking an extremely
light, buttery dough called *croûte,* but never before had
I eaten *croûte* that almost dissolved in my mouth. When
I had finished, the first waiter replaced my plate, fork,
and knife with clean ones, and a third waiter served me
a slice of *foie gras naturel truffé* embedded in a ring of
crème de foie gras. The ritual of changing plates and
silver was repeated after each hors-d'oeuvre—hot sausage
baked in a light pastry shell, accompanied by delicious
sauce piquante; a *pâté* of pheasant; crackling hot
cheese croissants; fresh asparagus (which M. Mercier
must have bought in Lyon that morning), set off by a
truly perfect *sauce hollandaise.*

A bottle of wine—an elegant, airy Montrachet—was
brought in an ice bucket; the waiter filled my glass
half full and gave it a gentle swirl to spread the bouquet.
It was a great show and a fine wine. The last hors-
d'oeuvre was followed in person by M. Point, who informed me that I had now completed the "overture."

"The overture merely indicates the themes that will
turn up later," he said. "A good meal must be as well

constructed as a good play. As it progresses, it should gain in intensity, with the wines getting older and more full-bodied."

Having delivered himself of this pronouncement, he returned to the kitchen.

Whenever I think back to that lunch, I feel contentedly well fed; the memory of it alone seems almost enough to sustain life. The next course was *truite au porto*, which, the headwaiter told me, had been prepared by M. Point himself; brook trout boiled in water to which vinegar, pepper, salt, and bay leaf had been added, and then skinned, split in half, and filled with a ragout of truffles, mushrooms, and vegetables. With it came a sauce made of butter, cream, and port wine.

It was a masterpiece. I was by then entirely willing to take the word of my friends in Paris that Fernand Point is today France's greatest chef. The trout was followed by a breast of guinea hen with morels, in an egg sauce; a splendid Pont-l'Evêque; strawberry ice-cream, made of *fraises de bois* that had been picked the same day; and an array of pâtisserie.

M. Point had chosen as a wine for the guinea hen a rich, full-bodied Château Lafite-Rothschild '24. And at the end of the meal, with my coffee, there was a Grande Fine Champagne '04, the taste of which I still remember vividly.

Later M. Point sat down at my table.... "Of course, I know that there is no such thing as perfection. But I always try to make every meal"—he closed his eyes, searching for the right words,—"*une petite merveille.* Now, you won't believe it, but I gave a lot of thought to your lunch."

In America it is most rare to find a meal, either in a private home or in a restaurant, that could be classed as *"une petite merveille"; "un petit catastrophe"* would better describe most of them. Because of our pragmatic indifference to the finer things of life, we simply do not "give a lot of thought" to what we eat, even though eating constitutes one of the major activities of life. Peter Hunt quotes from an essay in which André Simon, founder of the International Wine and Food Society, applied to our eating habits Theodore Dreiser's expression, "An American Tragedy":

The average American probably spends more than the average citizen of any other country in the world upon food and drink, but he certainly is less well nourished than the ordinary peasant class in any part of Europe. To say

nothing of the little French bourgeois whose income is
half that of a New York elevator boy, and yet feeds far
better than a Chicago packing millionaire. . . .

Of course, your belly must not be your god. You
should have no false gods. The average American's gods
are speed, shows and sugar. They are the first loves of
most children; they are desirable in themselves, and in
moderation. They are all very well so long as you cannot
or do not care to think. There is no exhilaration comparable to that of speed, nor any greater relaxation than
a well acted play or even film, no surer way to forget
one's worries or one's unsatisfactory self. But if it is
good to forget sometimes, it is better to remember and
to think: to remember others and to think of so many
people and so many things so well worth thinking about.
To think of others is what matters most, and that is not
done on a doped stomach or closed-up bowels; it is not
done on ice water any more than on fire water, "hard
liquor". That is what the new generation needs to be
taught in America, and maybe elsewhere as well. Food
is a very important matter and so is drink. Too few
Americans realize it at present. Too many eat what happens to be at hand, good or bad. It is all the same. They
have no time to think about it.

Again we arrive at a spiritual problem: we "have
no time" to think about food because our value system
excludes it, as it does so many of the cultural benefits
God has bestowed on the world out of His creative goodness. We prefer to bypass His gifts in order to give ourselves more time to carry out our self-made struggle
for "success." And evangelicals—as I have stressed in
an essay on "Transcendental Gastronomy"—instead of
serving as models of the well-balanced life, frequently
are the worst offenders because of their misconceived,
pietistic, monkish "denial of the flesh," which reduces
to a denial of God's creative work in the (supposed)
interests of His redemptive activity. As I declared in the
peroration of my inaugural lecture at the Académie de
Gastronomie "Brillat-Savarin" in Paris, we too easily
forget "la vérité fondamentale que les festins de ce
monde préfigurent le 'festin des noces de l'Agneau' à
la fin des temps"—the basic truth that the banquets of
this world prefigure the Marriage Supper of the Lamb
at the end of time.

*   *   *   *   *

Additional light on the good and the bad in American

society is shed by the exceedingly important cross-
cultural studies of Laurence Wylie, Professor of the Civilization of France at Harvard. In an essay on "Youth
in France and the United States," contributed to Erik
Erikson's symposium on *Youth: Change and Challenge,*
Wylie describes the openness and progress-orientation of
his own upbringing in a midwestern Methodist parsonage:
"I knew I should not accept life as it is but should act
so that I might help change things in preparation for
God's earthly kingdom. In school . . . I learned by heart:
'Let the Past bury its dead! Act, act in the living present!
Heart within, and God o'erhead!' " He then contrasts the
French experience:

> The French child learns that life has been compartmen-
> talized by man and that the limits of each compartment
> must be recognized and respected. The American child
> learns that life is a boundless experience. The Frenchman
> recognizes that rules are a convenience, but that they
> are man-made and therefore artificial. The American
> believes he has discovered his rules for himself and that
> they reflect the essential structure of reality. For the
> Frenchman, reality is dual: there is the official reality of
> man-made rules, but it is only a façade concealing a deep-
> er, more mysterious reality which may be felt by the in-
> dividual in moments of introspection or revealed by art
> and religion. For the American, reality is a unity, and
> any apparent discrepancy between the ideal and the
> actuality is essentially immoral. . . .

> There is a tendency in France to assume that one's
> position in the social structure is fixed. Just as Americans
> assume there is more mobility in their society than there
> is, the French assume that there is less chance for change
> than there actually is. . . .

> To fulfil his self-image, the French adolescent must learn
> to fit into the limits prescribed by society, and having
> accepted these boundaries, he utilizes the means avail-
> able to express his individuality outside these limits.
>   The American adolescent is in a quite different predica-
> ment as he strives to achieve the ideal image he has
> formed of himself. His difficulty lies not in living up to
> expectations but in discovering what they really are. The
> only system of rules he has been taught is a Sunday-school
> sort of code, and as he grows up he learns little by little
> that it is not the code by which people actually live. The
> real code exists, but no one defines it openly.
>   Confronted by the fact that this double standard
> exists, American adults beat their breasts and admit their

sins. Still they insist that the ideal code is the right one. Failure to live up to it is attributed only to the weakness of human beings who hopefully merit forgiveness when they confess their sins and show their good intentions. The adults' need to believe that everything will come out for the best in the long run is satisfied by placing the responsibility on the adolescents to make the ideal code function as it should. "Our generation has gotten the country into trouble, and we want you to get us out," Senator Barry Goldwater tells an audience of Young Republicans, just as every adult speaker has told every adolescent audience in which I have been present since I was a child. Adolescents are not told how to do a better job, however. When they ask for advice, they are merely given further indoctrination in the ideal code. Middle-aged professional adolescents continue to insist at Sunday-evening meetings, summer conferences, in discussion groups and recreational organizations that the ideal is attainable.

Which of these two world-views is correct? Neither—or both! The Frenchman is profoundly right in recognizing that in a fallen world the rules of society are largely man-made, that they are nonetheless ordinarily to be followed to prevent anarchy, and that the realm of ultimate values lies far deeper (cf. Romans 13). His failing is either too readily to fit in with the man-made structures, thereby preserving "the moss on the old oaken bucket along with the bucket itself" and not exercising his talents to change society for the better, or too skeptically to view all structures, considering them no more than arbitrary human creations. Politically, when the Frenchman makes the former error, he worships a Napoleon; when he commits the latter mistake, he becomes an insane revolutionary Jacobin—and oscillation between these two extremes has been the history of French politics in modern times (cf. the May "Revolution" of 1968 and de Gaulle's return to power, stronger than ever, as a result of it).

The American properly recognizes that there must be a connection between eternal values and societal structures—that a dualism between them can never be ultimately satisfying. But he makes the colossal blunder—based on his New Edenic, chosen-people, Promised Land, utopian mythology which we have analyzed in detail—of assuming *that he himself can build this unified value-system by his own rugged, frontier efforts.* "Let the Past bury its dead": he will create value from scratch, out of a wilderness if not *ex nihilo*! Of course, the resulting Promethean values (inevitable progress, rags-to-riches, "God helps them that help themselves," "honesty means success," etc.) will fail him, for they are not eternal truths, and in the attempt to force them on each younger generation, we breed hypocrisy, disrespect for all values, societal neurosis, and running Rabbit finally immobilized without knowing why. The only answer is (1) to recognize that reality and eternal value are not something *we* create, but a *given*—a gift from God, for which we are utterly dependent on Him, (2) to distinguish properly between human structures and divine structures (as the Frenchman haltingly tries to do, but is stymied by his Catholic culture that neglects to point him to Scripture as the single valid source of eternal truths), and (3) to devote our American ingenuity and energy not to "self-development" but to bringing our societal patterns more into line with biblically revealed standards. But how to achieve this in a pluralistic society, where the majority are no longer experientially Christian?

The Perils of Pluralism

The dilemma for today's American Christian is most acute: he knows that "except the Lord build the house, they labour in vain that build it"—that the very survival of our nation depends upon its alignment with eternal values—yet he knows equally well that our country stands for freedom in matters of religion as in other matters, so that he cannot impose particular religious beliefs (even though they actually represent divine truth) on his fellow citizens. In the earlier days of our nation's history, this dilemma, though always present in theory, was not especially troublesome in practice, since the vast majority of people—the "men on the street"—at least gave lip service to the biblical faith. But now religious and philosophical diversity has reached such a point in the United States that attempts to promote any particular religious position are sure to draw fire from adherents of other views. And the Supreme Court, in its school prayer decisions and other similar judgments, has made plain that it will not tolerate even indirect means of "establishing religion" in subversion of the First Amendment.

This is precisely the agonizing situation which en-

courages Professor Singer in his *Theological Interpretation of American History* to argue that in choosing democracy we departed from biblical faith and that the only
genuinely scriptural form of government is theocracy!
Earlier in the present book the difficulties with Professor
Singer's position were discussed; here we would only note
that he at least recognizes a very real problem: in any
democratic society, the number of non-Christians can con-
ceivably come to exceed the number of Christians, thereby
permitting the democratic elimination of biblical standards and the inevitable collapse of that society. Even
the constitutional exclusion of "certain unalienable
rights" from democratic revision does not solve the problem, for—as in the *Roe v. Wade* abortion decision, where
the Court redefined "person" in nonbiblical terms so as
to exclude the unborn child from constitutional protection of his right to life—a non-Christian Supreme Court
can reinterpret the Constitution so as to alienate the very
rights supposedly removed forever from alienation. The
answer, however, is hardly a theocracy, for the problem
of "watching the watchers" is just as real there, and
the possibilities of hypocrisy are considerably greater.
But how can we deal with the secularization process in
our existing democratic society, where the climate of
opinion becomes less distinctively Christian as every day
passes? I suggest three fundamental ground rules.

(1) *It is no solution to institutionalize Christian values,
even if our Constitution permitted it, which it does not.*
Our previous chapters have demonstrated that America
cannot be considered a Christian land in the sense that
a specific Christian corpus of doctrine has been incorporated into its founding documents: these documents
establish a concept of freedom and of inalienable rights
which is thoroughly biblical, but they expressly disavow
the establishment of religion. If, therefore, misguided
rightist Christians try to argue that nonetheless the founding documents do make Christianity our national faith
(on the basis of general references to the "Supreme
Being" and eternal principle), they end up promoting,
not historic, biblical Christianity at all, but what Robert
Bellah calls "civil religion," a vague national cult virtually indistinguishable from Deism—and that does
Christianity more harm than good, for it obscures the
uniqueness and finality of Jesus Christ (John 14:6; Acts
4:12). Moreover, as such widely diverse writers as Cush-

ing Strout, Martin Marty, and Justice William O. Douglas have observed, the establishment of Christianity in England and elsewhere has done Christianity irreparable harm, since people no longer come to regard Christianity as a matter of free decision but as a state obligation, and therefore turn from it.

In *The Bible and the Schools*, Douglas noted quite properly that "what the Roman Catholics, the Baptists, or the Presbyterians can command of the public treasury or in other public support, so in time can the Moslems or the Mormons as they grow politically stronger." A few years ago I gave politically conservative Harold John Ockenga some worrisome moments when at his "historic Park Street Church" in Boston I declared, as a Christian Education Conference speaker, that I fully agreed that prayers in the public schools should be banned. It is perfectly obvious that such prayers either open up the possibility of Moslem and Mormon prayers, or promote "non-sectarian" prayers which are just as bad, since they are not Trinitarian prayers in the Name of Jesus (Col. 3:17). If we want to integrate historic Christian worship with the educational task, the parochial school is the remedy. We cannot expect the state to do the church's business. Where it attempts to do so or is made to do so, the result is utter confusion of Law and Gospel and the mixing of the Two Kingdoms. In C. S. Lewis' terms, Aslan (the Christ-symbol) and Tash (the Antichrist) are syncretically blended into the monster "Tashlan." Marty is correct that ours is no longer the "placed" Christianity of Constantine or of the medieval "Corpus Christianum"; we have both the agony and the privilege, like the early Christians, of functioning in a pluralistic society as "strangers and pilgrims on the earth," having "here no continuing city, but we seek one to come."

(2) *It is no solution to legislate non-revelational mores in the name of revelation, or to legislate even genuinely scriptural moral teachings when they do not have direct and demonstrable social necessity.* Christians have as much a right as non-Christians to speak out and to influence legislation in our democratic society. The question is: how far should they go in exercising this right? On the negative side, they do neither the society nor the Gospel any service when they endeavor to legislate their own temporal values (such as prohibition, local liquor

options, Sunday closing laws, and the like) as if these derived from Scripture. The result can only be a loss of respect on the non-Christian's part for the Scripture if he becomes convinced that the non-revelational idea really does come from the Bible, or a loss of respect for professing Bible-believers if he discovers it doesn't. And if Christians employ their majority status to legislate genuine biblical teaching which, however, cannot be demonstrated to the non-Christian to have social necessity (such as anti-profanity ordinances), they will surely drive the unbeliever away from the Cross by giving him the impression that Christianity is a religion not of Gospel but of tyrannical legalism in which Christians force their peculiar beliefs on others whenever the political opportunity arises.* As I stress in my book, *The Law above the Law*, Christians often forget that there is a Last Judgment coming that will right the wrongs which human legislation is incapable of rectifying; we must not get the idea that every moral truth in Scripture is to be implemented on earth by human sanctions. Our task in a secular society is not to force the society, come what may, into the framework of God's Kingdom, but rather to bring it as close as we can to divine standards *consistent with effective Gospel preachment to the unbeliever.*

(3) *We should actively strive to legislate all revelational standards whose societal importance can be demonstrated to our fellow citizens, and where we are unsuccessful in legislating them we should do all in our power to create a climate of opinion in which they will eventually become acceptable.* In many instances not only are the ethical concerns of the day pronounced upon by Scripture,

---

*We do not mean to give the impression that *any* biblical truth is undemonstrable. However, there is a clear distinction between those truths (e.g., "God's name is holy") which are provable only by way of a general demonstration of the truth of the Bible (the historical data show that Christ rose again; He is therefore divine and His stamp of approval on the Bible establishes its total truth), and those truths (e.g., "Thou shalt not steal") whose social utility or necessity can be demonstrated to the non-Christian on independent grounds. To accept the former truths, one must, if sceptical, first be led by apologetic evidence to accept Christ (i.e., one must become a Christian); to accept the latter is possible apart from Christian profession. We must not force non-Christians to agree to peculiarly Christian moral values prior to accepting Christ; otherwise Gospel will inevitably be turned into Law and the non-Christian will refuse to consider Christianity on Gospel grounds.

but the validity of the scriptural position on them is independently demonstrable to a non-Christian audience. Thus, for example, open housing and equal pay for equal work (Acts 17:26; Gal. 3:28), stringent narcotics laws and rigorous enforcement of them (I Cor. 6:19-20), antiabortion laws (Ps. 51:5; Luke 1:15, 41, 44)—in all these instances a powerful case can be made on scientific, social, and ethical grounds meaningful to the non-Christian, apart from the biblical justification for these same values.* Christians have a holy responsibility to serve as lights in the world in such instances, and where they succeed in bringing about an elevation of societal standards they can point the non-Christian to the revelational source of their beliefs, thereby creating a powerful impetus for the unbeliever to consider the claims of Christ: seeing their light so shining, the non-Christian will be impressed by their good works and glorify their Father which is in heaven (Matt. 5:13-16).

Tension remains, however, and it cannot be overcome in a secular society; it is the price of living in a fallen world. On the one hand, we must not permit the non-Christian to conclude from our political or social actions that Christianity is a religion of legalistic compulsion. Thus, in matters such as divorce legislation, we may well conclude, as I have argued elsewhere, that a parallel no-fault divorce ought to be available to those who want it, since to compel non-Christians to divorce according to Christian standards when they have married according to pagan standards is to lay upon them a burden they may not be able to bear. "Moses because of the hardness of your hearts suffered you to put away your wives: but from the beginning it was not so." Yet, on the other hand, short of creating a stumbling block to the non-Christian that would keep him from the Cross, we need to push pluralistic America toward biblical values until it says "uncle"—for only by the maintenance of God's standards can we counteract the "leveling" process which brings us to lowest-common-denominator secularity and jeopardizes our very survival as a free people.

---

* For examples of such argumentation relative to the abortion issue—which Professor Witherspoon of the University of Texas School of Law rightly considers the gravest moral and constitutional issue of our day—see the *Human Life Review*, and my contributions to *Birth Control and the Christian*, the *Journal of the American Medical Association*, and *The Jurist*.

We must not, for example, conclude that because Christianity cannot be preached in the public schools, we can do nothing to prevent the preaching of Deistic civil religion, evolutionary secularism, Transcendental Meditation, or the latest religio-cultic fad. The same Constitution that protects obnoxious Mrs. O'Hair from having Christianity rammed down the throats of her offspring protects the Christian school child from metaphysical poison. Christians should scream bloody murder at school board meetings where their constitutional rights are being trampled and should litigate the issues in the courts when they do not obtain satisfaction. Positively, Christian teachers in the public schools have every right, as well as a clear moral obligation, to introduce the facts of biblical history and the objective accomplishments of the Christian church into their instruction, and they should encourage open, free, and non-evangelistic discussion of religious issues (in which the merits of Christ's Way will readily surface!) as a necessary part of liberal education. After a careful discussion of the legal and constitutional issues involved, attorney Christopher Hall rightly argues:

> The manner in which educators evade a discussion of values indicates that there is danger of overemphasizing discretion. Given the nation-wide misunderstanding of the nature and extent of the court rulings in this area, it is all too easy for the Christian teacher to utterly fail to share his or her faith because they "do not want to stir up trouble." *Put in these words,* no Christian anywhere would want to "stir up trouble." Had the early Church thought of it in that way, Peter would not have defied the Sanhedrin (Acts 4:1-20 and 5:27-29) and Paul would not have offended the "devout and honorable women, and the chief men" of Antioch in Pisidia (Acts 13:46-50).

Harold O. J. Brown does not exaggerate when he speaks of "the passivity of American Christians": the gutless manner in which so many professing evangelicals abrogate their responsibilities to their society in the interests of "not offending." We shall see in our next and final chapter how the ingrown, sanctimonious pietism characteristic of evangelical circles has contributed to this unfortunate result; for the moment, let us simply take Brown's words to heart:

> Christians must acknowledge that if God has placed them in a largely non-Christian society (at least in the sense

of genuine commitment, as opposed to merely nominal Christianity), it is not in order that they be transformed by it, but for its healing and transformation by them. Can God expect less of Christians than that they at least have the courage to attempt to *persuade* non-Christians that the organization of society according to Christian, biblical principles is to the advantage of all?

Conversely, if Christians, who through our historical development have been the trustees of most of the ethical and moral wisdom of our civilization—for it has come to us through Christian sources—refuse or are too timid to share it with others, they are depriving the whole nation and all its people of a good of which they are supposed to be stewards and disseminators, not mere warehousemen. What this simply means is that it is a Christian duty to proclaim to all society, not just to the like-minded, the social value of the laws, principles, and insights that we derive from our biblical heritage, but that correspond in their ultimate validity to the nature of man as a creature made in the image of God.

Exporting the American Way

Analogous to the question which the Christian American must face as to how far scriptural values are to be pushed in a secular America is the general question as to how far American values are to be pushed in the world at large. And just as American evangelicals manifest a "passivity" in expressing their convictions in the domestic marketplace of ideas, so the country in general seems more and more reticent to export its national values beyond its own boundaries.

True, with our Promised Land mythology, we have had a history of "carrying the big stick," and if we have seldom engaged in political imperialism we have more than once made up for it by extending our economic tentacles around the globe. We have exported coca cola, cheap jazz, and jeans until it is small wonder that countries with a modicum of taste and culture have not established aesthetic tariff barriers to keep us out! The universal appreciation for Puccini's *Madame Butterfly* quite clearly shows that our worldwide adventures have left a trail of broken hearts, whatever else they may have accomplished.

Moreover, a special danger is now seen to attach to crusades in behalf of "western values": the danger of letting the end justify the means. Hochhuth's drama

The Deputy and Carlo Falconi's *Silence of Pius XII* tell the sobering story of a pope who, because of his crusade against Russian Communism as the greatest of all evils, compromised his spiritual authority by not speaking forthrightly against the genocidic activities of the Third Reich, in the vain expectation that Hitler would at least save Europe from Marxism. Such a fundamental blunder easily leads to a reconsideration as to whether ideological crusades do not often do more harm than good.

But again the drunken man staggers to the opposite wall. Just as we petulantly fell into an irresponsible isolationism after our World War I disenchantment, so today we run every danger of abrogating our responsibilities as bearer of the torch of freedom now that our enemies have castigated us and our friends misunderstood us for our tragic involvement in Vietnam. William Lederer, in a book published as long ago as 1961, characterized us as *A Nation of Sheep* for our irresponsiveness in foreign policy.

On the day before Christmas, 1975, a Religious News Service release announced:

> The number of people in the world living in a democratic society reportedly dropped by 40 percent in 1975 —the sharpest dip recorded by Freedom House since it began assessing the trend 24 years ago.

> Freedom House, an independent organization here devoted to the strengthening of free societies, said its 20-foot "map of freedom" has been "darkened as never before." The map depicts free nations in white, partly free in grey and the not free in black.

> Led by India with 619.6 million citizens, eight nations with a combined population of 743.2 million experienced sharp declines in freedom as measured by the Freedom House ratings. Freedom expanded in only five nations in 1975, with 60 million citizens.

> The 1975 Comparative Survey of Freedom lists 57 nations with 803.6 million population as Free, 84 nations with 1,435.8 million people as Partly Free, and 68 nations with 1,823.4 million people as Not Free.

> This means 19.8 per cent of the world's population is now living in freedom, 35.3 per cent are partly free and 44.9 per cent are not free.

> Last year, the comparative study showed 35 per cent of the world's people free, 23 per cent partly free and 42 per cent not free.

> The annual survey covers the level of individual freedom in 156 nations and 51 dependent territories, based on criteria developed for the survey.

That this is a horrifying situation goes without saying. What responsibility do we have as a nation to prevent or to reverse such trends?

Our current foreign policy of détente, as expressed most eloquently by Secretary of State Kissinger, would appear to offer little response to this question beyond maintaining defensive strength in our own right and continuing to voice our historic beliefs in the value of free society. This seems hardly enough when, as Kissinger's even more eloquent adversary Solzhenitsyn has rightly maintained, the free world has a holy responsibility to relieve the miseries of the millions of people suffering under totalitarian governments with neither the possibility of legal redress of grievances in their own homeland nor the possibility of emigrating to a life of dignity elsewhere. We grant that full-scale offensive war against totalitarian powers could be suicidal in a nuclear age, but was there sufficient excuse for not responding to the Czechoslovakians when, like Paul's Macedonians, they pleaded, "Come over and help us"? And is there any way to justify our not attaching rigorous conditions (release of those jailed or confined to "psychiatric hospitals" because they exercised freedom of speech; permission for Jews and others desiring to emigrate to do so; etc.) when we agree to supply totalitarian countries with the raw materials, products, or food supplies they request of us?*

Novelist Jean Dutourd, in his *Taxis of the Marne,* reminded his own people of the contrast between the France of 1914, which had the dynamism to use taxis to get its reinforcements to the front to save the country, and the France of June, 1940, when "the Generals were stupid, the soldiers did not want to die," and the country, by trying to save its life with no higher purpose, lost it. Bruckberger, another clear-eyed French observer, applies the lesson to us:

---

*"We are slaves, but we are striving for freedom. You, however, were born free. If so, then why do you help our slave owners? In my last address I only requested one thing and I make the same request now: when they bury us in the ground alive—I compared the forthcoming European agreement with a mass grave for all the countries of East Europe—as you know, this is a very unpleasant sensation: your mouth gets filled with earth while you're still alive—please do not send them shovels. Please do not send them the most modern earth-moving equipment."—Solzhenitsyn, speaking under AFL-CIO sponsorship in New York City on July 9, 1975.

What ill luck, how great a misfortune it is for us all, that it should be the ideology of the Communist Manifesto, and not that of your Declaration of Independence, which is now conquering so large a part of the world and firing the imagination of the colored races. Americans, for this you may well be to blame, just as undoubtedly all Christians are to blame for the fact that today the name of Lenin is held in greater veneration in the world than the name of Jesus. We Christians have failed in missionary spirit. And you, Americans, have been too ready to look upon the Declaration of Independence as a document designed for yourselves alone and not for other nations. How fatal an error.

Americans, it is time to admit that you have erred; it is time to recognize that the Declaration of Independence is not yours alone. That solemn Declaration was made not just for you, but for everyone; not just for the men of one time, the eighteenth century, and one place, America— but for the whole world and for all the generations of mankind.

It is perhaps worth emphasizing at a time when the idea of détente carries such a positive connotation and so much stress is placed on not interfering with the internal affairs of other nations, that the National State is not the end-all and be-all of human existence, much less its highest value. The National State is a relatively modern development, and the notion of its absoluteness comes from such doubtful sources as realpolitiker Machiavelli (*Il Principe*) and atheist Thomas Hobbes (*The Leviathan*). Scripture insists that states, no less than individuals, are subordinate to God's laws. When Christian apologist Hugo Grotius became the "father of international law" by creating that discipline through his great work, *De jure belli et pacis,* his fundamental principle was that nations are subject to higher laws than the ones they themselves deign to create.

If we have any reason for existence as a nation, it is surely our historic stand for freedom—freedom without which living becomes mere existence—that freedom which is a necessary condition for the meaningful proclamation of the eternal riches of Christ. In Lincoln's most famous evocation of freedom, he did not limit himself to his own country, but declared: "Government of the people, by the people, for the people, shall not perish *from the earth.*" And Julia Ward Howe, a year earlier, made the essential connection between God's redemptive work in Christ and the national purpose to which we are (or should be) committed: "As He died to make men holy, let us die to make men free." When we no longer are willing to die for the freedom of others, we shall no longer merit freedom for ourselves.

3

The Gospel Vision

In his *Growth of American Thought*, the great American intellectual historian Merle Curti writes:

> The Christian tradition, introduced by the first comers, reinforced by nearly all their European successors, and perpetuated by conscious effort, was the chief foundation stone of American intellectual development. No intellectual interest served so effectively as Christian thought to bring some degree of unity to the different classes, regions, and ethnic groups. Whatever differences in ways of life and whatever conflicts of interest separated the country gentry and great merchants from the frontiersmen, poor farmers, artisans, and small shopkeepers, all nominally subscribed to Christian tenets and at least in theory accepted Christianity as their guide.

This impressive testimonial to the importance of Christian thought in American history leads naturally to the question: what can contemporary Christianity offer the Concentric, Melancholic American at Bicentennial time to assist him in solving the grave problems he faces? The American church today is most easily understood in terms of its two major foci, the "liberal" and the "evangelical," and we shall pose this vital concluding question to each, and then endeavor to offer suggestions going beyond the weaknesses of both these movements.

Modern Religiosity in Collapse

Very little space will be devoted here to today's "liberal" wing of the American church. Though the larger denominations, especially the Methodist, Presbyterian, and Episcopal churches, are administratively in the hands of theological liberals, their divinity schools almost one

hundred percent liberal, and their local churches ener-
vated by liberal clergy, the movement they represent
is a dying phenomenon. The more theologically liberal
a denomination, the slower its growth rate and the less
its per capita contributions. Many liberal denominations
have kept a façade of growth only by ecumenical union
with other liberal churches. Most indicative of all, the
nondenominational liberal seminaries, which have always constituted the prime prestige symbols of the movement, are in serious trouble. A *Time* report (October
9, 1972) sketched the national picture:

> For much of its 136-year history, New York's pres-
> tigious Union Theological Seminary has been the largest
> interdenominational divinity school in North America.
> This fall, however, as Union opens its academic year,
> its enrollment is down 227 students from a peak of 665
> four years ago, dropping the school to sixth in size. More-
> over, Union is currently operating on a budget deficit
> ($390,000 last year) and, as President J. Brooke Mosley
> candidly admits, is undergoing an identity crisis. Says
> Mosley: "The school has not been clear about its prior-
> ities in the past several years."
>
> Union's troubles are variously shared by other lead-
> ing liberal seminaries. The University of Chicago Divin-
> ity School has suffered a net loss of 200 students in the
> past four years, reducing its enrollment almost by half.
> Harvard's enrollment for its Master of Divinity pro-
> gram is also down. Yale Divinity School has had its
> university subsidy cut from $300,000 a year to $30,000,
> mandating the school's recent merger with the well-
> endowed (though ailing) Berkeley Divinity School in
> New Haven.

It is estimated that if Union Seminary's enrollment continues to drop at the same rate for the next twenty years
that it has for the last twenty years, the school will simply
die a natural death.

Why this decline of liberal Christianity? *Time* accurately observes that an "evangelical renascence" is
in progress and that "many liberals have become dis-
illusioned with the church as an instrument of social reform and have redirected their money to secular organizations." These considerations point to the central
problem in theological liberalism: it has always, by definition, endeavored to relate itself first and foremost
to the trends of the time. The origins of liberal American Protestantism can be traced back to 18th-century

Deism and its milder Unitarian counterparts, as we have seen, but the movement attained unified, national significance only in the late 19th century, when its fortunes rose in direct proportion to the success of the progress myth. Hard on the rise of Darwinianism came English Neo-Hegelian theologians (such as T. H. Green, and Edward Caird, author of *The Evolution of Religion*) who declared that Christianity was really an evolutionary faith! In America, as Irvin Wyllie has already taught us, liberal religion put Christianity at the service of the self-made-man ideology, big business, science, and the philosophy of pragmatic success. When Charles Clayton Morrison refounded *The Christian Century* in 1908 (a journal whose dissemination and influence are now minuscule in comparison with evangelicalism's *Christianity Today*), the title conveyed the popular secular dream, which we have examined in detail, that the new century would usher in an epoch of millennial progress consistent with man's inherent moral evolution.

The collapse of the progressivistic mirage due to the World Wars only caused liberal theology to change horses: when Existentialism became the prevailing secular philosophy of despair, the liberals suddenly announced that Christianity was at root a theology of existence, *Angst,* and self-authentication. With increasing secularism during the Cold War came liberalism's "theologies of secularity." When Vietnam protest became general, the liberals developed corresponding theologies of protest; the struggles for racial justice led to the creation of "black theology." Most recently, interest in Whitehead and Hartshorne's process philosophy has brought about a Protestant process theology (John B. Cobb, Jr., Shubert Ogden, Norman Pittenger); revolutionary political interests, a theology of liberation; and increasing leisure time, a concern with developing a "theology of play" (Harvey Cox).

Elsewhere I have plotted this regressive demise as *The Suicide of Christian Theology.* Its practical effects on the church have been devastating. Writes convert-to-historic-Christianity Malcolm Muggeridge, who "rediscovered Jesus" not because of, but in spite of, liberal clergy:

> It is not surprising that the ministry should attract crackpots, eccentrics and oddities who in happier times would have appeared as characters in Waugh's earlier novels rather than as beneficed clergymen.

Scarcely a day goes by but some buffoon in holy orders makes an exhibition of himself in one way or another, more often than not on the subject of sex—that *pons asinorum* of our time. Can it be wondered at, then, that the Church's voice, when heard, is more often than not greeted with derision or just ignored?

In practice, very few clergy trained in the liberal tradition had the traumatic benefit of experiencing an Indian Mutiny (as did Farrell's fictional Padre in the *Siege of Krishnapur*), so as to disabuse them of their naïve and antiscriptural view of human goodness and inevitable progress. For every Karl Barth who saw hell in the trenches of World War I, there have been thousands like John Updike's Rev. Mr. Eccles, who are incapable of ministering with any effectiveness to the disorientated, aimlessly running Rabbits of 20th-century America, since they lack that confidence in Scripture which alone permits one to declare, "Thus saith the Lord."

Protestant liberalism offers no answers because its interest is limited to the questions. Like the proverbial chameleon, it changes color according to the cultural surface it sits upon. Afraid at root that secularism has all the cards, it prefers to "fold" rather than to run the risk of losing the game. Its motto might well be: *If you can't beat 'em, join 'em.* But in joining the spirit of the age, it sells the Christian birthright for a mess of secular pottage, and offers only a counterfeit religion to the American seeking answers at Bicentennial time.

The Evangelical Dilemma

American evangelicals, in contrast, are growing in numbers and influence daily. Their churches are filled; their budgets are high; their seminaries are crowded; their student organizations are recording impressive numbers of conversions on secular campuses; their world and regional congresses on evangelism are of global significance; and here in America their prime spokesman, Billy Graham, is probably the single individual most respected by the majority of his fellow citizens. Moreover (and this is surely the major reason for the "evangelical renascence"), evangelicalism maintains without compromise the "faith once delivered to the saints": an authoritative Scripture, the biblical Gospel of Christ's death for our sins and resurrection for our justification,

and the teachings of the historic Christian church as summarized, for example, in the Apostles' Creed. Here, therefore, one should certainly expect to find religious answers on one's 200th birthday.

And evangelicalism does indeed provide answers, if
only by pointing with an unwavering finger to Holy Scripture and its divine Christ. But the effectiveness of evangelical proclamation is very seriously blunted by certain
grave sociological difficulties to which we must give our
attention.

American evangelicalism did not grow directly from
the soil of the Protestant Reformation. Nor did it arise
from the 17th-century Puritan heritage, which, as we have
seen, was a reflection of the last great period of Classical-Christian integration. From the Reformation to
modern evangelicalism the path wends its way through
"left-wing," Anabaptist-Mennonite, "believers' baptism"
theology, Moravian Pietism, the English Arminian-Wesleyan movement, and—of principal interest to us here,
since it constitutes such a vital aspect of religious history—Great-Awakening revivalism. From the Anabaptist-Mennonite tradition came a powerful stress on "personal religious decision" and serious doubts as to the
adequacy of any gradual coming-to-faith through cate-
chetical or other formalistic instruction. The Moravian
Pietists added a deep-seated suspicion toward the propositions of orthodox theology taken by themselves, and
the conviction that an identifiable "experience" and a
certain quality of life are as important as doctrine in
the makeup of the true believer. Wesley (who was converted in a Moravian meeting) reinforced these emphases
with strong insistence on man's act of faith (the human
contributory response to God's grace) and on the theoretical possibility of living a sanctified life of "Christian perfection." All of these elements came together in
the Great Awakening of the 1740's: the necessity for a
radical, personal, identifiable experience of salvation in
order to consider oneself saved; the essentiality of the
sinner's own volitional contribution* to this experience;
and the blending of justification and "holiness" in the
same general operation (as suggested by the strange use

---

*Less emphasis was of course placed on man's contributory act by
Calvinist preachers of revival such as George Whitefield. But the pre-
dominant American revivalistic theology has always been that of the
Arminian-Wesleyan Methodist circuit riders.

of the word "revival" to cover the preaching of both original commitment and *re*commitment).

American revivalism deserves the highest praise for stressing the central biblical truth that Christian faith does neither the individual nor society any good if it does not become a genuine reality in people's lives; one thinks in this connection of Augustine's insistence that Christ be the center and the circumference of every true believer's existence, and Luther's reminder that becoming a Christian is like dying: no one can do it for you. However, at the same time, we must recognize the extra-biblical elements in the theology and practice that gave birth to revivalism and came to define it.

First, though the Bible insists that there is no salvation unless Christ becomes experientially real in a man's life, no single psychological avenue to that reality is set forth in Scripture: Peter's gradual growth in grace is as real as Paul's unique, dynamic experience on the Damascus road. The theological tradition from Anabaptism to the Great Awakening tended to absolutize a single, stereotyped variety of conversion experience.

In the second place, Pietism's emphasis on one's response to the Gospel rather than on the Gospel itself and its suspicion toward formal doctrine tended to move Christians in a subjective, anti-intellectual direction, cut them off from the theological sources of their strength, remove them from the chastening control of earlier church history, and open them to the wild "reinterpretation" of the Bible in terms of their own experiential lights. The Pietists in Europe had created *ecclesiolae in ecclesiis* ("little churches in the churches")—groups of "true" believers as distinct from the "unregenerate" mass of professing church members—and this fostered attitudes of sanctimonious self-righteousness based on superficial, observable life-style, in contradiction to our Lord's insistence that the tares must be allowed to remain with the wheat until the judgment, "lest while ye gather up the tares, ye root up also the wheat with them" (Matt. 13:24-30).

Thirdly, in the Arminian-Wesleyan teaching that a man contributes his act of decision to the gracious work of God in salvation, the Protestant dog was permitted to return to synergistic Catholic vomit: Luther's "Copernican revolution in theology" was reversed so as to put man again in the position to trip the switch of salvation;

such a teaching flies in the face of Eph. 2:8-9, and offers the most dangerous possibilities of reintroducing a subtle form of works-righteousness into the church. Wesley's preoccupation with sanctification and with the conditions of "Christian perfection" reinforced the existing pietistic tendency to stress observable conduct and "good works" and to deemphasize the cardinal Reformation teaching of forensic justification; the eventual path of American Methodism would lead, by way of these themes, directly into the arms of Rauschenbusch's social gospel and G. Bromley Oxnam's liberal ecumenism. In sum, the several influences just mentioned gave American revivalism a unique focus on "religious experience" which has no direct parallel either in Scripture or in the teachings of the Reformers.

THEOLOGICAL MOVEMENT	SPECIAL EMPHASIS
1) The main-stream Reformation	The Word (Law & Gospel)
2) Anabaptist-Mennonite tradition	"Believers' baptism"
3) The Moravian Pietists	Demonstrable Christian life
4) Arminian-Wesleyan tradition	Contributory act of faith & growth in empirical holiness
5) American Revivalism & today's Evangelicalism	Religious experience

To understand American revivalism—which, more than any other single factor, has created the tone of modern evangelicalism—it must be seen in frontier context. The Great Awakening of the 1740's occurred very largely under frontier conditions, and the Methodist circuit riders and Baptist preachers of revival that followed in its wake took the Gospel to those who were steadily pushing the frontier boundary farther westward. Here is Thomas Low Nichols' contemporary description of a typical revival meeting in 1835:

> The camp meetings are mostly held by the Methodists. They gather from a wide district, with tents, provisions, and cooking utensils; form a regular camp in some picturesque forest, by some lake or running stream; a preacher's stand is erected, seats are made of plank, straw laid in a space railed off in front of the preachers for those who are struck with conviction or who wish

to be prayed for to kneel upon, and then operations com-
mence.

Ten or twelve preachers have collected, under the
leadership of some old presiding elder or bishop, who
directs the proceedings. Early in the morning, the blow-
ing of a horn wakes the camp to prayers, singing, and
a bountiful breakfast: then the day's work begins. People flock in from the surrounding country. Sonorous
hymns, often set to popular song-tunes are sung by the
whole congregation, pealing through the forest aisles.
Sermon follows sermon, preached with the lungs of Sten-
tors and the fervour of an earnest zeal. Prayer follows
prayer. The people shout, "Amen!" "Bless the Lord!"
"Glory to God!" "Glory! Hallelujah!" They clap their
hands, and shout with the excitement. Nervous and hyster-
ical women are struck down senseless, and roll upon the
ground. "Mourners" crowd to the anxious-seats, to be
prayed for. There is groaning, weeping, shouting, praying, singing. Some are suddenly converted, and make the
woods ring with joyful shouts of "Glory!" and these ex-
hort others to come and get religion. After three or four
hours of this exciting and exhausting work, a benedic-
tion is given, and all hands go to work to get dinner.
Fires are burning behind each tent, great pots are smoking
with savoury food, and, while spiritual affairs are the
main business, the physical interests are not neglected.
After dinner comes a brief session of gossip and repose.
Then there are prayer meetings in the different tents, and
the scenes of the morning are repeated at the same time
in a dozen or twenty places, and the visitor who takes a
place in the centre of the camp may hear exhortations,
prayers, and singing going on all together and on every
side, while at times half a dozen will be praying and ex-
horting at once in a single group, making "confusion
worse confounded." . . .

Then the horn blows again, and all gather before the
preacher's stand, where the scenes of the morning are
repeated with increased fervour and effect. A dozen
persons may be taken with "the power"—of the Holy
Ghost as believed—falling into a state resembling cat-
alepsy. More and more are brought into the sphere of the
excitement. It is very difficult for the calmest and most
reasonable person to avoid its influence.

Now there is no doubt that such revivalistic evangelicalism did bear positive fruit. The genuine piety
exemplified in David Brainerd's *Diary*, edited by no less
distinguished a figure in the Great Awakening than Jonathan Edwards, demonstrates that fact, as does the preach-

A camp meeting in southern New York in 1836.

ing of Edwards' grandson Timothy Dwight, who literally rechristianized Yale College during his presidency at the turn of the 19th century. In *Revivalism and Social Reform,* Timothy L. Smith has definitively shown the extensive influence of the revivalists on social service and eleemosynary activity (reminding one, by contrast, of Malcolm Muggeridge's classic comment that he had yet to hear of a Unitarian leper colony). A little-known laboratory example of the positive effect of American evangelical revival was the missionary conversion of Hawaii in the 19th century; in his testimonial to Loomis' *Grapes of Canaan: Hawaii 1820,* refuting James A. Michener's unfounded accusations, Abraham Akaka declares:

> I am glad that these missionaries, so often ridiculed and maligned, came to our islands and to our people. Because of them, we native Hawaiians have fared much better over the past one hundred and fifty years than "discovered" natives in Africa, India, the Americas and other areas of the world. Rather than bringing extinction and extermination, the missionaries were a people who, like grapes of Canaan long ago, brought joy of heart and gladness of soul to my people. Their lives and labors are the foundation for Hawaii's eventual [now actual] statehood.

But there is another, far less attractive side to revivalism, as Nichols' account of a typical frontier camp meeting makes plain. Revivalism picked up the unfortunate qualities of the frontier (its theology had already prepared it to do so) and it injected these qualities into the lifeblood of American evangelicalism. In his essay on "The Ohio Valley in American History," Frederick Jackson Turner touches on "such democratic and emotional sects as the Baptists, Methodists and the later Campbellites, as well as Presbyterians," stressing that their frontier mentality provided "a foundation of emotional responsiveness to religion and a readiness to find a new heaven and a new earth in politics as well as religion." Frontier revivalism accepted the American Edenic dream, giving it an emotional, pietistic twist: the Promised Land was indeed available in America, but only those who had the proper conversion experience and led the right kind of sanctified lives could truly enter it. Revivalistic evangelicalism developed an *ecclesiola in patria*—a little church within the nation—a "true Israel" that alone represented the divine promise. The characteristics of this "peculiar people" (peculiar in more ways than one!) were anti-intellectualism (opposition to "the wisdom of this world"), moralistic legalism (do's and don't's—but chiefly don't's—served as identifying marks of the sanctified ingroup), and, perhaps most significant and unfortunate of all, cultural insolation.

In the face of increasing secularism in the late 18th and the 19th centuries and the growing complexity of life, revivalistic evangelicalism took the easy way out: *If you can't beat 'em, separate from 'em.* In a sense, even towering evangelists of the Great Awakening had contributed to the pattern, for most of them preached the "simple Gospel" without attempting to deal in any profound way with the Deistic philosophy of the time. One recalls Whitefield's correspondence with Franklin: "As you have made a pretty considerable progress in the mysteries of electricity, I would now humbly recommend to your diligent unprejudiced pursuit and study the mystery of the new birth": Franklin should study the new birth, but Whitefield does not seem to help him by studying, so as effectively to refute, the contemporary Deistic ideas that drew Franklin away from the Gospel. For every Jonathan Edwards or Timothy Dwight there were hundreds of revivalists who made no effort to understand the secular thought of their day, to say nothing of giving an answer to it. When a recent article by an evangelical seminarian (Mark Shaw's "Spirit of 1740") claims that the Great Awakening was the real birthday of our nation, the result is merely whistling in the dark: after all is said that can be said for the revivalists of that era, one cannot possibly maintain that they met head-on the controlling secular ideas of their day or in fact dominated the climate of opinion.

And subsequent generations of revivalistic evangelicals did far less in this respect. It was too easy to maintain the pietistic ingroup on the basis of superficial outward expressions of holiness and limit evangelism to snatching brands from the secular burning. Thus particular attention was given to the condemnation of "worldly" practices—while the great ethical, philosophical, scientific, and cultural issues of the day were left to go begging. Charles J. Stewart's study of contemporary sermonic reactions to Lincoln's assassination by Northern clergy reveals that a full third of them condemn in some fashion or other Lincoln's presence at Ford's Theatre; for example:

>Would that he had fallen elsewhere than at the very
>gates of Hell—in the theatre, to which through persuasion,
>he so reluctantly went. But, thus a stain has been put
>upon that so falsely called school of virtue. How awful
>and severe the rebuke, which God has administered to
>the nation, for pampering such demoralizing places of
>resort! The blood of Abraham Lincoln can never be ef-
>faced from the stage. . . .

Such preaching compares favorably with those Deistic
sermons of the Enlightenment which took from the resurrection text, "Very early in the morning the first day
of the week, the women came unto the sepulchre at the
rising of the sun," the theme: "The Virtues of Early
Rising." The fact that the latter derives from Bible-
doubters while the former comes from Bible-believers
is inconsequential, since both involve the preaching of
an extrabiblical, non-revelational message and the consequent avoidance of the real issue. But these examples
are a useful reminder that evangelicals, no less than liberals, can and do bypass Scripture and substitute their
own ideas for its teachings—regardless of their theoretical
beliefs and formal protestations to the contrary.

Such negativistic revivalism is sadly characteristic
of American evangelicals through most of their history.
Here is a by-no-means atypical example of late 19th-
century revivalistic preaching—by Evangelist Martin
Wells Knapp (thoughtfully preserved in book form by
the M. W. Knapp Revivalist Office, Cincinnati, Ohio):

>The humblest pupil who is really in the school of
>Christ is "wiser" than the profoundest sage whose eyes
>have never been opened to the realities of eternity and
>things divine. As one has said, it were better to be
>"learning the alphabet in heaven than reading Greek in
>hell." . . .
>Continually supplied by the King from the chalice of
>divine truth with the crystal soul inspiring water of life
>there is no craving for the putrid, slimy waters from
>the stagnant pools where deluded worldlings attempt to
>slake their thirst.
>It has been truthfully said that: "Dancing, rink going,
>card playing, theater going, horse racing, novel reading,
>and circus-loving professors are doing vastly more harm
>than open infidelity." They do double harm, they ruin
>their own souls and give the lie to our religion by act-
>ing as if its fruits were unsatisfactory and less desirable
>than these "rotten apples" of "Sodom." Worldly amuse-

ments, much loved as they might have been, seem like flickering tallow candles of satan's own lighting, and are forever rejected when the "Son of Righteousness" is shining in the soul. Listening to the soul entrancing melodies of the Divine Music-maker who henceforth makes the heart His conservatory of music, the croaking jargon of the frogs of worldliness which ever haunt the dismal swamps of sin, becomes inexpressibly repellant.

The most damning aspect of such preaching lies not so much in its tragic rhetoric or even its blatantly unscriptural moralism and anti-intellectualism, but in the fact that while such revivalism went on, the secular, evolutionary progressivism of the century was left with neither prophetic opposition nor reasoned, scripturally based refutation. America was allowed to descend into the secular abyss while evangelicals ranted and raved about dancing and the theatre. A descendant of Cotton Mather, Roger Williams, and Francis Asbury—one Herbert Asbury—described in a humorous but tragic book, *Up from Methodism,* how such evangelical "proclamation" drove him to reject the Christian faith altogether.

But surely today's evangelicalism cannot be placed in this category? One would fervently hope not, and encouragement comes from the mere existence of learned, cultured representatives of it such as Wilbur M. Smith, whose autobiography, *Before I Forget,* is a blueprint of what evangelicalism ought to be. However, the revivalist, frontier mentality continues to play a powerful role. A hoopla cult of personality still features "name" revivalists and entertainment acts that are supposedly free of "worldliness" (for example, the magician-convert who now puts on magic shows for evangelistic purposes). A bulletin of October 22, 1972, from the First Baptist Church of Spring Lake, Michigan, announces: "SUNDAY SCHOOL—next week is the final of our fall promotion, 'Fishing For Families.' IF WE HAVE 500 present, the pastors and S. S. Superintendent will swallow live goldfish. EVERY CHILD present (5th grade and under) will receive a goldfish." (Considering the childishness of the operation, it seems unfair not to give goldfish to the "adults" as well.) Ingroup language ("fellowship" employed as a verb, etc.) is used to create an evangelical subculture; bumper stickers declare: "In case of Rapture no one will be driving this car." (This sticker well illustrates the utter obtuseness of many evangelicals to the needs of today's unbeliever. The obscure dispensational eschatology of the sticker wouldn't be clear to one non-Christian out of a million; as a matter of prurient fact, "Rapture" will suggest to today's pagan something quite different from I Thess. 4:17!) That the Blue Laws are still very much with us is clear from the number of Bible schools and Christian colleges that still make their students and faculty sign an anti-dancing, anti-card-playing, anti-theatre "pledge"; one distinguished evangelical college which still requires such an affirmation admits on the form itself that the rules are not derivable from Scripture but maintains lamely that they are in the spirit of doing nothing "whereby the weak brother is offended." (Evangelicals reveal their ingrownness in regularly choosing the interests of their hypothetically weaker brethren over the Great Commission—the need for maximum witnessing contact with the unbelieving world.) Evangelical bookstores are generally non-controversial places where insipid but "radiant" clerks sell insipid but "radiant" publications that will make *your* life more well-adjusted, joyous in the Lord, and generally sanctified. (Even Marxist bookstores have more teeth in them—displaying far more concern to bite into the prevailing mind-set of the day and change it.)

The central evangelical difficulty is its "experience" focus, to which the individualistic, anti-intellectual frontier revivals contributed so much. The Reformation had made *doctrine* central (the formal principle of Scripture alone and the material principle of grace alone), and Christian "experience" came about derivatively, when one responded to this divinely revealed truth. But modern evangelicalism, on the basis of its frontier inheritance, has very largely reversed the picture, making *experience* central and using scriptural teaching to bolster and illustrate what it has already "felt." As A. H. Ackley's popular gospel song puts it: "You ask me how I know He lives? He lives within my heart"—thereby making the resurrection Gospel depend on religious experience instead of serving as its only proper basis. In my *Inerrant Word of God* I have illustrated how this fundamental error has led more than one prominent evangelical theologian and institution to give up belief in a totally reliable, inerrant Scripture. The mere fact that so many American evangelicals can class Helmut Thielicke among them (he appreciates Spurgeon!) is a sufficient indicator of the theological sloppiness on the evangelical scene—Thielicke who has expressly disavowed the Reformers' belief in an error-free Bible and has made the hideous public statement that those in the Lutheran Church-Missouri Synod who insist on that historic view are like the Nazi bigots who persecuted the confessing church.

The same overemphasis on experience leads many of today's evangelicals into will-o'-the-wisp quests for "second blessings" and other evidences of the "deeper life"—i.e., deeper experience. My book *Principalities and Powers* suggests that this is one of the reasons why not a few members of evangelical churches have fallen into the grip of the occult, since occult practices invariably appeal to the desire for the most remarkable spiritual jolts. And while such irrelevant experientialism goes on, the evangelical remains blind to the overarching moral issues of the day, where the Christian faith should be altering the climate of opinion. Thus a recent textbook on Christian ethics by an evangelical seminary professor takes a weak position on abortion, paralleling the remark of a very prominent Southern Baptist church leader a few years ago that "we have never regarded the unborn child as fully human."

Two brief personal examples may be in order. While chairman of the Church History Department of the Trinity Seminary, I created a European Graduate Theological Study Program in cooperation with the Faculty of Protestant Theology at the University of Strasbourg, France. Our students were able to spend an academic quarter at the university, sitting under its distinguished professors, and at the same time they received full credit toward their degree at home. Such a program is of course quite common in other scholarly fields, but to my knowledge it was the only regular resident program organized by an American seminary, liberal or evangelical, at the theological faculty of a European university. (As alluded to in an earlier chapter, the existence not only of Harvard Divinity School but also of "Joybells Bible Institutes" on the American educational scene gives European universities pause before hooking up with our theological schools!) The Trinity program put five missionaries on the field in Francophonic parts of the world and two of our students later took French doctorates in theology. But after seven years I gave the program up. Why? Lack of support and appreciation from my home institution. I tried in vain to get a budget for the program (it had none, but was supported entirely by the contributions of student participants); I had to fight like a tiger to get student monies extricated to pay the bills abroad during most of the years I conducted the program; and I was unable to persuade my home administration to give the program semi-independent status so that it would not constantly be subject to harassment from jealous colleagues who wanted to alter its character. Finally the effort required to maintain the program exceeded what I could constructively accomplish through it, and I gave it up. Why is this worth mentioning? Because it illustrates the priorities even at a better-than-average evangelical institution of higher learning. If impact on the climate of opinion in our day were half as important to evangelicals as pietistic self-sanctification, the growth of a program to influence a foreign theological faculty and give our students exposure in such an environment would have been foremost on the list of priorities. As it was, it hardly made that list at all, and did so only by special pleading.

Second example, already mentioned in our Preface: the demise of the International School of Law as a distinctively Christian institution, just when an evangelical response to the corruption and legal hanky-panky of Watergate was most needed. What could possibly have convinced evangelical Trustees and Administrators whose names are recorded here (the list is a sober reminder that history occasionally catches up with people for what they do) to throw founder John W. Brabner-Smith out of his office and his professorial chair,* remove all Jurisprudence from the curriculum, and embrace the philosophy that what makes a law school evangelical is merely the presence of some "pious" individuals on its staff?

*He still remains on the Board of Trustees, but his influence, needless to say, has been reduced virtually to nil.

C. Robert McBrier
Curran Tiffany

George L. Powell, acting
administrative dean
Ralph Norvell, dean

Jacques Ellul of the Bordeaux University Law Faculty and other only slightly less stellar international figures had agreed to associate their names with ISL on my personal recommendation; I had prepared (and used for one year) a Jurisprudence casebook interrelating positive law and historic Christian theology and dealing with such central ethical issues as the Supreme Court's abortion decision; and I was in a position actively to recruit law students from the better Christian colleges. The Trustees and Administration threw all this over, ostensibly because there wasn't enough money both to satisfy American Bar Association accreditation requirements and to maintain a Christian content in the curriculum, and because Christian content would offend the A.B.A. Such reasons can hardly be dignified as rationalizations. The Christian Legal Society offered a momentary gift to assist in keeping Jurisprudence in the curriculum; the gift was not accepted. The Rev. Richard Halverson of Fourth Presbyterian Church, Bethesda, offered to solicit funds for the same purpose; the Trustees would not give him the green light to do so. And the A.B.A. has not hesitated to accredit distinctively Catholic law schools! The real reason behind the Trustees' actions was, again, the frontier pietistic syndrome: the conviction that Christian faith doesn't require any serious theological content, that it is a matter of feeling, sentiment, emotion, and experience, not a matter of doctrine. Powerfully indicative of the problem was one ISL administrator's penchant for the writings of Watchman Nee: Nee who, in such works as *Spiritual Knowledge,* advocates special renewing of the "Nous" (mind) subsequent to salvation, thereby permitting evangelicals an even wider opportunity to denegrate the intellectual efforts of other evangelicals as representing no more than what Nee calls "fleshly, natural wisdom."* After the ISL débacle I wrote a *Christianity*

---

*Writes Nee (note *inter alia* his horrendous misuse of the term "revelation"): "Today's defect lies here: at the moment we are saved we receive a tremendous revelation, yet after being saved our nous is not renewed. . . . I am afraid many do not have any further great revelations after that of salvation. . . . Your progress has nothing to do with your natural wisdom. If your nous has been renewed, you will be able to know God and the things of God; the cleverest person beside you may not comprehend what you have comprehended."

Today article relating it to the general superficiality of Washington evangelicalism (with which most of those responsible for the ISL mess are associated); Editor Harold Lindsell sent me the following note: "I read with interest your last 'Current Religous Thought' column on the Law University.* It's the same old story. One almost gives up hope about the possibility of having distinctively Christian institutions on the graduate school level, both with respect to the composition of the student body and also to the integration of faith and learning in the discipline. Keep plugging away." But it's sad that "plugging away" is so difficult in evangelical circles where so many varieties of pietistic sanctimoniousness blind the believing community to the crying needs of America in her Bicentennial year.

Aux Armes, Citoyens!

The collapse of religious liberalism and the weaknesses of evangelicalism may again suggest the possibility of flirting with secular solutions to America's problems on her 200th birthday. But as soon as one begins to consider such proposals as Robert Theobald's "invention of the future to insure survival," one recognizes the same self-made man image that created most of the problems we now need so desperately to solve. And the Bicentennial advocates of secularized "civil religion" only remind us of Ethelbert Stauffer's thesis that as soon as Rome began to regard herself as the highest value and to worship her emperors as personal symbols of her ultimacy, the kiss of death was upon her.

Any answer to our problems worth talking about will be a genuinely religious answer. But where will it arise if the respresentative movements in today's church disqualify themselves from providing it? One can, of course, look for direct divine intervention. Plato tells us that when the Atlanteans "being unable to bear their fortune, became unseemly, and to him who had an eye to see, began to appear base, and had lost the fairest of their precious gifts, but to those who had no eye to see the true happiness, still appeared glorious and blessed at the very time when they were filled with unrighteous avarice and power, Zeus, the god of gods, who rules with law, and is able to see

---

*The essay is reprinted below as Appendix B.

into such things," destroyed them. That immanent judgment occurs from time to time, even in the midst of the "Buy-Centennial sellebration," seems clear from such an unlikely source as the *Saturday Review's* classified page (issue of August 23, 1975):

COMPUTER-ERROR MERCHANDISE

COMPUTER ERROR has resulted in 600,000 Declaration of Independence medallions with likeness of King George instead of Thomas Jefferson. Would like to dispose of entire lot quietly. SR Box T.J.

But for those not wishing to await the expansion of such judgments, a reconsidering of our biblical responsibilities is mandatory. Writes Bruckberger with characteristic perception:

> The West launched Marxist Communism upon the world, as it also introduced industrial enterprise with all its fabulous efficiency. If the West were one day to rediscover a spiritual unity, that unity might encompass the world as swiftly as has the heresy. After all, the first centuries of Christianity were filled with heresies long since forgotten. There was a time, for instance, when Arianism swept over the East, yet afterward the Christian world rebuilt its unity. But to wipe out a heresy, to recreate a unity, more than authority, more than force is needed; there must be an immense intellectual effort. Perhaps what the Western world most lacks today is a clear and wholly comprehensible doctrine of man's earthly salvation, a doctrine not opposed to Christianity but inspired by it.

Fully consistent with this French interpretation is Picard's rally cry to his fellow Germans after the fall of the Third Reich (*Hitler in Our Selves*):

> There must be restored to the Germans an inner continuity, an inner personal history, and a center of personality where the good can dwell lastingly, independent from external elements. This restoration can be effected solely by Christianity.
>
> It has been through Christ's coming to man that everything human was firmly jointed; it was only through the figure of Christ that man became firmly founded in himself.
>
> An abysmal discontinuity did exist before that time; it was between God and man, between the infinite and

the finite, between the eternal and the mortal, between divine love and human frailty. This discontinuity was greater than any possible discontinuity in the human and mortal world.

But in that Christ became man and in that man believes in Christ, this discontinuity is abridged. Divine love and human faith not only abolish discontinuity; they also create between themselves the greatest continuity. Thus, from the greatest discontinuity there emerges the greatest continuity.

If Picard's thesis is correct that the evils of Nazism "as a disposition exist within all nations" (and can we really doubt it?), then his claim to national restoration solely through Christ deserves equal consideration on this side of the Atlantic.

Of the options so far considered, evangelicalism brings us closest to the kind of model faith Bruckberger and Picard regard as essential to survival. But why does evangelicalism not offer more practical help to our nation at the level of its most pressing problems? As I have maintained in my contribution to Gary Collins' *Our Society in Turmoil,* the reason in large part is that evangelicalism's biblical resources are continually being diffused on pseudoproblems—on issues that may once have been of ethical moment, but which today are trivial in comparison with the overarching national problems we face. On the frontier, immorality was especially concentrated in the saloon: there card-playing, dancing, theatrical entertainment, and alcohol were linked with gambling, prostitution, and immoral excess in general. Frontiersmen used the saloon as an emotional catharsis in the midst of a life of backbreaking hardship and loneliness. So frontier evangelicalism fought fire with fire by offering the emotional catharsis of the revivals (cf. the battle cry of the Jesus People today: "Get high on Jesus"). The revivalists lumped all saloon activity together— whether it was in fact condemned by Scripture or not—and thereby transmitted to the modern evanglical church a set of Blue Laws that only very tangentially represent biblical teaching or the key ethical issues of our day.

In this respect, as in its anti-intellectualism, its overstress on sanctification and separation ("a peculiar people"), and its general ingrownness, evangelicalism is the victim of its history. While (rightly) criticizing religious liberalism for accommodating to the "spirit of the age," evangelicalism does the same thing—but generally accommodates to an age which has long since passed! It appears that even avant garde evangelicals, like their liberal opponents, only condemn immorality in Vietnam or strive for women's liberation after the secularists have piped the tune. Belief in an inerrant Word from God should make a man prophetic; he should be impelled by it to speak forth (*pro-phesy*) relative to the evils of his day. Evangelicals, however, have been so tainted by the frontier element in their own history that they find it almost impossible to speak out meaningfully against the evils of American frontier adolescence. Their remedy, like that of the liberals, has been contaminated by the very disease that should be treated. What is needed is an evangelical community that is not itself such an adolescent reflection of frontier values that it aids and abets the country's problems instead of solving them.

But how can such maturity be arrived at? We must begin where the evangelicals are, but not end there. We must trace back through their history to the real source of their strength, leaving by the wayside the unfortunate accretions and sociological hangups which have emasculated the basic evangelical message. In a word, in order to reverse the great evangelical heresy of experience-first, Bible-second, we must cut behind not only the American frontier but even the period of the English evangelical revival—to Reformation sources. The Reformers, whose teachings were at the heart of the Puritan faith that gave substance to the American mind in its formative years, insisted on God first, man second; revelation first, response second; Gospel first, faith second; justification first, sanctification second—in a word, the Bible in first position and man's religious experience secondarily related to it.

In focusing attention on God's Word instead of man's situation, the Reformers found the true content of divine revelation: Law and Gospel. If Law and Gospel are unreservedly applied to the life of an individual or of a nation, the result is a concern for biblically revealed, eternal standards of righteousness (the Law) rather than ephemeral human mores and traditions, and a concern for Jesus Christ as the only Way by which, to use Picard's fine phraseology, human discontinuity can be replaced by continuity (Gospel). Corresponding to the Reformation focus on Law will be implementation of scriptural principle; corresponding to the Reformation centrality of Gospel will be the effort to preserve and extend freedom, the *sine qua non* of meaningful decisions for Christ.

The return to these sources, therefore—as we have previously emphasized—does not in any way detract from the Founding Fathers' emphasis on limited government under law or the essentiality of liberty. Since the Founding Fathers actually acquired their values from Christian revelation (in spite of their protestations to the contrary), a return to biblical Law and Gospel serves as no less than a fulfillment of the national heritage. Indeed, as C. S. Lewis emphasized in the last of his Narnian Chronicles, insofar as our earthly country operates according to the divine pattern, it is a "real" country where "no good thing is destroyed." Acceptance of the biblical message never means the loss of genuine values; quite the opposite: they are raised to proper significance by way of it. If like the children in Narnia who found a "real England" present even in the eschaton, we long someday to find a "real America" there, we should recognize that national reality, like personal reality, is directly dependent on the extent of participation in God's Kingdom. May we someday indeed be able to say, paraphrasing one of the creatures in Lewis' *Last Battle:* "I have come home at last! This is my real country! I belong here. This is the land I have been looking for all my life, though I never knew it till now. The reason why we loved the old America is that it sometimes looked a little like this."

Practically, however, how does a Reformation perspective aid us in the national melancholia of our 200th birthday? We have already offered illustrations of its applicability as we discussed such aspects of American "bad news" as New Edenic utopianism, leveling, parochialism, and cultural colorblindness. It is our contention that in contrast to liberal religion's "If you can't beat 'em, join 'em" and evangelicalism's "If you can't beat 'em, separate from 'em," a Reformation perspective can courageously say to such problems: *"Let's beat 'em"!* Here are some additional illustrations:

PROBLEM	REVELATIONAL/REFORMATION PERSPECTIVE
1. Technological idolatry & rampant consumerism	We are to "subdue the earth," not be subdued by it; we must look at possessions from an eternal standpoint, recog-

nizing that life's value does not consist in the abundance of things possessed, but that we are strangers and pilgrims on the earth.

2. Uncontrolled urban growth, destruction of historic buildings and traditions, urban fiscal irresponsibility

Size is not a positive value in itself: Bethlehem was not least among the cities of Judea. Newness is likewise not a value as such: treasure consists of things both new and old. The city, like the Sabbath, is built for man, not conversely; and cities, like individuals, should "owe no man anything" that cannot be responsibly repaid.

3. Pollution of environment

The earth is the Lord's and the fullness thereof, and must no more be prostituted than the human body. "Man's power over Nature is really the power of some men over other men, with Nature as their instrument" (C. S. Lewis, quoted by Peter Sand).

4. The arms race

He who lives by the sword, dies by it. The revelationally based common law rule should be strictly applied to our stockpiling of arms and development of weaponry: "The force used in defense must be in proportion to the force used or about to be used by the assailant." We must never again, as at Hiroshima, use an excessively destructive weapon against vastly lesser force.

5. Third World nations unwilling to cast their lot with us

We must first cast out the beam in our own eye: improve the level of our ethics both at home and abroad, cease our national hypocrisy in supporting repressive colonialistic regimes just because they are anti-Communist, and demonstrably show that we are willing to come to the aid of those, such as Czechoslovakia, who cry out to us for help in their struggles for freedom. In a word, if we get our own value system straightened out in terms of biblical standards, we will have no trouble securing the right kind of friends and followers.

But is not the advocacy of a Reformation perspective

of Law and Gospel hopelessly naïve as a solution to national problems when it is perfectly apparent that secularism is daily increasing and the proportion of Americans willing to embrace such a viewpoint daily decreasing? We grant that, in the large, the amount of empirical faith per cubic inch will have diminished virtually to nil by the time our Lord comes again (Luke 18:8); but it does *not* follow that at any given point in history or in any given country there must be a uniform diminution of faith. To think so is the grossest defeatism and plays right into the devil's paws. National revival is a theoretical possibility at any time, and the essential precondition for it is the introduction of the Word of God into all spheres of national life by those committed to the scriptural Christ.

Luther properly stressed not only the impossibility of our turning the kingdom of this world into the Kingdom of God (this requires the power of Christ's own Second Advent), but also the necessity of our personally serving as dynamic links between the two kingdoms in the present age. Christians are literally the connecting-point between God's Kingdom and the world—the channel by which the living water of His revelation spills onto the parched landscape of a secular society. A more than usually absurd *Christian Century* article several years ago maintained that our best presidents had been those who were neither strongly confessional nor strongly anticonfessional religiously, but who held to a mild and innocuous civil religion. What nonsense! The greatest president we have ever had, by universal agreement, was Abraham Lincoln, and he did not hesitate to declare (September 7, 1864): "I have but to say, it [the Bible] is the best gift God has given to man. All the good Saviour gave to the world was communicated through this book. But for it we could not know right from wrong. All things most desirable for man's welfare, here and hereafter, are to be found portrayed in it." Commitment to scriptural standards of right and wrong, to scriptural values as to what is in fact desirable for man's welfare, and to the scriptural Savior made Lincoln the president he was and bore direct fruit in his emancipation of the slaves.* A man's beliefs will

---

*On May 30, 1864, and on other occasions in substantially the same terms, Lincoln argued for emancipation on specifically biblical grounds: "To read in the Bible, as the word of God Himself, that 'In the sweat of thy face shalt thou eat bread,' and to preach therefrom that, 'In the

inevitably determine what he does—in public and national life as surely as in the private and personal realm. What do you suppose the effect on the Supreme Court's abortion decision would have been if at least five committed Christian judges had been sitting on the bench? The impact of committed Christian believers on a secular society can be incalculably great; like Churchill, they can walk with destiny and literally change the course of history.

On July 14, 1975 (the French National Holiday) I was privileged to hear a superlative sermon on Judges 9:7-16 at the Temple-Neuf, Strasbourg. Pastor Heinz noted that in Jotham's "last broadcast from Radio Free Israel" he declared parabolically that national chaos and revolution had come about simply by default: the competent refused to serve (out of self-interest but also for not unworthy independent reasons), so the incompetent took over and destruction became inevitable. Israel was unable to obtain the services of an olive-tree king, or a fig-tree king, or even a vine king, so she acquired a bramble-bush king who brought her to ruin. When Christians abrogate their responsibilities in national life, they present engraved invitations to non-Christians to enter the breach and impress their values on the nation. According to John 8, only Christians are "free indeed," because only they have been emancipated by Christ from debilitating slavery to sin; Christians, therefore, are just the indispensable people needed to articulate and implement the foundational American ideal of freedom.

What, in sum, is the root problem of American life to which the revelationally committed Christian must bend all his efforts to solve? What produces the melancholia so characteristic of our Concentric American as he faces the third century of his national existence? He fears that "things are out of control"—meaning out of *his* control—and thereby betrays the self-made-man syndrome which has corrupted so much of his history. Bertrand Russell, though hardly committed to Christianity, accurately describes this great failing:

The Christian religion, Christian art, and Christian

---

sweat of other men's faces shalt thou eat bread,' to my mind can scarcely be reconciled with honest sincerity. When brought to my final reckoning, may I have to answer for robbing no man of his goods; yet more tolerable even this, than robbing one of himself and all that was his."

literature are deeply impregnated with [a] spirit of humility. And even among those Europeans who think that they have forgotten religion, it is natural to feel that it is for man to adapt himself to his environment rather than to adapt his environment to himself. Where life is hard, and the medieval tradition is still strong, as in most parts of Europe, this outlook on life still dominates philosophy, literature, and the feelings of ordinary men and women.

In America hardly a trace of this outlook survives. True, the old pious formulas are repeated on Sundays, and are thought, by those who repeat them, to be still believed. But they have lost their grip: they have become only Sunday truths, and during the rest of the week other views prevail. Why bother with the stars? We never see them, because our street lighting is too bright, and in any case they do not have that influence upon human affairs that astrology ascribed to them.

Religion is regarded as a useful influence in human affairs, but its superhuman aspects are forgotten. There is truth in the jest about the newspaper which praised an eminent divine for "the finest prayer ever addressed to a Boston audience." In a modern great city, the works of God are much less noticeable than the works of man. If Job had been reincarnated as an inhabitant of New York, and had been twitted, as the original Job was, with the great size of Leviathan and Behemoth, he would have been unimpressed, and would have replied: "Gee, they ain't half as big as a skyscraper." And as for adaptation to the environment, how lazy and old-fashioned! Compare New York with Manhattan Island as it was when the first white settlers arrived. Is this adaptation of man to his environment? No, it is adaptation of the environment to man. Man is lord of the earth: what he wants, he can get by energy and intelligence. The Soviet government, using an American invention, boasts that it can 'remove mountains, but not by faith. True, the heavenly bodies remain, but why bother about them? And if, some day, we get tired of the moon, we shall find ways of disintegrating it by radioactive projectiles. To all intents and purposes, God is an adjunct of man, a help in Church work and in procuring victory in man-made wars. The Power that humbled Job out of the whirlwind no longer finds an echo in American mentality.

That this is no exaggeration is plain from many illustrations throughout our book—for example, Münsterberg's delight that his fellow Americans exhibit "self-direction, self-initiative, self-assertion, and self-perfection." Russell identifies this philosophy and life-style with the ancient Greek sin of *hubris* or pride: for the Greeks of classical time such self-assertiveness and defiance of any standard above themselves was "the most unforgivable and most swiftly punished of sins."

It may thus constitute a blessing in disguise that things no longer appear to bend to our control. Perhaps the way is now open to a national *re*birthday: a new era of dependence on the God of Scripture. If so, the proclamation of that wondrous option will depend squarely on the courageous entrance of Christian believers into all spheres of national life. The result could be the incarnation of Robert Payne's vision, offered at the end of his history of the baleful influence of human pride, and inspired by his friend Charles Williams:

> Once there were sanctuaries and holy places where men walked in delight of God, and the world was filled with a glory; all things were shining; the women came down to the wells in the evening, and there were flowers and food for the asking. Before pride came, there was no ruthless self-seeking, the humble were exalted, men loved one another and adored the earth and everything upon the earth, because life was almost too short for anything except adoration. Either those times are passed or they have never been. Occasionally in some villages of Asia it is still possible to come upon these patriarchs of another age, who behave with a simple dignity and friendliness which suggest that pride has never entered them; they live for the world alone. For them the earth is eternally being reborn and eternally perishing; the sun glows in their faces, and the white moon is a mysterious stone shedding a blessing. They do not fear themselves, and everything made by their hands is ennobled by the making; and though they have no desire to compete with the gods, they talk to the gods as familiars. The corn and the vine reach their fullness and are then destroyed; men also grow great and then weaken and die. They neither fear the lightning nor attempt to shine like flames, and are pleased with everything that is laid before them; these are the salt of the earth, adoring the earth, and they have turned away from pride, if pride ever entered them, because they know that "every good gift and every perfect gift is from above, and cometh down from the Father of lights, with whom is no variableness, neither shadow of turning."

An America recentered on scriptural Law and Gospel would be like that. Rx for the Concentric, Melancholic American on his 200th birthday: substitute *Christ-made* for *self-made* as a national image. Transformed by this vision, the people and their liberties shall not perish from the earth.

O blest the land, the city blest,
Where Christ the Ruler is confessed!
O happy hearts and happy homes
To whom this King in triumph comes!
Thy Holy Spirit guide us on
Until our glorious goal is won.
    Eternal praise and fame
    We offer to Thy name.

      —Georg Weissel, *Macht hoch die Tür*
      (1642). Trans. Catherine Winkworth

APPENDICES

Appendix A

From Enlightenment to Extermination*

On what has become an annual pilgrimage to the Reformation sites of East Germany during the week after Christmas, my tour group and I revel in the heroic actions of Luther at the Erfurt monastery, the Wartburg fortress, and the Wittenberg castle church; and on New Year's Eve we meet the shade of J. S. Bach as his chorales resound through St. Thomas Church, Leipzig, announcing another year of grace. But along the way we have contact with two places whose associations are very far from the Reformation era and the great period of Baroque orthodoxy.

These two historical sites are Weimar and Buchenwald, one the center of the eighteenth-century German "Enlightenment," the other perhaps the most horrible of the death camps of World War II. Buchenwald is on a hill just above Weimar. Thus the epitome of man's inhumanity to man was demonstrated just a few kilometers from the city that lauded man's perfectibility. A chance irony? On one level, yes, but on another (the level where the Lord "laughs them to derision"?), a parable of the history of a fallen race.

Even today, in the suffocating embrace of the totalitarian-Marxist German Democratic Republic, Weimar is a perfect physical expression of the eighteenth-century "Age of Reason." Its broad streets and rationally placed buildings impress the visitor with a sense of order and humanistic self-satisfaction. It is as if eighteenth-century Freemasonry's Great Architect of the Universe had himself been hired to lay out the town. Here Goethe, Schiller, and Herder gave expression to the German Enlightenment and to its Classical-Romantic worship of man.

As the greatest literary representative of the era, Goethe serves as our best introduction to its central beliefs—and myths.

---

*Originally published in *Christianity Today*, October 11, 1974, and here reprinted by permission.

While a law student at Strasbourg, in contact with Herder, Goethe concentrated more on mystical flights of fancy (alchemy and occultism) than on the rigors of the Justinian Code, for he saw in the occult a possible means of romantic self-salvation. (During my doctoral time at Strasbourg, when I was preparing a theological dissertation involving the study of alchemical and Rosicrucian mysticism, I was amused by the non-romantic use the pigeons make of the statue of Goethe in front of the Palais Universitaire. Ironies of history abound everywhere!) In Goethe's early *Sturm und Drang* ("storm and stress") period, human emotions were elevated to the status of means of grace. Subsequently, Goethe's travels to Italy introduced him to the Classical ideal of eternal beauty and order and the Renaissance motif of the universal man.

Goethe's house in Weimar is the best possible illustration of the truth that architecture is physical liturgy. The house was built and furnished as an extension of the world-view of its famous occupant. Virtually every inch of wall space is covered with paintings, classical objets d'art, and evidences of man's accomplishments—as if Goethe (a bit unsure of himself, like Faust?) had to remind himself continually that man was indeed the apex of the universe. (In this respect, the contrast with Luther's humble quarters at the Wartburg castle and at Wittenberg could not be more striking.) The height of the steps of the main stairway is abnormally low, even when the small stature of eighteenth-century people is taken into account; the psychological effect is to give one the feeling of a Gulliver striding into Lilliput. There is even a hallway, extending from one end of the house to the other, in which the door frames at intervals along it are so constructed that each is slightly larger than the one before it; as one walks along this hallway, he sees a full-length portrait of himself in the mirror at the end of the hall, framed in a series of enlarging frames: bigger and more important than life!

Theologically, Goethe embraced the eighteenth-century rejection of biblical revelation. He said of the crucifix that it was "the most repugnant thing under the sun," and the idea of miracles was a "blasphemy against the great God and his revelation in nature." But unlike the Deists of his time, such as Thomas Paine, Goethe did not merely substitute "Nature" for "Scripture" as the source of truths about God; Goethe regarded Nature *as* God. One of his most famous aphorisms was: "When we study nature we are pantheists; in our poetry we are polytheists; in our morality, monotheists."

Arnulf Zweig has summed up Goethe's theology in terms that show its influence on and alignment with later evolutionism, Bergson's *élan vital,* and contemporary process thinking:

Since every man is part of nature and, hence, of the divine,
he shares the basic impulses of all natural things—specifically,

> the urge to develop upward and outward, the striving for an ideal.... Since there is no goal for man apart from his life, man struggles, like Faust, with the fear of life (*Lebensangst*) and is tempted by care (*Sorge*).

Thus the German Enlightenment rejected the Bible and the Cross, substituting for them nature and man. Man's striving quickly became the only ultimate value, and he himself took on the functions of pantheistic Deity. His morals became the "monotheistic" reflection of himself as sole arbiter of value.

A hundred years after Goethe's death (we are told that the clock in his house in Weimar stopped ticking when he died, and its hands still point to that moment), the inheritors of the German Enlightenment pushed tens of thousands of Jews, political opponents, and evangelical Christians through the iron gates of the concentration camp in the beech forest just above Weimar; most of them never came out again. On that iron gate, the camp motto remains: "Jedem das seine"—"To each his own," i.e., "Each man gets what he deserves." Note the logical (and inevitable) sequence: The Enlightenment makes man the measure of all things; modern man establishes the measure as he wills; and the strong, having devalued the weak, exterminate them. From Goethe to Nietzsche to Hitler is as short a step as from Weimar to Buchenwald.

The only counteractive to such a hideous sequence is a thoroughgoing rejection of the fundamental premise of the German Enlightenment. Man is *not* God; and fallen humanity is without hope apart from a clear scriptural word as to who God really is and as to the miraculous means He has provided for man's salvation. "Fear of life" (*Lebensangst*) and the "temptation of care" (*Sorge*), when made ends in themselves, reduce to meaninglessness and the annihilation of human value. Only the Gospel—as the Reformers taught from the *Angst* of their experience in the light of Scripture—is capable of *Seelsorge:* the binding up of fractured souls.

Appendix B

Washington Christianity*

Few would deny that the evangelical Christianity of the Ozark "Bible belt," with its hillbilly gospel singers, is identifiably different from the Boston evangelicalism classically described in John P. Marquand's *The Late George Apley.* It is my thesis that the metropolitan area of Washington, D.C., has its distinctive evangelical theology as well, and that this theology leaves much to be desired. Readers from this area will doubtless be appalled at what follows, discounting it as the product of too brief contact with Washington-area complexities, but let them remember De Tocqueville, whose to-the-mark portrait of the American character was in large part the result of observation from a foreign perspective.

In baldest terms, Washington Christianity is *superficial, non-doctrinal,* and *experientialistic.* It lacks theological substance. Like the church at Thyatira (Rev. 2:18 ff.), it is activistic, displaying "service and works," exhibits some genuinely spiritual personality characteristics ("charity," "patience"), but is relatively unconcerned with issues of sound doctrine versus false teaching, and is in consequence easily seduced by misdirected spirituality. To employ St. Paul's "milk and meat" analogy (1 Cor. 3:2), Washington is a dairy farm, not a cattle ranch, and the milk is dilute at that.

Hard words! But the evidence is not difficult to come by. Can one, for example, read Wesley Pippert's journalistic *Faith at the Top* (David C. Cook, 1973) without becoming aware of just how superficial Washington evangelicalism is? Discounting Mark Hatfield, whose sound theology manages to transcend even the turgid reportorial treatment of him, the portraits are of Washington Christian "heroes"—a former assistant director of the Secret Service, a player for the Redskins, etc.—most of

---

* Originally published in *Christianity Today,* August 8, 1975, and here reprinted by permission.

whom once led appropriately gross pagan lives (smoking, drinking, and swearing), went through an interminable series of "personal encounters" with warm Christian personalities, suffered backslidings and conversions, and now are successful, radiant, beautiful Christians themselves.

I have attended some of the "prayer breakfasts" and "professional luncheons" organized by these Christians-at-the-top: the praying is minimal, often of doubtful biblical substance, and childishly stereotyped ("Lord, just make us more loving when we just fellowship together here and just help us just to . . ."). There is almost never deep and penetrating study of scriptural teaching. One gets the unshakable impression that those who attend do so not so much to grow as to identify with others at their own experience level. The same can be said of most of the prestigious evangelical churches. Where are the Spurgeons in Washington? And if they were here, how long would they survive?

One of the classic essays in contemporary religious sociology is Robert Bellah's "Civil Religion in America" (*Daedalus,* Winter, 1967). Bellah correctly observed that in our national life we have created a generalized religion ("In God we trust") that is more deistic than Christian and that attempts to link our country's aspirations with eternal values. Washington evangelicals are by no means Deists, but they have been infected by the amorphous, undefined character of civil religion.

Washington evangelicals dislike doctrine (what a *cold* word!). At the Law School where I taught this year, the trustees—all Washington Christians—finally managed, after three years of operation, to introduce a single "doctrinal" reference into faculty contracts. The reference? Faculty must pledge not to disparage the "Judeo-Christian" heritage for which the school stands. My children, on the basis of their Lutheran confirmation instruction, know more theology and are deeper into God's Word than those guiding and directing an institution that was supposed to reintroduce the great profession of the Law to its revelational origins and biblical justification.

The real center of Washington religion is "personal experience." One local pastor has dignified the phenomenon with the expression "relational theology." Here I do not refer primarily to the Pentecostal, second-blessing, deeper-life movements that are strong in Washington as they are elsewhere in the seventies; the problem is more fundamental even than that. In general, one's own style of spirituality or that of one's group is made the norm to which others must conform to be a "beautiful Christian." Scripture is subordinated to an allegedly normative Christian experience, instead of being allowed to set the standards itself.

To use another personal example: the young acting dean at our Law School seems to have a fixation about humility and meekness; he can spot "spiritual frauds" among his faculty by such tests as whether one refuses to paint one's own office. Meanwhile, no systematic recruitment of Christian students goes on, so the 90 percent non-Christian student body has virtually no objective witness presented to it. Biblical teaching goes by the board, while an extrabiblical standard of piety is pharisaically and sanctimoniously elevated to authoritative status.

Why has Washington Christianity become this way? Here are some reasons:

1. The Washington area has a transitory life-style, with politicians and the military constantly moving in and out; such an atmosphere is not conducive to depth in any area.

2. The government and the armed forces dominate Washington, and their bureaucracies are concerned with pragmatic success. Therefore little emphasis is placed on serious study of what is foundational—whether the Bible or anything else. Add to this a Virginia anti-intellectualism that goes back to antebellum days (maxim: "What Virginia needs is less Ph.D.'s and more F.F.V.'s [First Families of Virginia]"—see Marshall Fishwick's *The Virginia Tradition* [1956]) and you have an atmosphere of façades, not substance.

3. The predominant "influential" churches in the area are Presbyterian and Episcopal, and these denominations have never recovered from their disastrous fall into liberalism. Therefore even when individual congregations have come under evangelical influence, there is no established tradition of sound doctrinal teaching, and Barthian-subjective attitudes are rife. Many lay leaders—"at the top" and otherwise—were converted late in life and still operate with essentially non-Christian value systems and attitudes.

Is there an answer to this sad state of things? There is indeed, and some valiant, scripturally oriented pastors of the Washington area are putting it daily into practice (one thinks immediately of Dick Halverson of Fourth Presbyterian). The answer is to teach the *Bible's doctrinal content,* so that both secular social patterns and personal religious experience will continually be tested against that fundament. Even at the top, faith comes only by hearing the Word of God.

Appendix C

The Colonial Parish Library of
Wilhelm Christoph Berkenmeyer *

Historical Background

WILHELM Christoph Berkenmeyer (1686-1751) has been described as "the most influential spirit among the Lutherans of colonial New York" (Wentz, p. 10).[1] When this learned clergyman arrived in New York in 1725, "He brought with him a library for [his] congregation, bought with funds which he had collected, which would be beyond the capacity not only of the most of the congregations, but even most of the pastors of the present day" (Jacobs, p. 122). According to Gräbner (p. 170), the collection was "eine Kirchenbibliothek von 20 Bänden in Folio, 50 Quart-, 23 Octav- und 6 Duodezbänden, ... unter denen sich Werke wie Calovs *Biblia Illustrata,* Baldvins *Commentar zu den paulinischen Briefen,* Dedekenns *Consilia,* Hülsemann *de auxiliis gratiae* und Brochmands *Systema* befanden, Bücher, deren Charakter uns schon erkennen lässt, wie die Theologie des Mannes geartet war, der sie ausgewählt hatte" (cf. Hart, pp. 13, 15, 153, 225-26, 336, 339-40). Berkenmeyer may well have brought with him even more than these 101 volumes, for Evjen (p. 137) has shown that by the time of his death his congregational library at Loonenburg (now Athens), New York, contained at least 367 volumes, not including his private book collection.

The whereabouts of this historically important church library was in doubt for many years. Writing in 1893, Jacobs asserted (*loc. cit.*) that "the remnants of this library are said to be in Wittenberg College,

---

*Reproduced from the *Papers of the Bibliographical Society of America*, Volume Fifty-three, Second Quarter, 1959.

[1] See list at end of this section for complete data on the works here cited.

Springfield, O." In 1902, Grace Prince, librarian at Wittenberg, ventured the following opinion: "The fact that a good edition of Baldwin's *Commentaries on St. Paul's Epistles*, bearing the date of 1664 and printed at Frankfort,[2] is in the library would indicate that Dr. Jacobs' statement may be correct and perhaps the remnants of Mr. Berkenmeyer's library of ninety-nine volumes [*sic*; based on Jacobs' misreading of Gräbner] have at last found a permanent home" (p. 258). Not until 1925, however, was it definitely shown that about sixty per cent of the above-mentioned 367 books in Berkenmeyer's church library had become part of the Wittenberg College library. Dr. John O. Evjen made the discovery as a result of his knowledge of Berkenmeyer's handwriting, and then went on to isolate the collection by observing three unique series of ownership marks on the books. It thereupon became evident that the Berkenmeyer collection had provided much of the original core of the Wittenberg College library. Indeed, in the first annual faculty report to the Board of Directors (1 September 1846), Ezra Keller, Wittenberg's first president, had referred to what was actually the Berkenmeyer library: "The College Library has now 354 volumes. The thanks of the Board are due to the donors of these books, especially to Rev. T. Lape of New York, and congregation [here we have the Berkenmeyer donation], who sent us 295 volumes and Brother Lape himself eleven volumes, together with 56 copies of his excellent Manual on Baptism, to be sold for the benefit of the Institution" (Board Minutes, vol. 1; quoted in Lentz, pp. 44-45).

During the years from 1925 to the present, the Berkenmeyer library was again dispersed among Wittenberg's general book collection. The effects of heat and dampness in the Zimmerman library building necessitated the discarding of a number of old volumes which had become unreadable—and presumably some Berkenmeyer items were among these. With the construction of the new chapel-library, the entire college book collection was moved from Zimmerman to its present location. The importance and intrinsic interest of the Berkenmeyer library led me early in the 1957-58 academic year to retrieve the collection once again, and to give it its first bibliographic description. Evjen provided only a partial and frequently inaccurate list of the authors represented in the collection. The books have never been classified or catalogued by the library. By familiarizing myself with the script of Berkenmeyer and of his later successor at Loonenburg, the Rev. J. C. Leps; by studying the ownership marks employed in the collection; and by utilizing the first volume of the earliest surviving

---

[2] Entry number 16. This is the only volume in Gräbner's above-quoted list which may still be found at Wittenberg.

Accession Record of the Wittenberg library, I have been able to isolate all the Berkenmeyer items which remain at Wittenberg. The total number of physical volumes is 226, but these are not precisely identical with the "about 225" volumes which Evjen found in 1925. Evjen missed a number of books, and during the last thirty years all trace of some Berkenmeyer volumes has disappeared. Separate bibliographical items in the collection now number 434 (Evjen stated that his 225 or so physical volumes contained "about 450" separate publications).

The significance of Wittenberg's Berkenmeyer library can hardly be overestimated. It is true that Berkenmeyer's private book collection never came to the college, but Evjen has shown that the books which did arrive were collected for the Loonenburg church library during Berkenmeyer's lifetime and were personally used by him. In his will Berkenmeyer refers to these books as "my whole stock" and bequeaths them "in Trust only, for the use of the succeeding minister at Loonenburgh and his successors" (quoted in Evjen, p. 139). Thus we have at Wittenberg a sizable portion of one of the most important colonial parish libraries, and a lasting record of the *Weltanschauung* of its pastor. The poor physical condition of a number of the volumes should not obscure the intrinsic value of the 434 works in the collection. Here one finds books on geographical, scientific, philosophical, and literary matters; pamphlets and periodicals recording the theological controversies of the time; sermons delivered by prominent pastors and theologians; and bibliographic, exegetical, and dogmatic publications of permanent value. The mere fact that many of the items in this collection of sixteenth-, seventeenth-, and eighteenth-century books cannot be found in the British Museum's *Catalogue of Printed Books* indicates the potential wealth of material now made available through the present bibliographical description.

A Selected List of Works Containing Information on Berkenmeyer or His Library

"Berkenmeyer, Wm. C." *Lutheran Cyclopedia.* Ed. by Erwin L. Lueker. St. Louis, Concordia, [1954]. Pp. 105-06.

Evjen, John O. "The Berkenmeyer Library." *The Lutheran Quarterly,* LV, 132-47 (April 1925).

Genzmer, George H. "Berkenmeyer, Wilhelm Christoph." *Dictionary of American Biography.* New York, Scribner, 1928-45. II, 218-19 (includes bibliography).

Gräbner, A. L. *Geschichte der lutherischen Kirche in America.* Th. 1. St. Louis, Concordia, 1892. See index under Berkenmeyer.

Hart, Simon and Kreider, H. J., trs. and eds. *Protocol of the Lutheran Church in New York City, 1702-1750.* New York, The Synod [i.e., The United Lutheran Synod of New York and New England], 1958. See index under Berkenmeyer.

Jacobs, Henry Eyster. *A History of the Evangelical Lutheran Church in the United States.* (The American Church History Series, vol. 4). New York, Christian Literature Co., [1893]. Pp. 117, 121-29, 177, 250, 310, 523.

Lentz, Harold H. *A History of Wittenberg College (1845-1945)*. [Springfield, Ohio], Wittenberg Press, 1946. P. 45.

Prince, Grace. "Zimmerman Library, Wittenberg College." *Sketches of Ohio Libraries*. Ed. by C. B. Galbreath. Columbus, Fred. J. Heer, State Printer, 1902. Pp. 258-59.

Wentz, Abdel Ross. *A Basic History of Lutheranism in America*. Philadelphia, Muhlenberg Press, [1955]. Pp. 9-10, 26, 27.

Wolf, Edmund Jacob. *The Lutherans in America*. New York, J. A. Hill; Rostock (Germany), E. Volckmann, [1889]. Pp. 179, 209, 217, 219, 229, 253f., 287f.

The Nature of the Bibliographical Description

The bibliographical entries to follow are arranged not by subject, but by "main entry" only, i.e., by author (personal or corporate), or, if authorship has not been readily ascertainable, by title. In the case of a work of joint authorship, the name of the first author listed on the title page is used for the main entry. Where a pseudonymous publication is involved, entry is made under the author's real name (if definitely known), or under the pseudonym (if identification is problematical). When initials are employed on the title page of a book to conceal the author's identity, and the author's name remains in question, entry has been made under title. Library catalogues are entered under the name of the personal or corporate owner of the library. Cross-references from variant forms of a name have not been given, since these can be obtained in standard biographical sources. Hebrew or Greek words in titles have been disregarded in filing. Alphabetization is word by word, then letter by letter, rather than by the reverse procedure.

A bibliographical citation can have as many as seven parts, and these will normally be given in the following order: entry number; author statement (personal authors are given with death date and reference to a standard biographical source if such information has been obtainable without undue effort; the spelling of personal names follows the biographical source employed, if one has been used); title (spelling as on title page; punctuation and capitalization often modernized; frequently only the first few significant words of the title are given—not necessarily a complete sentence or idea); edition or volume statement; imprint (place name as on title page; publisher [or printer if no publisher given] generally in vernacular or Latin nominative case form, with first and middle names sometimes reduced to initials or omitted;[8] date in arabic numerals); pagination or total number of volumes (pagination does not ordinarily include unpaged material except in the case of short, completely unpaged works; in the latter instance the total number of pages is given within square brackets);

---

[8] Publishers' or printers' widows are not indicated in the bibliographical citations. Thus, for example, "J. Meyers witwe" appears simply as "Meyer."

miscellaneous notes. When brackets appear in the author, title, edition or volume statement, or imprint, they indicate that the data within them were not obtained from the title page of the work being described.

Symbols for Biographical and Bibliographical Reference Works Employed Below in Verifying Data

AdB   *Allgemeine deutsche Biographie.* Leipzig, Duncker, 1875-1912. 56 vols.

D   *Dansk biografisk Leksikon.* Ed. by C. F. Bricka. København, Schultz, 1933-44. 26 vols.

G   Georgi, Gottlieb. *Allgemeines europäisches Bücher-Lexicon.* Leipzig, Georgi, 1742-58. 5 pts. and 3 suppl.

H   Heinsius, Wilhelm. *Allgemeines Bücher-Lexikon, 1700-1892.* Leipzig, Brockhaus, 1812-94. 19 vols.

H-B   Holzmann, M., and Bohatta, H. *Deutsches Anonymen-Lexikon, 1501-1910.* Weimar, Gesellschaft der Bibliophilen, 1902-28. 7 vols.

H-B (pseu)   Holzmann, M., and Bohatta, H. *Deutsches Pseudonymen-Lexikon.* Wien, Akad. Verlag, 1906.

J   Jöcher, C. G. *Allgemeines Gelehrten-Lexicon.* Leipzig, Gleditsch, 1750-51. 4 vols.

Js   Jöcher, C. G. *Allgemeines Gelehrten-Lexicon. Fortsetzung und Ergänzungen.* Ed. by J. C. Adelung, *et al.* Leipzig (vols. 1-2, 7), Delmenhorst (vol. 3), Bremen (vols. 4-6), 1784-1897. 7 vols.

L   *Lutheran Cyclopedia.* Ed. by Erwin L. Lueker. St. Louis, Concordia, [1954].

N   *Nouvelle biographie générale.* Ed. by Hoefer. Paris, Firmin Didot, 1853-66. 46 vols.

My thanks to the University of Rochester for permitting me to use D, H-B, H-B (pseu), and J there; to the Ohio State University for giving me access to their copies of D, G, H, H-B, and H-B (pseu); and to the University of Chicago for making J and Js available to me.

Main Entry Listing of the Berkenmeyer Collection at Wittenberg College

1. Acker, Johann Heinrich, d. 1719 (AdB). Trauer-Blätter. [Altenburg?, To. Richt.?, 1710?]. 78 pp. T.-p. mutilated; data from G.

2. Acta historico-ecclesiastica, oder gesammlete Nachrichten von den neuesten Kirchen-Geschichten. 1-[-6.] Th. Weimar, S. H. Hoffmann, 1735-38. 972, 156 pp. Includes the separately paged Anhang to this Bd. 1. Th. 1-2, 3. ed. (1737-38); Th. 3, 2. ed. (1736); Th. 4-6 (1735-36); Anhang (1736).

3. Acta historico-ecclesiastica, oder gesammlete Nachrichten von den neuesten Kirchen-Geschichten. 7.[-11.] Th. Weimar, S. H. Hoffmann, 1737-38. 862 pp.

4. Acta historico-ecclesiastica, oder gesammlete Nachrichten von den neuesten Kirchen-Geschichten. 19.[-24.] Th. Weimar, S. H. Hoffmann, 1740. 1161 pp. Includes the whole of Bd. 4, with Anhang.

5. Acta historico-ecclesiastica, oder gesammlete Nachrichten von den neuesten Kirchen-Geschichten. 28.[-30.] Th. Weimar, S. H. Hoffmann, 1741. 467-962 pp. T.-p. of Th. 28 missing; first leaf of Th. 28 badly mutilated.

6. Acta historico-ecclesiastica, oder gesammlete Nachrichten von den neuesten Kirchen-Geschichten. 31.[-36.] Th. Weimar, S. H. Hoffmann, 1742-44. 1100 pp. Includes the whole of Bd. 6, with Anhang. Th. 31-32, 2. ed. (1744, 1743); Th. 33-36 (1742-43); Anhang (1743).

7. Ammersbach, Heinrich, d. 1691 (AdB), ed. Der heilige kluge und gelehrte Teuffel. Halberstadt, 1675. 223 pp.

8. Amyraldus (Amyraut), Moses, d. 1664 (J). Von Religionen . . . aus dem Frantzösischen übersetzt durch Adrian Stegern. Leipzig, Johann Grosse, 1667. 934 pp.

9. Arndt, Johann, d. 1621 (L). Vorrede über die teutsche Theologia; gedruckt zu Halberstadt durch Georg Koten/anno 1597. 2. ed. 1660. 16 pp.

10. Auserlesene theologische Bibliothec. 37.[-48.] Th. Leipzig, J. F. Braun, 1729-30. 1194 pp. This comprises Bd. 4.

11. Auserlesene theologische Bibliothec. 55.[-60.] Th. Leipzig, J. F. Braun, 1731-32. 571-1098 pp. The unpaged indexes at the back cover the whole of Bd. 5.

12. Avenarius, Johann, d. 1739 (AdB). Epistolischer Christen-Schmuck. Arnstadt, Ernst Ludwig Niedt, 1722. 3 vols. in 1.

13. Baier, Johann Wilhelm, d. 1695 (L). Compendium theologiae moralis. Jenae, E. C. Bailliar, 1697. 572 pp.

14. Baier, Johann Wilhelm, d. 1695 (L). [Compendium theologiae positivae]. [3. ed.]. [1693]. 1047 pp. Most annotated volume in the collection.

15. Balduin, Friedrich, d. 1627 (L). Brevis institutio ministrorum verbi. Wittebergae, Müller & Helwig, 1623. 308 pp.

16. Balduin, Friedrich, d. 1627 (L). Commentarius in omnes epistolas beati Apostoli Pauli. Index Balduinianus generalis . . . autore Johanne Oleario [Johannes Olearius, d. 1684 (AdB, J)]. Francofurti ad Moenum, B. C. Wust, 1664. 1652, 510 pp. Cf. 299.

17. Balduin, Friedrich, d. 1627 (L). De communione sub utraq; specie disputatio Martini Becani [Martin Becanus, d. 1624 (AdB)]. Wittebergae, Paul Helwich, 1610. 332 pp.

18. Balduin, Friedrich, d. 1627 (L). Diatribe theologica de Antichristo. 2. ed. Witebergae, Paul Helwich, 1615. 292 pp.

19. Balduin, Friedrich, d. 1627 (L), praes. Disputatio ordinaria, de verbis testamenti Jesu Christi. Witebergae, Joh. Gorman, 1609. [30] pp.

20. Balduin, Friedrich, d. 1627 (L). Epistola apologetica . . . in qua respondetur ad epistolam Martini Becani [Martin Becanus, d. 1624 (AdB)]. Wittebergae, Johann Gormann, 1610. 110 pp.

21. Balduin, Friedrich, d. 1627 (L). Idea dispositionum biblicarum. Wittebergae, J. W. Fincel, 1666. 331 pp.

22. [Balduin, Friedrich], d. 1627 (L). [Passionis typicae liber unus]. [Wittebergae, Selfisch & Helvvig, 1614?]. 512 pp. T.-p. missing; data from G.

23. Balduin, Friedrich, d. 1627 (L). Passionis typicae liber alter. Wittebergae, Selfisch & Helvvig, 1616. 551 pp.

24, 24a. Balduin, Friedrich, d. 1627 (L). Solida refutatio catechismi Ariani, qui Rackoviae in Polonia anno 1608. excusus. Wittebergae, Paul Helwig, 1620. 549 pp. Originally published in German; here translated into Latin. 2 cop.

25. Bartholinus, Caspar, d. 1629 (J). De studio theologico. Hafniae, Henricus Waldkirch, 1628. [44] pp.

26. Baxter, Richard, d. 1691 (L). Nun oder niemahls. Lübeck und Franckfurt, Otto und Wiedemeyer, 1688. 358 pp. Tr. from the English.

27. [Bentheim, Heinrich Ludolf], d. 1723 (AdB). [Neu-vermehrter Engelländischer Kirchen- und Schulen-Staat]. [Bremen, Sauerm., 1732.]. 1288 pp. T.-p. missing; data from J and G.

28. Berckenmeier, Paul Ludolph, fl. 1720 (J). Vermehrter curieuser antiquarius. 5. ed. Hamburg, Schiller und Kissner, 1720. 936 pp. Pp. 29-44, 651-52 badly mutilated.

29. Berger, Theodor, d. 1773 (AdB). Die durchlauchtige Welt. 3. ed. Hamburg, Johann Christoph Kissner, 1730. 976 pp.

30. Besold, Christoph, d. 1638 (AdB). Christlich und erhebliche Motiven. Ingolstatt, Gregory Hänlin, 1639. 253 pp.

31. Betke, Joachim, d. 1663 (AdB). Mensio Christianismi et ministerii Germaniae, das ist: geistliche Abmessung des heuttägigen Christenthumbs. 1648. 184 pp.

32. Bibliander (Buchmann), Theodor, d. 1564 (AdB). Deliciae ebraeo-homileticae, das ist: Ergetzligkeiten der ebräischen Sprache. Th. 1. Dressden und Leipzig, J. C. Mieth, 1705-06. 1322 pp. Editorial work by Kaspar Neumann, d. 1715 (L), and Johann David Schwertner, d. 1711 (AdB).

33. Bleu, Jacobus le, d. 1668 (J). Tractatus de instructione futuri consiliarii. Gissae, J. D. Hampel, 1652. 352 pp.

34. Blumberg, Christian Gotthelf, d. 1735 (J). Rhat der Meissheit. Chemnitz, Conrad Stössel, 1707. 204 (i.e., 304) pp. Tr. from the French (only in part?).

35. Bödiker, Johann, d. 1695 (AdB). Grund-Sätze der teutschen Sprache. Berlin, C. G. Nicolai, 1723. 400 pp.

36, 36a. Bohse (Talander), August, d. 1740 (AdB). Die lebenden Todten. Leipzig, J. L. Gleditsch, 1705. 738 (i.e., 538) pp. Pp. 368-538 contain material from Philip Picinelli's [b. 1604 (N)] "Mundus symbolicus: oder die in mannichfaltigen Sinn-Bildern vorgestellte Welt." 2 cop. The 36a copy lacks t.-p., and is a different printing from (but apparently the same edition as) the 36 copy; its final page is correctly numbered 538.

37. Bostel, Lucas von, d. 1716 (AdB). Catalogus librorum . . . in aedibus . . . domini Lucae à Bostel. Hamburgi, literis Königianis, 1724. 286, 31 pp.

38. Botsack, Johann, d. 1674 (AdB). Fürbild der heilsamen Worte vom Glauben und der Liebe in Christo Jesu. Dantzig, Christian Mansklapp, 1676. 736 pp. Ed. by Nathanael Dilger, d. 1679 (AdB).

39. Breckling, Friedrich, d. 1711 (AdB). Excidium . . . darin dem Thier dieser vierten Monarchi. 1661. 24 pp.

40. Broitzem, Bruno von. Decas concionum poenitential: das ist: zehen christliche Buss Predigten. Zell, Elias Holwein, 1637. 214 pp.

41. Buddeus, Johann Franz, d. 1729 (AdB). Bedencken über die wolffianische Philosophie mit Anmerckungen erläutert von Christian Wolffen [Wolff, d. 1754 (L)]. Franckfurt am Mayn, Andreäischen Buchhandlung, 1724. 136, [12] pp.

42. Burchard, Georg Heinrich, d. 1701 (J). Christliche gründliche Anmerckungen. Hamburg, Gottfried Schultz, 1674. 240 pp.

43. Calov, Abraham, d. 1686 (L). Paedia theologica. Wittebergae, Andrea Hartmann, 1652. 392 pp.

44. Calov, Abraham, d. 1686 (L). Die völlige vom Gest Gottes eingegebene Beschreibung/der heilwertigen Historien . . . Christi Jesu. Wittenberg, Christian Schrödter, 1680. 829 pp.

45. Carolus, Philipp. Animadversiones . . . in Noctes Atticas Agellii, et Q. Curtii Historiam. Noribergae, Michael & J. F. Endterus, 1663. 656 pp.

46. Carpzov, Johann Benedikt, the elder, d. 1657 (J). Hodegeticum. Lipsiae, Tobias Riesen, 1656. 62 pp.

47. Carpzov, Johann Benedikt, the younger, d. 1699 (J). Auserlesene Tugend-Sprüche. Leipzig, Johann Grosse, 1717. 1232 pp.

48. Carpzov, Johann Benedikt, the younger, d. 1699 (J). Ausserlesene Trost und Leichen-Spruche. 7. und letzter Th. Leichenpredigt von Gottlob Friedrich Seligmann [d. 1707 (J)]. Leipzig, Friedrich Lanckisch, 1700. 988 pp. Latin funeral orations for Carpzov included at end.

49. Carpzov, Johann Benedikt, the younger, d. 1699 (J), and Rappolt, Friedrich, d. 1676 (AdB). [Commentatio in epist. Joannis de charitate & veritate (by Carpzov); Scripta theologica & exegetica (by Rappolt)]. Lipsiae, haeredes Lanckisianorum, 1693. 2 vols. in 1. T.-p. partially missing; data from J and G. Indexes missing.

50. Carpzov, Samuel Benedikt, d. 1707 (AdB). Der (1.) eligirte und ausgelesene (2.) vocirte und ausgeschickte (3.) ordinirte und ausgerüstete Jeremias. Dresden, Melchior Bergen [1674?]. 204 pp.

51. [Cellarius, Christoph], d. 1707 (AdB). [Curae posteriores de] barbarismis et idiotismis sermonis latini. 5. ed. Jenae, J. F. Bielcke, 1718. 432 pp. T.-p. and first prefatory leaf mutilated; verified in G.

52. Cellarius, Christoph, d. 1707 (AdB), ed. Appendix ad Curas posteriores. Jenae, J. F. Bielcke, 1718. 120 pp. Contains material by "A.B.", identified by a MS. note on t.-p. as Andreas Borrichius (cf. 53).

53. Cellarius, Christoph, d. 1707 (AdB). Discussio Appendicis Danicae ad Curas

suas posteriores. 2. ed. Jenae, Bielcke, [1695]. 72 pp. Contains material by Andreas Borrichius (see pp. 13, 16). Date verified in G.

54. Cellarius, Christopher, d. 1707 (AdB). De latinitate mediae et infimae aetatis liber, sive antibarbarus. 5. ed. Jenae, J. F. Bielcke, 1723. 268 pp.

55. Christliche und notwendige Verantwortung der Prediger zu Rostock auff M. Nathanis Chytraei [Nathan Chytraeus, d. 1598 (AdB)] gedruckte Glaubens Bekentnis. Gryphisswaldt, Augustin Ferber, 1593. Unpaged. Cf. 57.

56. Der christliche Vermahner zum heiligen Leben. Hamburg, Thomas von Miering, 1723. 166 pp.

57. Chytraeus, Nathan, d. 1598 (AdB). Christliche und richtige Glaubens Bekentnuss. 1593. [15] pp. Cf. 55.

58. Clauberg, Johann, d. 1665 (AdB). Logica vetus & nova. 2. ed. Amstelaedami, Elzevier, 1658. 463 pp.

59. Colbe, Georg, d. 1670 (AdB). Abscheulicher Missbrauch der Beicht und Communion ... Nun wiederum der Gemeine in Altona zum Besten zum Druck befordert ... allerunterthänigst übergeben von Daniel Sass. Altona, Christian Reymer, 1711. 140 pp.

60. Colberg, Ehregott Daniel, d. 1698 (AdB). Das Platonisch-hermetisches Christenthum. Franckfurt(h) und Leipzig, M. G. Weidmann, 1690-91. 2 vols. in 1.

61. Colerus, Johann Christoph, d. 1736 (AdB). Historia Gothofredi Arnoldi [Gottfried Arnold, d. 1714 (AdB)]. Vitembergae, Theophil Ludovicus, 1718. xlviii, 301 pp. The Prolegomena consist of a "Dissertatio critica de corruptoribus historiae ecclesiasticae."

62. Collin, Friedrich Eberhard, d. 1727 (Js). Die Gemeinschafft der Schmach Christi. Franckfurt am Mayn, W. C. Multz, 1723. 192 pp.

63. Compendieuse Priester-Bibliothec. Jena, E. C. Bailliar, 1711. 220 pp. Interleaved throughout with blank sheets.

64. [Conring, Hermann], d. 1681 (J). Rettung dess Osnabruckischen und Münsterischen Friedens wieder Papst Innocentii x. Nulliteths Erklärung. Erstlich zu Londen in Engelland Lateinisch getruckt. [N.p., n.d.]. 141 pp. Published under the pseudonym Ludovicus de Monte Sperato (Montesperato).

65. Copia. Eines Send-Briefes/An Se. königl. Maj. von Preussen/ Betreffend der Juden und Christen Bekehrung. 1704. 16 pp.

66. Creide, Hartmann, d. 1656 (AdB). Postilla epistolica. Das ist: schrifftmässige Erklärung aller sontäglichen Episteln. Franckfurt am Mayn, Johann Beyer, 1649. 3 vols. in 1. Vols. 1 & 2 are 2. ed. T.-p. of vol. 3 varies slightly from those of vols. 1 & 2.

67. Cyprian, Ernst Salomon, d. 1745 (L). Abgetrungener Unterricht von kirchlicher Vereinigung der Protestanten ... mit historischen Original-Documenten. 2. ed. Franckfurth und Leipzig, M. G. Weidmann, 1726. 2 vols. in 1. Vol. 2 entitled "Documenta und Nachrichten."

68. חק, d.i. Da hast Dus/Mag. Leidings ... jetzo Kusters/ auffgestreckter Pfauen-Schwantz/mit tausend pedantischen Augen/wider Oliger Paulli. 1704. 32 pp. Cf. 311.

69. Dannhauer, Johann Konrad, d. 1666 (AdB). Apologia pro Tractatu de syllo-

gismo infinito. 2. ed. Argentorati, Josias Staedel, 1654. 34 pp.

70. Dannhauer, Johann Konrad, d. 1666 (AdB). Collegium psychologicum. 4. ed. Argentorati, Josias Staedel, 1660. 220 pp.

71. Dannhauer, Johann Konrad, d. 1666 (AdB). Decas diatribarum logicarum in sex syllogas distributa. 4. ed. Francofurti, C. J. Klein, 1653. 123 pp.

72. Dannhauer, Johann Konrad, d. 1666 (AdB). Elementa dialectica ex Commentario logico . . . Dannhaweri . . . ad discentium faciliorem captum formata à Johanne Henrico Rapp. Argentorati, Josias Staedel, 1667. 84 pp.

73. Dannhauer, Johann Konrad, d. 1666 (AdB). Epitome dialectica. 4. ed. Argentorati, Josias Staedel, 1663. 200, 39 pp.

74. Dannhauer, Johann Konrad, d. 1666 (AdB). Hodomoria spiritus papaei, duodecim phantasmatis. Argentorati, Friedrich Spoor, 1653. 1476 pp.

75. Dannhauer, Johann Konrad, d. 1666 (AdB). Idea boni interpretis et malitiosi calumniatoris. 5. ed. Argentorati, Josias Staedel, 1670. 266 pp.

76. Dannhauer, Johann Konrad, d. 1666 (AdB). Tractatus de syllogismo, ut vulgò dicitur, infinito. Argentorati, W. C. Glaser, 1630. 22 pp.

77. Deutsche acta eruditorum. 117.[-120.] Th. Leipzig, J. F. Gleditsch, 1726. 589-886 pp.

78. Deutsche acta eruditorum. 145.[-156.] Th. Leipzig, J. F. Gleditsch, 1729-30. 904 pp.

79. Deutsche acta eruditorum. 162.[-168.] Th. Leipzig, J. F. Gleditsch, 1731-32. 381-906 pp. The Registers at back cover Th. 157-168.

80. Deutsche acta eruditorum. 205.[-216.] Th. Leipzig, J. F. Gleditsch, 1736-37. 889 pp.

81. Deyling, Salomo, d. 1755 (AdB). Christliche und moralische reflexiones über die Passions-Historie. Leipzig, Friedrich Lanckisch, 1724. 104 pp.

82. Diecmann, Johann, d. 1720 (AdB). Catalogus bibliothecae Johannis Diecmanni. Bremae, H. C. Janus, 1721. 484 pp.

83. Dippel, Johann Konrad [Democritus, Christianus, pseud.], d. 1734 (AdB). Ein Hirt und eine heerde. Amsterdam, Henrich Betkius, 1706. 100 pp.

84. Döring, Paul, d. 1727 (Js). Wohlgemeynte Buss-Vermahnungen. Dresden, Zimmermann und Gerlach, 1720. 400 pp.

85. Donatus, Johann Jacob. Der muhsame, darbey erbauliche Catecheta. Dresden, J. C. Zimmermann, 1716. 967 pp.

86. Dorn, Johann Christoph, d. 1752 (Js). Bibliotheca theologica critica. Francofurti et Lipsiae, E. C. Bailliar, 1721-23. 2 vols. in 1.

87. [Dranckmeister, Albrecht] (Js). [Geistlicher Hoffarth, mit Gottfried Arnolds Vorrede]. [Hamburg, Heyl, 1712]. 55 pp. T.-p. missing; data from G. On Arnold, see entry 61.

88. Ebart, Johann, fl. last half of 17th C. (J). Enchiridion theologicum positivo-polemicum. 4. ed. Jenae, J. T. Fleischer, 1685. 718 pp.

89. Ebart, Johann, fl. last half of 17th C. (J). Supplementum Enchiridii theologici

positivo-polemici. Jenae, J. T. Fleisher, 1685. 82 plus pp. All pages after 82 missing.

90. Eckard, Melchior Sylvester, d. 1650 (J). Genuinus christianismus, in cujus descriptione praeter doctrinam de fide, traditur ethica christiana. Ulmae, Balth. Kühn, 1668. 352 pp.

91. Eckard, Melchior Sylvester, d. 1650 (J). Pastor conscientiosus. Ulmae, Balth. Kühn, 1668. 332 pp.

92. Eckard, Melchior Sylvester, d. 1650 (J). SS. theologiae studiosus, hoc est: fidelia monita. Ulmae, Balth. Kühn, 1668. 12, 245 pp.

93. Edzardus, Esdras Heinrich, d. 1733 (N). Abgedrungette Vertheidigung wider den ströhernen Goliath in Holland. 1720. 85 pp.

94. Edzardus, Sebastian, d. 1736 (AdB). Erwegung der Motiven und Promessen, mit welchen die Reformirten zu B. eine Lutheris. Kirche an sich zu ziehen trachten. 1707. 142 pp.

95. Edzardus, Sebastian, d. 1736 (AdB). Der Geist des Irrthums. [Hamburg?], 1711. 80 pp. At the end is an unpaged "Kurtze Abfertigung D. Jo. Franc. Buddei [Buddeus, d. 1729 (AdB)], und seines Licht-scheuenden Vor-Fechters des falschgenannten Friedrich Gottwalts."

96. Edzardus, Sebastian, d. 1736 (AdB). Mataeologia Romelingiana. [Hamburg?], 1711. 126 pp.

97. Edzardus, Sebastian, d. 1736 (AdB). Widerlegung der abscheulichen und höchstärgerlichen Sacramentschänderey. 1707. 109 pp.

98. Elswich, Johann Hermann von, d. 1721 (AdB). De reliquiis papatus ecclesiae Lutheranae temere afficits commentatio. Hamburgi, J. W. Fickweiler, 1721. 398 pp.

99. Engelschall, Karl Gottfried, d. 1738 (AdB). Derer praejudiciorum vitae. Th. 2. Leipzig, August Martin, 1724. 1299 pp.

100. Engelschall, Karl Gottfried, d. 1738 (AdB). Das doppelte Ubel der Sünder. Dressden und Leipzig, J. C. Mieth, 1712. 55 pp.

101. Engelschall, Karl Gottfried, d. 1738 (AdB). Die heuchlerische Frömmigkeit des Volckes Israel. Dressden und Leipzig, J. C. Mieth, 1712. 64 pp.

102. [Erasmus, Desiderius], d. 1536. [Apophthegmata, ac lepide dicta, principum, philosophorum, ac diversi generis hominum, ex Graecis pariter ac Latinis scriptoribus selecta, cum interpretatione commoda, dicti argutiam aperiente]. 926 pp. The work includes 8 books. T.-p. missing. On authorship identification, see MS. notes on p. 1, and the British Museum's *Catalogue of Printed Books*.

103. Ermisch, Christian Ludwig, d. 1722 (Js). Quadragena, das ist: XL. einfältige/doch schrifftmässige Quatember-Sermones ... Die erste Abtheilung/Bestehend in XX. Quatember-Sermonen. Braunschweig, C. F. Zilliger, 1692. 557 pp.

104. Ermisch, Christian Ludwig, d. 1722 (Js). Quadragena, das ist: XL. einfältige/doch schrifftmässige Quatember-Sermones ... Die andere Abtheilung/Bestehend in XX. Quatember-Sermonen. Braunschweig, J. G. Zilliger, 1708. 577 pp.

105. Erörterung dreyer Fragen/zum ersten Ob Christus die völlige Macht gehabt habe den Menschen die Sünde zu vergeben? 1705. 71 pp.

106. Espagne, Jean d', d. 1659 (N). Gemeine Irthümer . . . übersetzt von Adrian Stegern. Leipzig, Johann Grosse, 1667. 249 pp.

107. Extract zweyer Schreiben/ den Begriff und das Bekentnis der lutherischen Kirche. 1721. 32 pp.

108. Faber, Zachaeus, the elder, d. after 1607 (J). 100. Unwarheiten. Welche die Calvinisten begehen an der H. Schrifft. Wittemberg, Johann Crafft, 1598. 391 pp.

109. [Fecht, Johannes], d. 1716 (AdB). [Historia & examen novae theologiae in-differentisticae]. [Rostochii, Russw., 1721]. xxiv, 476 pp. T.-p. missing; verified in G and H. The last four (unpaged) leaves of Index IV. are mistakenly bound after prefatory pages xviii and xxii.

110. Feinler, Gottfried, d. 1704 (J). Biblische Schau-Bühne bekehrter Sünder; d.i. auserlesene Buss-Exempel. Leipzig, Friedr. Lanckisch, 1704. 387 pp.

111. [Feurborn, Justus], d. 1656 (J), praes. [Disputatio theologica prima, de dicto Joh. 16. v. 7.8.9.10.11]. [Gissae Hessorum, J. D. Hampel, 1651]. 48 pp. T.-p. missing. This work and 112 may have been published under a common t.-p.

112. Feurborn, Justus, d. 1656 (J), praes. Disputatio theologica secunda, de dicto Joh. 16. v. 7.8.9.10.11. Gissae Hessorum, J. D. Hampel, 1651. 48 pp.

113. Feurborn, Justus, d. 1656 (J), praes. Succincta epitome errorum calviniano-rum. Giessae Hessorum, typis Chemlinianis, 1651. 209 pp.

114. Finck, Kaspar, d. 1631 (AdB). Giessischer ausserlesener Leichpredigten. Gies-sen, Nicolaus Hampel, 1613 (vol. 1); Marpurg, Nicolaus Hampel, 1625 (vol. 2). 2 vols. in 1.

115. Forster, Johann, the younger, d. 1613 (J), praes. Exercitationum theologi-carum disputatio 1.[-xvi.]. Witebergae, Joh. Gorman, 1608-09. Unpaged. The various disputations involve different respondents.

116. Forster, Johann, the younger, d. 1613 (J). Hohe Festtagsschreinlein/in welchem auff ein jedes hohes Fest fünfferley zu finden. Wittenberg, Clement Berger, 1628. 730 pp.

117. Forster, Johann, the younger, d. 1613 (J). Nervosae, elegantes ac singulariter methodicae homiliae seu dispositiones concionum . . . nunc secundò . . . in lucem editae, curâ M. Johannis Seubothii. Noribergae, Simon Halbmayer, 1631. 795 pp.

118. Fortgesetzte Sammlung von alten und neuen theologischen Sachen . . . u.d.g. Ertheilet von einigen Dienern des göttlichen Wortes. Auf das Jahr 1721. Leip-zig, Joh. Friedr. Braun. 1126 pp.

119. Fortgesetzte Sammlung . . . auf das Jahr 1722. 1130 pp.

120. Fortgesetzte Sammlung . . . auf das Jahr 1723. 1118 pp.

121. Fortgesetzte Sammlung . . . auff das Jahr 1725. 95-346 pp. Includes part of the "Erster Beytrag. Neues" (Section 15 to end), and all of the "Zweyter Bey-trag." T.-p. of 1st Beytrag, and general t.-p., missing.

122. Fortgesetzte Sammlung . . . auf das Jahr 1727. 340 pp.

123. Fortgesetzte Sammlung . . . auf das Jahr 1729. 1318 pp.

124. Fortgesetzte Sammlung . . . auf das Jahr 1731. 1066 pp.

125. Fortgesetzte Sammlung . . . auf das Jahr 1732. 1052 pp.

126. Fortgesetzte Sammlung . . . auf das Jahr 1735. 844 pp.

127. [Fortgesetzte Sammlung]. Frühaufgelesene Früchte der theologischen Sammlung von Alten und Neuen . . . Abgefasst von einigen Dienern des göttlichen Worts . . . auf das Jahr 1735. Leipzig, J. F. Braun. 264 pp.

128. [Fortgesetzte Sammlung]. Frühaufgelesene Früchte der theologischen Sammlung von Alten und Neuen . . . Abgefasst von einigen Dienern des göttlichen Worts. 1.[-6.] Beytrag. Auf das Jahr 1738. Leipzig, J. F. Braun. 292 pp.

129. [Franckenberg, Abraham von], d. 1652 (J). Einige Gewissens-Gründe und Fragen. Amsterdam, 1692. Unpaged. May be incomplete; 12 pp. including t.-p. are present; last paragraph of text is no. 26. Author identified in H-B.

130. Franz, Wolfgang, d. 1628 (AdB), praes. Disputatio theologica ordinaria de baptismo. Wittebergae, Johan. Gorman, 1609. Unpaged.

131. Franz, Wolfgang, d. 1628 (AdB). Historia animalium sacra. Wittenbergae, Schurer & Gormann, 1616. 888 pp.

132. Frauen-Zimmer-Bibliotheckgen/oder thuelicher Vorschlag. Güstrau, Rüdiger. 1705. 130 pp.

133. Freylinghausen, Johann Anastasius, d. 1739 (AdB). Betrachtungen von der Gnade des Neuen Testaments. Halle, Wäysenhaus, 1714. 158 pp.

134. Freylinghausen, Johann Anastasius, d. 1739 (AdB). Grundlegung der Theologie. 6. ed. Halle, Wäysen-Haus, 1721. 487 pp.

135. Freylinghausen, Johann Anastasius, d. 1739 (AdB). Schriftmässige Einleitung zu rechter Erkäntniss und heilsamen Gebrauch. 2. ed. Halle, Waysenhaus, 1715. 208 pp.

136. Frisch, Johann Leonhard, d. 1743 (AdB). Specimen lexici germanici, oder ein Entwurff samt einem Exempel wie er sein teutsches Wörter-Buch. Berlin, C. G. Nicolai, 1723. 61 pp.

137. Gebhard, Hermann, fl. middle of 17th C. (Js). Zwey Hundert Kerm- und Macht-Spruche der alten h. Kirchen Väter von den Häuptwercken unser Erlösung. Gosslar, Nicolaus Duncker, 1651. 136 pp.

138. Geier, Martin, d. 1680 (L). Allgegenwarth unsers allsehenden Gottes. 2. ed. edited by Martin Gabriel Hübner. Leipzig, Christian Michael, 1674. 896 pp.

139. Geier, Martin, d. 1680 (L). Liebe zu Gott und dem Nähesten. Dressden, Fritzschen und Günther, 1677. 64, 629 pp.

140. Gerhard, Johann, d. 1637 (L). Sacrarum homiliarum in pericopas evangeliorum. Jenae, Johannes Naumann, 1656. 2 vols. in 1.

141. Gerhard, Johann, d. 1637 (L). Scholae pietatis liber 1.[-111.]. Das ist: Christlicher und heilsamer Unterrichtung. Jehna?, Ernest Steinman, 1633. 3 vols. in 1. Running title: "Von Ubung der wahren Gottseligkeit." T.-p. of vol. 1 missing.

142. Gesenius, Justus, d. 1673 (AdB). Catechismus-Fragen/über den Catechismum D. M. Lutheri . . . Auch . . . einige Gebeter . . . aus dem Stadischen Gesang-Buche. Stade, Hinrich Brummer, 1723. 288 pp.

143. Gesner, Johann Matthias, d. 1761 (AdB). Institutiones rei scholasticae. Jenae, J. F. Bielcke, 1715. 286 pp.

144. [Gessner, Salomon], d. 1605 (AdB). [De persona Christi]. [Witebergae?, 1595?]. 334 pp. T.-p. missing.

145. Giese, Joachim. Der christliche Freyer/und Ehedan. Kiel, Joachim Reumann, 1682. 271 pp. Includes music, pp. 261-62.

146. Gisenius, Johannes, d. 1658 (AdB), praes. Calvinismus, hoc est, errorum Zwinglio-Calvinianorum methodica enumeratio. 2. ed. Giessae Hessorum, Nicolas Hampel, 1620. 115 (i.e., 335) pp. Each of the 21 disputations included has a different respondent.

147. Glass, Salomon, d. 1656 (AdB). Enchiridion S. Scripturae practicum. Biblisches Hand-Buchlein. Leipzig und Gotha, J. H. Klossen, 1700. 1086 pp. Includes material by Johann Saubert [d. 1646 (AdB)].

148. [Glass, Salomon], d. 1656 (AdB). [Philologia sacra]. [2. ed.]. [Jenae, 1643]. 532 pp. T.-p. and all but the last leaf of the unpaged prefatory material missing; identification and data from T. H. Horne's *Introduction to the Critical Study and Knowledge of the Holy Scriptures*, 7th ed., vol. 2, Pt. 2 (London, 1834), p. 152.

149. Goetten, Gabriel Wilhelm, d. 1781 (AdB). Das jetzt-lebende Gelehrte Europa. Braunschweig, Ludolph Schröder, 1735. 824 pp.

150. Goetten, Gabriel Wilhelm, d. 1781 (AdB). Das jetztlebende Gelehrte Europa. Th. 2. Braunschweig und Hildesheim, Ludolph Schröder, 1736. 818 pp.

151. Goetten, Gabriel Wilhelm, d. 1781 (AdB), ed. Das jetztlebende Gelehrte Europa. Th. 3, Stück 1. Zelle, J. A. Deetz, 1737. 224 pp.

152. [Goetten, Gabriel Wilhelm], d. 1781 (AdB), ed. Das jetztlebende Gelehrte Europa. Th. 3, Stück 2. Zelle, J. A. Deetz, 1739. 225-400 pp.

153. Goetze, George, d. 1699 (J). Leich-Abdankungen/nebenst einem Anhange ezzlicher deutscher Reed-Ubungen. 3. ed. Jena, Mattheus Birkner, 1665. 239 (i.e., 263), 80 pp.

154. Goetze, George Heinrich, d. 1728 (J). Miracula Catechismi Lutheri, oder sonderbare Denckwürdigkeiten des Catechismi D. Martini Lutheri. Lubeck, Samuel Strucke, 1717. 96 pp.

155. Gottfried, Christian Georg, fl. end of 17th C. (J). Einfältige doch gründliche Erläuterung der jüdischen Irrthüme. Hamburg, 1698. 46 pp.

156. Grape, Zacharius, d. 1713 (AdB), praes. Compendii theologiae positivae universae . . . specimen. Rostochii, Nicolas Schwiegerovius, 1706. 280 pp.

157. [Gregorii (Melissantes), Johann Gottfried], d. 1770 (AdB). [Geographia novissima generalis, specialis et specialissima, oder Welt-, Land- und Städtebeschr. in Frag.]. [4. ed.]. [T. 1.]. [Erffurt, Stössel, 1722?]. 1078 pp. T.-p. missing; data from G and H.

158. Grot, Adolph, d. 1739 (Js). De benedictione speciatim sacerdotali. Lipsiae, Jacob Schuster, 1721. 141 pp.

159. Gryphius, Andreas, d. 1664 (AdB). Verlibtes Gespenste/Gesang-Spil. 3. ed. Bresslaw, Jesaias Fellgibel, [1660]. 75 pp.

160. Gude, Friedrich, d. 1753 (N). Nützliches Lehr- und Lebens-Buch. 2. ed. Budissin, David Richter, 1721. 658 pp.

161. Güttner, Johann Gabriel, d. 1740 (Js). Die kräfftigen Hülffs-Mittel zum Wahren Christenthum. Dresden, Zimmermann und Gerlach, 1729. 1224 pp.

162. Gunther, Cyriacus. Latinitatis restitutae pars altera . . . Cura et studio Gothofredi Vockerodt. 2. ed. Jenae, J. F. Bielcke, 1734. 1124 pp.

163. Haas, Nicolas, d. 1715 (L). Drey geistliche Passions-Hütten. Leipzig, Gleditsch und Weidmann, 1711. 404 (i.e., 304) pp.

164. Haas, Nicolas, d. 1715 (L). Der getreue Seelen-Hirte. Leipzig, Joh. Ludwig Gleditsch, [1706?]. 4 vols. in 1. Bottom of t.-p. cropped; date from G.

165. Haas, Nicolas, d. 1715 (L). Wohlgemeinte Vorstellung: was bey der Vier-Brau- und Schenck-Nahrung wider Gottes Wort und gutes Gewissen sey? . . . Dabey mit angehänget wird . . . Joh. Jacobi . . . Christliche Erinnerung von dem so genannten guten Montag. Dressden, J. C. Zimmermann, 1710. 78 pp.

166. Haberkorn, Peter, d. 1676 (AdB), praes. Disputatio sexta, et quidem praeliminaris, tendens ad demonstrationem sacrosanctae Trinitatis. Gissae Hessorum, J. D. Hampel, 1651. 592 pp. May have been published under a common t.-p. with 167.

167. Haberkorn, Peter, d. 1676 (AdB). Syntagma secundum dissertationum theologicarum. Gissae, J. D. Hampel, 1652. 504 pp.

168. Haenichen (Henichen), Daniel, d. 1619 (J). Das schöne und trost-reiche Agnus Dei, Iohan. 1. Leipzig, Abraham Lamberg, 1612. 319 pp.

169. Hahn, Hermann Joachim, d. 1726 (Js). Vorschlag eines unfehlbahren und handgreiflich Richtigen Mittels. 2. ed. Dressden und Leipzig, J. C. Mieth, 1719. 322 plus pp. All pages after 322 missing.

170. Hallbauer, Friedrich Andreas, d. 1750 (AdB). Nöthiger Unterricht zur Klugheit. Jena, J. B. Hartung, 1723. 559 pp.

171. Hamburg. Cathedral library. Bibliopolium Königianum, sive catalogus librorum . . . quae in Cathedrali Hamburgensium Templo publicae ritu auctionis d. Aug. A. C. 1722. . . . distrahentur. Hamburgi, literis Königianis. 948 pp.

172. Hamburg. Mary Magdalene Cloister library. Catalogus curieuser, hochteutscher und holländischer Bücher . . . welche . . . auf dem Mariae Magdalenen Kloster verauctioniret werden sollen. Hamburg, Conrad König, 1724. 204 pp.

173. Hamburg. Ministerium. Abfertigung der falschen Auflagen/mit welchen E. Ehrw. Ministerium zu Hamburg/in dem zu Halle gedruckten Langischen Lebenslauff/Freuentlich Angetastet worden. 1723. 61 pp.

174. Hamburg. Ministerium. Des Ministerii in Hamburg Christliches Bedencken. Hamburg, Conrad Neumann. 64 pp. Date cropped.

175. Hamburgische Auszüge aus neuen Büchern. [Bd. 1.]. 1.[-12.]Th. Ham-

burg, C. W. Brandt (1.-4. Th.), Peter Heuss (5.-12. Th.), 1728. 887 pp. T.-p. of Th. 6 missing.

176. Hederich, Benjamin, d. 1748 (AdB). Progymnasmata linguae Graecae, oder Vor-Ubungen zur griechischen Sprache. Wittenberg, Gottfried Zimmermann, 1717. 230 pp.

177. Hederich, Bernhard, d. 1605 (AdB). Libellus astronomicus, de anno, eiusque partibus & accidentibus . . . in usum Scholae Suerinensis collectus. Lübeck, Laurentius Albertus, 1598. Unpaged. Printed at Rostoch by Stephan Myliander.

178. Helmich, Johann Albrecht von. Christliche Kinder-Zucht. Giessen, Henning Müller, 1704. 64 pp.

179. Hoffmann, Gottfried, d. 1712 (L), ed. Aerarium Biblicum, oder tausend Biblische Sprüche. Leipzig, Friedrich Lanckisch, 1706. 955, 34 (i.e., 43) pp.

180. Hoffmann, Gottfried, d. 1712 (L). Ausserlesene Kern-Sprüche Heiliger Schrifft. Leipzig, Friedrich Lanckisch, 1705. 704 pp.

181. Hoffmann, Gottfried, d. 1712 (L). Erbauliche Denck-Zettel. Hrsg. von Christian Altmann. [Budiss., Richter, 1717]. 404 pp. T.-p. mutilated; imprint obtained from G.

182. [Hoffmann, Gottfried], d. 1712 (L). Der gute Schul-Mann/Das ist: Wolmeynende Bedancken. Leipzig, Lanckisch, 1695. 593 pp. On the author of this work, see the last page of the "Vorrede," and the MS. note on the verso of the front cover.

183. Hoffmann, Gottfried, d. 1712 (L). Lebens-Beschreibung. Budissin, David Richter, 1721. 798 pp.

184. Hoffmann, Gottfried, d. 1712 (L). Nöthiger und nützlicher Unterricht/ Wie der Grund zu der Erziehung der Kinder. Lauban, August Vogel, [n.d.]. 323 pp.

185. Hoffmann, Gottfried, d. 1712 (L). Wohlmeynende Vorschläge/Wie christliche Eltern/die ihre Kinder in die Schule schicken. Zittau, David Richter, 1711. 96 pp.

186. Hoffmann, Gottfried, d. 1712 (L). Das Zittauische dic cur hic und hoc age. Zittau, J. J. Schöp, 1709. 162 pp.

187. Der homiletischen Studier Stube. 1.[-12.] Oeffnung. Saalfeld u. Leipzig, J. M. Kauffmann, 1720 (1.-5. Oeffnung); Rudolstadt, Tobias Friderici, 1721-23 (6.-12 Oeffnung). 1286 pp. T.-p.'s of the various parts vary slightly.

188. Hoornbeek, Johann, d. 1666 (AdB). Tractatus elegantissimus de ratione concionandi. Francofurti, 1703. 180 pp.

189. [Hübner], Johann, d. 1731 (AdB). [Kurze] Fragen aus der politischen Historia Biss auf gegenwärtige Zeit continuiret, und mit einem vollständigen Register versehen. 1. Th. Neue Aufl. [Leipzig], J. F. Gleditsch, 1723. 1192 pp. T.-p. mutilated; author's name supplied from Wittenberg library's Accession Record, vol. 1.

190. Huelsemann, Johann, d. 1661 (L). Manuale Augustanae Confessionis. Witt-[enberg], Clement Berger, 1631. 1311 pp.

191. Huelsemann, Johann, d. 1661 (L). Methodus concionandi. 3. ed. Wittebergae, Johannes Berger, 1648. 448 pp. Includes material by Johann Forster, the younger, d. 1613 (J), Leonhard Hutter, d. 1616 (L), and Balthasar Meisner, d. 1626 (L).

192. Huelsemann, Johann, d. 1661 (L). Myrtus Lipsiensis tam patricia quàm plebeja, das ist: Leipziger Myrten-krone. Franckfurt und Leipzig, T. M. Götz, 1665. 1312 pp.

193. Hunnius, Aegidius, d. 1603 (AdB). Calvinus Iudaizans. Witebergae, Matthaeus Welacus, 1593. 189 pp.

194. Hunnius, Nikolas, d. 1643 (L). Epitome credendorum, oder Inhalt Christlicher Lehre. Wittenberg, J. W. Fincel, 1683. 638 pp.

195. Hunnius, Nikolas, d. 1643 (L). Kurtze Anweisung zum Wahren Christenthumb. Wittenberg, 1683. 132 pp.

196, 196a. Hunnius, Nikolas, d. 1643 (L). Nothwendige/und gründliche Beantwortung der fürwitzigen. Lübeck, Johann Emb, 1640. 190 pp. 2 copies.

197. Hutter, Leonhard, d. 1616 (L). Epitome analytica locorum theologicorum, in Compendio D. Leonhardi Hutteri comprehensorum . . . Studio et labore M. Caspari Heunischii. Norimbergae, W. E. Felsecker, 1674. 368 pp.

198. Informatorium maternum, der mutter Schul. Nürnberg, Wolffgang Endter, 1636. 167 pp.

199. Irenaeus, Amynta. Justa bilanx. Veronae, 1722. 39 pp.

200. Jahn (Janus), Fridrich August, d. 1716 (Js). Drey Leichen-Reden/so bey Beerdigung zweyer Söhne und einer Tochter/des . . . Herrn Johann Petersohns. Leipzig, Friedrich Lanckisch, 1692. 32 pp.

201. Jan, Johann Lorenz, d. 1741 (J). Gott-geheiligte Passions-Andachten. Nürnberg und Altdorff, J. D. Tauber, 1721. 525 pp.

202. Jever, Johann, fl. 1st half of 18th C. (Js). Confutatio invectivae quam irae ridiculae homo Petrus Zornius Bibliothecae suae antiquariae temere & dementer inseruit. 1725. 14 pp. Cf. 203, 432.

203. [Jever, Johann], fl. 1st half of 18th C. (Js). Des ertz-lästerers Petri Zornii Urtheil über sich selbst/Aus seinen so genannten opusculis sacris vorgestellet: Von einem, der nicht zugeben kan, Dass . . . Theodori Dassovii [Dassovius, d. 1721 (AdB)], Seliger Gedächtniss, Ohnverwelcklicher Ehren-Ruhm Von diesem Freveler geschändet werde. 1723. 29 pp. On authorship identification, see verso of t.-p. Cf. 202, 432.

204. [Kapp, Johann Erhard], d. 1756 (AdB). Schauplatz des Tezelischen Ablass-Krams. Erffurt und Leipzig, J. C. Martin, 1717. 88 pp.

205. Kerler, Johann Christopher. Catechismus Iohannis Brentzii [Johann Brenz, d. 1570 (AdB)] . . . elegiaco carmine redditus & editus per Iohannem Christophorum Kerlerum. Heilbronnae, Christopher Kravsius, 1632. 20 pp. The date appears on the t.-p. in the form of a chronogram.

206. Kerler, Johann Christopher. Hortus cereris: et viridarium gratiarum. Ulmae Suevorum, Jona Saurius, 1628. 48, 33 pp.

207. Kerler, Johann Christopher. Liber epigrammatum. Tubingae, Joh. Conrad Geysler, 1629. 106 pp.

208. Kerler, Johann Christopher. Lucas anagrammaticus. Tubingae, Theodoricus Werlin, 1622. 92 pp.

209. Kerler, Johann Christopher. Poëmatum libri quatuor. Stutgardiae, Johann Wyrichius Rösslinus, 1625. 100 (i.e., 110) pp.

210. Kesler, Andreas, d. 1643 (AdB). Logicae Photinianae examen. 2. ed. Wittebergae, Johannes Berger, 1642. 429 pp. On Photinus, bp. of Sirmium, see L.

211. Kesler, Andreas, d. 1643 (AdB). Metaphysicae Photinianae partis generalis examen. 3. ed. Wittebergae, Friedrich Berger, 1648. 382 pp.

212. Kesler, Andreas, d. 1643 (AdB). Metaphysicae Photinianae partis specialis examen. 3. ed. Wittebergae, Friedrich Berger, 1648. 287 pp.

213. Kesler, Andreas, d. 1643 (AdB). Physicae Photinianae examen. Erffurti, Johannes Birckner, 1631. 256 pp.

214. Knauer, Johann, d. 1709 (Js). Ausgefertigte trauer und freuden Glocken. Jena und Leipzig, Michael Keyser, 1698. 310 pp.

215. König, Georg, d. 1654 (AdB). Casus conscientiae. Noribergae, Wolffg. Jun. & Johan. Andreas Endterus, 1654. 813 pp.

216. König, Georg, d. 1654 (AdB). Heptas casuum conscientiae miscellorum. Norimbergae, Wolfgang Jun. & Johann Andreas Endterus, 1655. 132 pp.

217. Koenig, Johann Friedrich, d. 1664 (L). Theologia positiva acroamatica. 8. ed. Lipsiae, Joachim Wild, 1691. 291 pp.

218. Kohlreif, Gottfried, d. 1750 (AdB). Chronologia sacra. Hamburgi, T. C. Felginer, 1724. 481 pp.

219. Kortholt, Christian, d. 1694 (AdB). Theologische zu Befoderung der Gottseeligkeit angesehene Tractätlein. Kiel, Joachim Reuman, 1679. 543 pp.

220. Kortholt, Christian, d. 1694 (AdB). Treuhertzige Auffmunterung. Kiel, Joachim Reuman, 1669. 96 pp.

221. Kromayer, Johann Abraham, d. 1733 (AdB). Dispositiones memoriales librorum & capitum Biblicorum tum V. tum N.T. 3. ed. Francof., Lipsiae & Jenae, Autor (prostat apud H. C. Crökerum), 1707. 336, 356 (i.e., 381), 295 pp.

222. Krüsike, Paul Georg, d. 1723 (AdB). Index vocum Graeco-Latinarum, in Matthaeo & Johanne obviarum. Hamburgi, Conrad Neumann, 1697. 42 (i.e., 46) pp.

223. Kunad, Polycarp, d. 1724 (Js). Schrifftmässiger Fest-Predigten. T. 2. Dressden und Leipzig, J. C. Zimmermann, 1719. 2016 pp.

224. Lange, Joachim, d. 1744 (AdB). Institutiones studii theologici litterariae. Halae Magdeburgicae, Orphanotropheus, 1724. 898 pp.

225. Laurentii Strandinger, Otto, d. 1724 (J). Bekänntnüs von dem kirchlichen/so genannten/ Gottesdienst im Lutherthum. [Flensburg?], 1708. 216 pp.

226. Laurentii Strandinger, Otto, d. 1724 (J). Die Heilsahme Warheit. 1717. 80, 512 pp.

227. Laurentius, Jakob, d. 1644 (AdB). Hugo Grotius [d. 1645 (AdB)] papizans. Amsteldami, Henricus Laurentius, 1642. 206 pp.

228. Laurentius, Jakob, d. 1644 (AdB). Hugonis Grotii [d. 1645 (AdB)] epistola ad Jacobum Laurentium anatomizata. Amstelredami, Henricus Laurentius, 1642. 48 pp.

229. Lauterbach, Samuel Friedrich, d. 1728 (J). Kleine fraustädtische Pest-Chronica. Leipzig, J. F. Gleditsch, 1710. 120 pp.

230. Lehmann, Johann Christoph, d. 1731 (Js). Gehaltene Kirchhoffs-Reden. Franckfurt, Johann Milisch, 1698. 648 pp. T.-p. and last leaf of Register mutilated.

231. Lehmann, Johann Christoph, d. 1731 (Js). Pentas epistolica, Die heiligen Episteln. 3. ed. Leipzig und Budissin, Johann Milisch, 1709. 896 pp.

232. Lehmann, Johann Christoph, d. 1731 (Js). Pentas evangelica, das ist: Die heiligen Evangelia. 5. ed. Budissin, David Richter, 1714. 1470 pp.

233. Leyser, Polycarp, d. 1610 (L). Catechismus Lutheri latino-germanicus, quaestionibus illustratus & ad praelum adornatus. 2. ed. Dresdae, Christian Bergen, 1610. 178 pp.

234. Lichtscheid, Ferdinand Hel(f)freich, d. 1707 (J, Js). Meditatio de iure vocationis ministrorum ecclesiae. [Leipzig, 1697]. 388 pp. T.-p. mutilated; imprint from Js.

235. Loescher, Caspar, d. 1718 (J). Der ehrwürdige Priester . . . Zum Druck befördert von M. Johann. Andr. Gleichen. Torgau, David Lötsch, 1691. 170 pp. Several pages of text badly mutilated.

236. Loescher, Caspar, d. 1718 (J). Neue(r) Absolution(s)-Formulen. Leipzig, Johann Herbordt Kloss, 1690. 2 vols. in 1. T.-p. of vol. 2 differs somewhat from that of vol. 1. Vol. 2 is 2. ed.

237. Loescher, Valentin Ernst, d. 1749 (L). Ausführliche historia motuum. T. 2. Franckfurt und Leipzig, Johann Grosse, 1723. 240 pp.

238. Loescher, Valentin Ernst, d. 1749 (L). Nöthige Reflexiones über das Anno 1722. zum Vorschein gebrachte Buch Pensées libres sur la religion &c. Wittenberg, Samuel Hannauer, 1724. 38 pp.

239. Loescher, Valentin Ernst, d. 1749 (L). Theologische Annales, das erste Decennium des 18. Seculi. Leipzig, J. F. Braun, 1715. 77, 919 pp.

240. Loescher, Valentin Ernst, d. 1749 (L). [Theologische Annales, das andere Decennium des 18. Seculi]. Leipzig, J. F. Braun, 1725. 152, 760 pp. T.-p. mutilated; verified in G.

241. Loescher, Valentin Ernst, d. 1749 (L). Vollständiger Timotheus verinus. Th. 1. Wittenberg, Samuel Hannauer, 1726. 851 pp.

242. Loescher, Valentin Ernst, d. 1749 (L). Vollständiger Timotheus verinus. Th. 2. Wittenberg, Samuel Hannauer, 1722. 546 (i.e., 456), 118 pp.

243. Lother (Lotter), Gabriel, fl. 1622 (J). Christlich Ehrengedächtnüs und Leichsermon. Jehna, Joh. Weidner, 1635. Unpaged (6 sermons by various divines).

244. Lübeck. Ministerium. Ministerii ecclesiastici zu Lübeck Bedencken/ auff drey Fragen/das Straff-Ampt betreffend. 2. ed. Lübeck, Ulrich Wetstel, 1668. 60 pp.

245. Lübeck, Hamburg, and Lüneburg. Ministerium. Das Predig-Ampt der Christlichen Gemeine zu Lübeck, Hamburg und Lüneburg. Kurtze nohtwendige[!]/in Gottes Wort gegründete Warnung für dem Gottes lästerlichen/ ergerlichen Schand-Buche/welches unter dem Nahmen Eliae Praetorii von den Missbreuchen dess Predig-Ampts herauss kommen. Hamburg, Zacharias Härtel, 1645. 518 pp. See 323.

246. Lütkemann, Joachim, d. 1655 (AdB). Harpffe von zehen Seyten/Das ist: Gründliche Erklärung zehen Psalmen Davids. Wolffenbüttel, Johann Bissmarck, 1658. 936 pp.

247. Lütkemann, Joachim, d. 1655 (AdB). Der vorschmack göttlicher Güte. Neue Aufl., vermehret von Philipp Julio Rehtmeyer [d. 1742 (AdB)]. Braunschweig, Ludolph Schröder, 1720. 792 pp.

248. Luther, Martin, d. 1546. Erbauliche Abhandlung von der Liebe und ihrer Vortrefflichkeit über 1 Johan. 4. v. 16. 17. 18. Hrsg. von Johann Jacob Rambach [d. 1735 (L)]. 2. ed. Jena, Joh. Friederich Ritter, 1725. 97 pp.

249. Luther, Martin, d. 1546. Erklärung des xiv. xv. und xvi. Cap. aus dem Evangelisten St. Johanne. Hamburg, Henning Brendeck(e), 1687. 1186 pp.

250. Luther, Martin, d. 1546. Geistreiche Auslegung der Fest-Epistel. Hrsg. von Johann Jacob Rambach [d. 1735 (L)]. 2. ed. Jena, Joh. Friederich Ritter, 1724. 48 pp.

251. M. G. Erklärung des ersten Psalms nach seiner richtigen Abtheilung . . . Abgefasset von A. H. O. [D.?]. Hamburg, Henning Brendeck(e), 1693. 115 pp.

252. [M. G. Kurtze Anleitung zur deutschen Poesie]. 220, 620 pp. The last 620 pp. comprise a "Reim-Register." Interleaved with blank sheets throughout. T.-p. missing. The work is bound as two vols.; the division occurs at p. 192 of the Reim-Register.

253. Marperger, Bernhard Walther, d. 1746 (AdB). Die eintzige Gewalt, welche die Christen gebrauchen dörfen. Dressden, J. C. Stössel, 1728. 245 pp.

254. Mauritius, Kaspar, d. 1662 (AdB). Exercitationes anti Socinianae. 2. ed. Hamburgi, Michael Pfeiffer, 1669. 768 pp.

255. Mayer, Johann Friedrich, d. 1712 (AdB). Bibliotheca Biblica. 3. ed. Lipsiae, Joh. Martinus Burckmannus, 1711. 164 pp.

256. Mayer, Johann Friedrich, d. 1712 (AdB). Bibliotheca Mayeriana seu apparatus librarius Io. Frid. Mayeri. [Berolini?], C. G. Nicolai, 1715. 1004 pp.

257. Mayer, Johann Friedrich, d. 1712 (AdB). Caroli Arndii [Carolus Arnd, d. 1721 (J)] Bibliotheca Biblica eaque continuata. Rostochii & Lipsiae, Christ. Gotthold Garmann, 1713. 162 pp.

258. Mayer, Johann Friedrich, d. 1712 (AdB). Hamburgisches Ninive. Fortgestellet von Erdmann Neumeister [d. 1756 (L)]. Hamburg, Samuel Heyl, 1721. 468 pp.

259. Mayer, Johann Friedrich, d. 1712 (AdB). Kurtze Anleitung/zu Erweckung heiliger Buss-Andacht. Stettin, Gabriel Dahl, 1709. 104 pp.

260. Meisner, Balthasar, d. 1626 (AdB). Brevis consideratio theologiae Pho-

tinianae, prout eam Faustus Socinus descripsit. Wittebergae, Caspar Heiden, 1619. 917 pp.

261. Meisner, Balthasar, d. 1626 (AdB). Hoseas novo commentario. Wittebergae, Caspar Heyden, 1620. 1300 pp.

262. Meisner, Balthasar, d. 1626 (AdB). Sechs Predigten/Von der sichtbarlichen aussgiessung Gottes des heiligen Geistes. Wittenberg, Johann Helwig, 1636. 405 pp.

263. Mentzer, Balthasar, d. 1627 (L), praes. De sacra domini nostri Jesu Christi coena. Giessae Hassorum, Nicolas Hampel, 1607. Unpaged.

264. Mentzer, Balthasar, d. 1627 (L). Erleutterung dess Communion-Streits/ Darin die zu Paderborn getruckte Lucerna evangelica. [Giessen?], Nicolas Hampel, 1616. 251 pp.

265. Meyfart, Johann Matthäus, d. 1642 (AdB). Teutsche Rhetorica oder Rede-Kunst . . . Neulichst übersehen und nach heutiger Reim-Art gesetzet von Johann Georg Albini [Albinus von Weissenfels, d. 1679 (AdB)]. Franckfurt am Mäyn, Georg Müller, 1653. 408, 48 pp.

266. Michaelis, Georg, d. 1718 or 1719 (Js). Teutonica dispositionum variatio. Das ist: Mannichfältige Veränderung derer nach deutzscher Reime-Art gesetzten Dispositionen. Eisenberg, J. C. Meise, 1688. 1322 pp.

267. M[ichaelis], J[ohann] H[einrich], d. 1738 (AdB). Der christliche Paedagogicus. Giessen, Henning Müller, 1699. 96 pp. MS. note on t.-p. identifies the author as Michaelis, and refers to p. 60 as basis for this assertion.

268. Michaelis, Johann Heinrich, d. 1738 (AdB). Gründlicher Unterricht von den Accentibus prosaicis u. metricis. Halle, Wäysen-Haus, 1700. 121 pp. Includes two folding accent charts.

269. Misander (Adami), Johann Samuel, d. 1713 (AdB). Deliciae epistolicae, oder Epistolische Ergetzlichkeiten. T. 1. Hamburg, Heyl und Liebezeit, 1711. 1248, 176 pp.

270. Misander (Adami), Johann Samuel, d. 1713 (AdB). Deliciae epistolicae, oder Epistolische Ergetzlichkeiten. T. 2. Hamburg, Samuel Heyl, 1712. 1406 pp.

271, 271a. Moeller, Johann, d. 1651 (J). Formulae, concionatoriae. 4. ed. Jenae, Peter Hendel, 1659. Unpaged. 2 cop.; t.-p. of 271 missing.

272, 272a. Moeller, Johann, d. 1651 (J). Loci communes cantionum ecclesiasticarum. Jenae, Peter Händel, 1653. Unpaged. 2 cop.

273. Moeller, Johann, d. 1651 (J). Sacer numerus, sive alvearium. Regiomonti, Peter Hendel, 1659. Unpaged.

274. Mosheim, Johann Lorentz, d. 1755 (L). Heilige Reden. Hamburg, T. C. Felginer, 1733-35 [vol. 3, 1733]. 3 vols. in 1. Vol. 1, 5. ed.; vol. 2, 4. ed.; vol. 3, 2. ed.

275. Müller, Johann, d. 1672 (J). Anti-Jansenius. Hamburgi, Jacob Rebenlinus, 1634. 797 pp.

276. [Müller, Johann], d. 1672 (J). [Comment. in Augustinam Confessionem oder

die Augspurgische Confession aus heil. Schrifft erkläret]. [Hamburg, Stanffenh., 1630]. 2 vols. in 1. T.-p.'s missing; data from J and G.

277. Müller, Johann, d. 1672 (J). Gründliche Antwort und Wiederlegung derer Einwürffe. Hamb[urg], Michael Hering, 1631. 606 pp.

278. Müller, Johann, d. 1672 (J). Judaismus oder Jüdenthumb. Hamburg, Zacharias Hertel, 1644. 1490 pp.

279. Müller, Johann, d. 1672 (J). Prodromus Anti-Janssenii. Das ist: Kurtzer und gründlicher Bericht. Hamburg, Heinrich Werner, 1632. 225 pp.

280. Mürdel, Johann Caspar (Js). Adeliche Knechtschafft/Und unadeliche Leibeigenschafft. Oder: Geistliche Betrachtungen. Ulm, G. W. Kühn, 1702. 2 vols. in 1.

281. Mürdel, Johann Caspar (Js). Göttlicher Glücks-Wechsel. Ulm, Anna Kühn, 1675. 693 pp.

282. Die murrende aussätzige Mirjam wider Mosen. Franckfurth und Leipzig, 1708. 39 pp.

283. Musculus (Meusel), Andreas, d. 1581 (I.). Der Jüngste tag/Wie nahe oder ferne er sey. Franckfurt an der Oder, Fridrich Hartman, 1603. Unpaged.

284. Naso, Joseph, d. after 1595 (J, Js). Bericht von der geistlichen Gegenwart dess Leibs Christi im Abentmale. Bremen, [15]88. Unpaged.

285. Naso, Joseph, d. after 1595 (J, Js). Historia des Abendtmals. [N.p., n.d.]. 65 leaves.

286. [Neumann, Kaspar], d. 1715 (AdB). [Trauer-Reden: Abdanckungen]. [Leipzig, Gleditsch, 1698]. 832 pp. T.-p. missing. Data obtained from G. On authorship identification, see spine.

287. [Neumeister, Erdmann], d. 1756 (L). [Andacht bey der 1. (-12.) Betrachtung der Leydens-Geschicht]. [Hamburg?, 1721?]. 159 pp. Pp. 135ff. consist of a "Zugabe einer Passion-Oede." T.-p. missing.

288. Neumeister, Erdmann, d. 1756 (L). Epistolische Nachlese. Hamburg, Liebezeit und Felginer, 1720. 416, 360 pp.

289. Neumeister, Erdmann, d. 1756 (L). Freytags-Andachten. Hamburg, Johann Christoph Kissner, 1724. 2 vols. in 1.

290. Neumeister, Erdmann, d. 1756 (L). Freytags-Andachten. 3.[-4.]Th. Hamburg, J. C. Kissner, 1726-27. 2 vols. in 1.

291. Neumeister, Erdmann, d. 1756 (L). Die Gestalt des Neuen Menschens in xxv. Predigten. Hamburg, Schiller und Kissner, [1719]. 628 pp.

292. Neumeister, Erdmann, d. 1756 (L). Heilige Wochen-Arbeit. Hamburg, J. W. Fickweiler, 1717. 2 vols. in 1. Pp. 99-110, 113-416 of vol. 1 missing.

293. Neumeister, Erdmann, d. 1756 (L). Heilige Wochen-Arbeit. Th. 3. Hamburg, J. W. Fickweiler, 1718. 1008 pp.

294. Neumeister, Erdmann, d. 1756 (L). Heilige Wochen-Arbeit. 4. und letzte Th. Hamburg, J. W. Fickweiler, 1718. 608, 302 pp.

295. Nöthiger und wolgemeinter Unterricht zur Information der zarten und anwachsenden Jugend . . . Auff Begehren gestellet vom christlichen Liebhaber

einer lobwürdigen Zucht. Braunschweig, Caspar Gruber, 1691. 24 pp.

296. Olearius, Gottfried, d. 1684 (J, Js). Aphorismi homiletici. Lipsiae, Johann Wittigau, 1658. 304 pp.

297. Olearius, Gottfried, d. 1684 (J, Js). Isagoge antipapistica. Lipsiae, Johann Wittigau, 1658. 137 pp.

298. Olearius, Gottfried, d. 1715 (J, Js). Anleitung zur geistlichen Seelen-Cur. Leipzig, Theophilus Georgi, 1718. 998 pp. Bottom of t.-p. cropped; date verified in G and Js.

299. Olearius, Johannes, d. 1684 (AdB, J). Methodus studii theologici, indici Balduiniano . . . adaptata. Halae Sax., Christopher Mylus, 1664. 227 pp. Cf. 16.

300. Olearius, Johannes, d. 1684 (AdB, N). Theologia exegetica. Francof. & Lipsiae, J. H: Ellinger, 1674. 305 pp.

301. Olearius, Johannes, d. 1713 (AdB). Synopses controversiarum selectiorum. [Ed. nova]. Lipsiae, Frider. Lanckisius, 1710. 836 pp.

302. Osiander, Lukas, the younger, d. 1638 (L). Theologisches Bedencken/und christliche treuhertzige Erinnerung. Tübingen, 1624. 448 pp.

303. Osterwald, Johann Friedrich, d. 1747 (J). Treu-gemeynte Warnung vor der Unreinigkeit. Hamburg, J. C. Kissner, 1723. 344 pp. Tr. from the French. Last leaf mutilated, with some loss of text.

304. Osterwald, Johann Friedrich, d. 1747 (J). Untersuchung der Quellen dess kläglichen Verderbens. Franckfurt und Leipzig, J. R. Dulssecker, 1716. 578 pp. Tr. from the French by Selintes (MS. note has Gottfried Heckingius).

305. Otto, Christian Caspar. Zween Predigten aus diesen zweyen Worten: Fürchtet Gott! I. Pétri am 2/17. Leipzig, Friedrich Lanckisch, 1723. 64 pp.

306. Palm, Johann Georg, d. 1743 (J). Betrachtungen über die Gleichnisse des Neuen Testamentes. Hamburg, J. C. Kissner, 1735. 874 pp.

307. Pape, Peter Sigismund, b. 1666 (Js). Pestologia homiletica, oder: Geistlich-gute Anstalten gegen die ietzt-grassirende Peste. 2. ed. Leipzig, J. F. Gleditsch, 1711. 294 pp.

308. Paulli, Holger, d. 1714 (D). ⁊ Das ist Jeoeva. 1704. 96 pp.

309. [Paulli, Holger], d. 1714 (D). David und Goliad/das ist/ alle Feinde Messiae uber einen Hauffen geworften. 1704. 16 pp. Author identified in H-B, vol. 6.

310. Paulli, Holger, d. 1714 (D). Es ist jedennoch wahr/ dass die fast todte Braut Christi, in einer Gemeinde. [N.p., n.d.] 32 pp.

311, 311a. Paulli, Holger, d. 1714 (D). Kommt jedennoch ins Weisse gekleidet zu Copenhagen an Durch ein Send-Schreiben . . . Dabey wird es auch wohl bleiben mussen. Wobey hinzu gesetzet aus Nicolao Hunnio [Nikolas Hunnius, d. 1643 (L)]. 1704. 16 pp. 2 copies. Cf. 68, 312, 404.

312. [Paulli, Holger], d. 1714 (D). Kurtzer Bericht/ An alle Puysancen von Europa, in deren Gebiet Juden sind/ wo jetzt von Oliger Paulli geredet wird. [1704]. 240 pp. Author identified in H-B, vol. 6. Imprint cropped; date from H-B. Cf. 311.

313. [Paulli, Holger], d. 1714 (D). Das wahre arcanum regium. 1704. 32 pp. Author identified in H-B, vol. 6.

314. Pelleprat, Pierre, d. 1667 (J, N). Prolusiones oratoriae. Parisiis, Jean Libert, 1644. 304, 107 pp.

315. [Pfefferkorn, Georg Michael], d. 1732 (AdB). [Etlicher Lutheraner, wie auch Widriggesinneter Religions-Verwandten gute Urtheile von Luthero]. [Gotha, 1717]. 94 pp. T.-p. missing; data from G and J.

316. Pfeiffer, Augustus, d. 1698 (AdB). Nuptialia, das ist: Zehen auserlesene Hochzeit-Predigten. Franckfurt und Leipzig, 1705. 221 pp.

317. Pfeiffer, Johann Gottlob, d. 1740 (J). Meditamenta homiletica. Lipsiae, sumtibus Lanckisianis, 1705. 288 pp.

318. Pietzschmann (Pitschmann), Georg Gottlob, d. 1703 (J, Js). Mit Gottes Gnaden-Pfande! Der Hochzeit-Redner. Leipzig, Friedrich Lanckisch, 1700. 3 vols. in 1. Vols. 2 and 3 have continuous pagination.

319. Pietzschmann (Pitschmann), Georg Gottlob, d. 1703 (J, Js). Mit Gottes Gnaden-Pfande! Leichen-Redner/welcher in dreyen Abtheilungen. Leipzig, Friedrich Lanckisch, 1702. 1232 pp.

320. Pipping, Heinrich, d. 1722 (AdB). Schrifftmässige Prediger-Gedancken. Leipzig, Gleditsch und Weidmann, 1711. 616 pp.

321. [Poetius, Johann Carl], d. 1706 (Js). [Bibliotheca portatilis exegetico-biblica]. [Lips., 1703]. 243 pp. T.-p. missing; data supplied by G and Js.

322. Poiret, Peter, d. 1719 (AdB). De christiana liberorum e veris principiis educatione libellus. Amsterdami, Henricus Wetstenius, 1694. 523 pp.

323. Praetorius, Elias, pseud. Apologia Praetoriana. Das ist: Spiegels derer Miss-bräuche beym heutigen Predig-ampt/Gründliche Verthedigung: Wider die lutherische Prediger in Lübeck/Hamburg und Lüneburg. [Lieflandt?], 1653. 630 pp. Cf. 245. Elias Praetorius was a pseudonym used both by Christian Hohburg, d. 1675 (J, AdB), and by Adolph Held, d. 1653 (J)—see H-B (pseu). J attributes the Spiegel and this work defending it to Held.

324. Praetorius, Johann, d. 1680 (AdB). Valedictorium exequiale: Oder hundert auserlesene Abdanckungen. Görlitz, Johannes Cundisius, 1663. 416, 101 pp. The final 101 pp. consist of additional laudations (in Latin), under the title: "Latinae gratiarum actiones & valedictiones sepulchrales."

325. Prückner, Andreas, fl. 1650 (J). Manuale mille quaestionum illustrium theologicarum. Ed. nova. Norimbergae, Endterus & Junius, 1668. 494 pp.

326. Prüssing, Joachim, d. 1715-20 (Js), ed. Unverfälschte lautere Reden zur Besserung über xxiii. Sprüche des Worts der Wahrheit an die werthe Christenheit. Rostock und Leipzig, G. L. Fritzsch, 1716. 2 vols. in 1. T.-p. of vol. 1 missing.

327. Pufendorf, Samuel, Freiherr von, d. 1694 (AdB). Compendium jurisprudentiae universalis. Francofurti, Friedrich Knoch, 1699. 316 pp. Excerpted from the author's De jure naturae & gentium.

328. [Pufendorf, Samuel, Freiherr von], d. 1694 (AdB). [De officio hominis et civis]. [Francofurti?, Friedrich Knoch?, 1673?]. 304 pp. T.-p. missing.

329. Quistorp, Johann, d. 1669 (AdB). Pia desideria. Rostochi, Johannes Kilius, 1663. 140 pp.

330. R[aken], B[usso] C[hn.], d. ca. 1722 (Js). Eines evangelischen Predigers B. C. R. Geistliches Journal oder Tage-Buch. Leipzig und Gardelegen, E. H. Campe(n), 1722. 260 pp. On authorship identification, see MS. note on t.-p., and also p. 224. Verified in H-B.

331. Rambach, Johann Jakob, d. 1735 (L). Betrachtungen über das Evangelium Esaiä von der Geburt Christi. Halle, Wäysenhaus, 1724. 144 pp.

332. Rambach, Johann Jakob, d. 1735 (L). Betrachtungen über die sieben Verheissungen. Halle, Waysenhaus, 1724. 142 pp.

333. Rambach, Johann Jakob, d. 1735 (L). Exegetische und moralische Betrachtungen über das aüsserliche Leyden Christi im Oelgarten. Jena, J. B. Hartung, 1723. 130 pp.

334. Rambach, Johann Jakob, d. 1735 (L). Exegetische und moralische Betrachtungen über das innerliche Leyden Christi im Oelgarten. Jena, J. B. Hartung, 1722. 132 pp.

335. Rambach, Johann Jakob, d. 1735 (L). Institutiones hermeneuticae sacrae. 2. ed. Ienae, Hartung, 1725. 822 pp.

336. Rambach, Johann Jakob, d. 1735 (L). Der wohl-informirte Catechet. 2. ed. Jena, J. F. Bielcke, 1723. 96 pp.

337. Rathlef, Ernst Ludwig, d. 1768 (AdB), ed. Geschichte jeztlebender Gelehrten. T. 1. Zelle, J. A. Deetz, 1740. 575 pp.

338. Rathlef, Ernst Ludwig, d. 1768 (AdB), ed. Geschichte jeztlebender Gelehrten, als eine Fortsetzung des jeztlebenden Gelehrten Europa. Th. 3. Zelle, J. A. Deetz, 1741. 282 pp. Pp. 129-256 missing.

339. Rauch, Christoph, fl. last half of 17th C. (J). Theatrophania. Entgegen gesetzet der so genanten Schrifft Theatromania. Hannover, Wolffg. Schwendimann, 1682. 150 pp.

340. Rechenberg, Adam, d. 1721 (AdB). De studiis academicis, liber singularis. 2. ed. Lipsiae, J. F. Gleditsch, 1692. 320 pp.

341. Rechenberg, Adam, d. 1721 (AdB). Lineamenta philosophiae civilis. 2. ed. Lipsiae, J. L. Gleditsch, 1696. 322 pp.

342. Regula divina, oder himmliche Richt-Schnur. Ratzeburg, Nicolaus Nissen [n.d.] [30] pp.

343. Reichhelm, Johann Jeremias. Jesus typicus, oder der in Vorbildern Altes Testamentes liegende Jesus. Leipzig, Friedrich Lanckisch [1689?]. 733 pp. T.-p. possibly cropped at bottom.

344. [Republyk der Geleerden . . . 1731]. [41. Deel]. [Amsterdam?, Gerrit de Groot?, 1731?]. 558 pp. T.-p. missing.

345. Republyk der Geleerden . . . 1740. Amsterdam, Gerrit de Groot, 1740. 561, 561 pp. T.-p. of the January-February section missing.

346. Rhenius, Johann, d. 1639 (J). Tirocinium linguae Graecae. Lipsiae, Schürer, Götz, & Lanckisch, 1638. 454 pp.

347. Riemer, Johannes, d. 1714 (AdB). Der von aller Welt beweinte Maccabeus. Merceburg, Christian Forberger [1689]. 78 pp.

348. Rolten, Johan Arnold. Einleitung zur Beweisung der Warheit der christlichen Religion. Berlin, Johann Andreas Rüdiger, 1721. 253 pp.

349. Rost, George, d. 1629 (J). Amica ac fraterna admonitio super controversiis. De Vero Dn. Joannis Arndten . . . Christianismo. Rostochi, Johann Hallervord, 1626. 287 pp. Cf. 398.

350. Rost, George, d. 1629 (J). Examen Brevis considerationis Varenianae apopologeticum[!]. Rostochi, Johann Hallervord, 1628 (colophon has 1627). 271 pp. See 398.

351. Roth, Georg von, d. 1723 (AdB). Compendium theologiae thetico-biblicae. 2. ed. Francofurti et Lipsiae, Jeremias Schrey, 1717. 556 pp. At back, unpaged, "Theologia in pagina."

352. [Rottmann, Friedrich Julius]. Die verthedigte Mägde-Heyrath . . . Nebst dem untrieglichen Meiber-Spiegel. Cölln, Peter Marteau, 1713. 48 pp. The date appears on the t.-p. in the form of a chronogram. Author identified in H-B.

353. Saltzmann, Johann Niclas. Unvernunfft der Thomasischen Gedancken und Erinnerungen über allerhand gemischte philosophische und juristische Händel. 1724. 45 pp.

354. Sammlung einiger evangelischen und päbstischen Geschicht-Schreiber. Franckfurt und Leipzig, 1728. 79, 167 pp. Includes, besides the brief anonymous selections, material by Stephan Kempe, d. 1540 (AdB), Johann Möller, and Adam Tratziger, d. 1584 (AdB).

355. Saubert, Johann, d. 1646 (AdB). Neu-Jahrs Geschencke von der neuen Creatur. Mühlhausen, T. D. Brückner, 1701. 128 pp. Contains material by Johann Arndt and Johann Adolph Frohn. Date verified in G.

356. Saubert, Johann, d. 1646 (AdB). Zuchtbüchlein der Evangelischen Kirchen/ Darinn mit gutem Grund erwiesen wird. Nürnberg, Wolffgang Endter, 1636. 432 pp.

357. Schamel, Johann Martin, d. 1742 (AdB). Vindiciae catecheticae, d.i. Gründliche Rettung und Beantwortung. Leipzig, Friedrich Lanckisch, 1713-15. 2 vols. in 1. Vol. 1 includes "Eine kurtze Historia catechetica" by Johann Franz Buddeus, d. 1729 (AdB). Vol. 2 has the title: "Fortsetzung der theologischen Vindiciarum und Beantwortung."

358. Schelwig (Schelwing), Samuel, d. 1715 (AdB). Denckmahl der Pestilentz. Dantzig, J.-Z. Stoll(e), [1710]. 191 pp.

359. Schickard, Wilhelm, d. 1635 (AdB). Analysis Hebraeo-grammatica. Hamburgi, Conrad Neumann, 1695. 64 pp. Includes material from Schickard's *Horologium Hebraeum* (Lipsiae, Daniel Wintzer, 1692).

360. Schipping, Petrus. Abgenöthigtes Gespräch von dem Bande der Religion und Societät. 1689. 71 pp.

361. Schmid, Sebastian, d. 1696 (J). Das Geheimniss von Jesu Christi Person/ Amt/Thun und Leiden. Lüneburg, Johann Stern, 1688. 465 pp.

362. Schmid, Sebastian, d. 1696 (J). Das jüngste Bericht. Lüneburg, Johann Stern, 1688. 262 pp.

363. Schmid, Sebastian, d. 1696 (J). Die Lehre von der Erb-Sünde. Lüneburg, Johann Stern, 1688. 383 pp.

364. Schoensleder, Wolffgang, d. 1651 (J). Apparatus eloquentiae. Ed. novissima. Lipsiae, M. G. Weidmann, 1698. Unpaged. Interleaved. 2 (physical) vols. ("Loq" being the division point).

365. Schröter, Johann Conrad. Die fünff leidenden Sinne unseres theuren Jesu. Leipzig, J. C. Coerner, 1724. 135 pp.

366. Scioppius, Caspar [Grosippus, Paschasius, pseud.], d. 1649 (J). Mercurius bilinguis, sive Nucleus linguae Latinae. 2. ed. Hamburgi, Thomas à Wiering, 1702. 184 pp. Latin and German; the German translation is by Johann Jacob Schürer.

367. Scriver, Christian, d. 1693 (L). Chrysologia catechetica, oder Boldpredigten. Leipzig, Johann und Friedrich Luderwald, 1690. 670 pp.

368. Scultetus, Daniel Severin, d. 1712 (AdB). Stereoma doctrinae evangelicae . . . in tria distincta opuscula congestum. Lipsiae, Gothofr. Liebezeit, 1692. 255, 106, 176 pp. Opusculum 1 is entitled "Testimonium Spiritus"; opusculum 2 (1689) is entitled "Judicium supremum"; opusculum 3 (1691) has the title "Panoplia sacra." Each opusculum has its own t.-p.

369. Selneccer, Nicolaus, d. 1592 (AdB). Calvinus redivivus, das ist: Zwinglii/ Calvini/Beze/etc. eigentliche Meinung . . . Uffs newe vom Authore ubersehen/Und an vielen Orten gemehret und gebessert. [Lübeck, Asswerus Kröger, 1592]. Unpaged. Tr. from Selneccer's *Examen theologicum* by Paul Heydenreich.

370. Sennert, Christopher. Erörterung vier theologischer Streit-Fragen. 1721. 77 pp.

371. Seybold, Johann Georg, d. 1677 (AdB). Minor silvula, exhibens phrases universales et Latinae linguae proprias. Norimbergae, W. M. Endterus, 1716. 377 pp.

372. [Siber, Justus], d. 1695 (AdB). De salute Christiana et philosophica . . . considerationes xxxiv. Auctore, J. S. P. L. Caes. Dresdae, Andreas Löffler, 1659. 372 pp. For authorship identification, see spine; verified in AdB.

373. Sibersma, Hero, d. 1728 (J). Fontein des Heils, aangewesen in den Heijdelbergsen Catechismus, nader geopend uit de Schriften. 3. ed. Leeuwaarden, Hero Nauta, 1703. 740 pp.

374. Sievers, Nicolaus. Die nach allen Umständen untersuchte und dennoch sehr practicable erfundene Quarre vor der Pfarre. Franckfurt und Leipzig, 1716. 195 (i.e., 196) pp.

375. Sirfius, Petrus. Entdeckung verschiedener in dem Rusmeyerischen so genannten Historischen Catechismo befindlichen Irrlehren. 1725. 16 pp. Cf. 400.

376. Sonntag, Christoph, d. 1717 (AdB). Horologium pestis nuntium, das ist: Geistliche Weck-Uhr. Hamburg, Hertel und Weyrauch, 1682. 248 pp.

377. Sonntag, Christoph, d. 1717 (AdB). Appendix Horologii de tempore pestis. Anhang der Geistlichen Weck-Uhr. Hamburg, Hertel und Weyrauch, 1682. 88 pp.

378. Sonntag, Christoph, d. 1717 (AdB). Wohl- und nützlich anzulegende müssige Sonntags Stunden. Nürnberg, Johann Hoffmann, 1696. 677 pp.

379. Spener, Philipp Jakob, d. 1705 (L). Der evangelische Glaubens-Trost. Franckfurt am Mäyn, J. D. Zunner, 1695. 1008 pp.

380. [Spener, Philipp Jakob], d. 1705 (L). [Predigten für Kirchenjahr]. [1679]. 2 vols. in 1. Pp. missing at front and back.

381. Spener, Philipp Jakob, d. 1705 (L). Tabulae catecheticae. 3. ed. Francofurti ad Moenum, J. D. Zunner, 1691. 303 pp.

382. Sperling, Johann, d. 1658 (AdB). Synopsis anthropologiae physicae. 4. ed. Wittebergae, Johannes Berger, 1671. 178 pp.

383. Sperling, Johann, d. 1658 (AdB). Synopsis physica. 11. ed. Wittebergae, Johannes Berger, 1678. 274 pp.

384. Struve, Burkhard Gotthelf, d. 1738 (AdB). Introductio in notitiam rei litterariae et usum bibliothecarum. Accessit dissertatio de doctis impostoribus. Et huic tertiae editioni accedunt supplementa necessaria et oratio de meritis Germanorum in historiam. 3. ed. Ienae, E. C. Bailliar., 1710. 576, 76, 176 pp.

385. Sturm, Leonhard Christoph, d. 1719 (AdB). Zufällige Gedancken von den gewöhnlichen weltlichen Ergötzlichkeiten /Ob/und wie weit sie indifferent seyn/Nach Veranlassung eines frantzösischen Gesprächs zwischen Ablancourt und Patrii. 1716. 64 pp.

386. Tappe, Sylvester, d. 1747 (J). Geographische und historische Beschreibung des Judischen Landes. Hildesheim, Ludolph Schröder, 1711. 87 pp. Pp. 1-6 badly mutilated.

387. Tappe, Sylvester, d. 1747 (J). Kurtze Anweisung wie die vier chronologische General-Tabellen über die Universal-Historie. Braunschweig und Hildesheim, Ludolph Schröder, 1721. 272, 38 pp.

388. Tappe, Sylvester, d. 1747 (J). Das Licht im Schatten. Hildesheim, Ludolph Schröder, 1721. 152 pp.

389. Taylor, Jeremy, d. 1667 (L). Christliche Lebens-Kunst. Zürich, J. R. Rahnen, 1681. 467 pp. Tr. from the English.

390. Taylor, Jeremy, d. 1667 (L). Christliche Sterb-Kunst. Zürich, J. R. Rahnen, 1682. 412 pp. Tr. from the English.

391. Textor, Conrad. Kahle und nichtige Entschuldigungen der Verächter dess hochheil. Abendmahls. Franckfurt am Mäyn, J. P. Andreas, 1688. 91 pp.

392. Thomasius, Christian, d. 1728 (AdB). Bedencken über die Frage: Wieweit ein Prediger gegen seinen Landes-Herrn/welcher zugleich Summus Episcopus mit ist/sich des Binde-Schlüssels bedienen könne? 3. ed. Wolffenbüttel, Freytag, 1707. 191 pp.

393. Thomasius, Christian, d. 1728 (AdB). Thummheit/Aus dem andern Theil seiner Gemischten Händel . . . In einem Gespräche vorgestellet von Johann Niclas Saltzmann. 1724. 46 pp.

394. Trublet [Nicholas Charles Joseph], d. 1770 (N). Pensées choisies sur l'incrédulité, a cause de leur justesse separement publiées par G. G. G. [Gabriel Wilhelm Goetten, d. 1781 (AdB)]. [Zelle, J. A. Deetz], 1737. 26 pp. Appeared originally as part of *Essais sur divers suiets de literature et de morale* (Paris, 1735).

395. Uhlich, Johann Elias, d. 1722 (AdB). Allernöthigste Beicht-Fragen. Wittenberg, C. G. Ludwig, 1714. 64 pp.

396. Umständliche Nachricht dessen, was sich mit einem Evangelisch-Lutherischen Prediger in Ost-Friessland begeben. Franckfurt und Leipzig, 1728. 724 pp. The Addenda at the back unpaged.

397. Unterricht von der Kinder-Zucht. Leipzig und Stendal, E. H. Campe(n), 1710. 336 pp.

398. Varenius, Henricus, d. 1635 (J). Brevis consideratio Admonitionis Georgii Rostii super controversiis de Vero B. Arndi Christianismo. Lunaeburgae, J. & H. Stern, 1626. 121 pp. See 349.

399. Varenius, Henricus, d. 1635 (J). Christliche/schrifftmässige/wolgegrundete Rettunge der vier Bücher vom Wahren Christenthumb. Luneburg, Johann und Heinrich Stern, 1624. 2 vols. in 1. T.-p. of vol. 2 varies from that of vol. 1.

400. Vereius, Johann. De superbia pietistica ad Michaelis [Christian] Rusmeyeri [Rusmeier, d. 1745 (AdB)] exercitationem academicam de Praejudiciis reformationem ecclesiasticam sufflaminantibus. 1724. 16 pp. Cf. 375.

401. Virginius, Andreas, d. 1664 (AdB), praes. Manipulus disputationum theologicarum. Dorpati Livonorum, Jacobus Pistorius, 1635. 400 pp. Various respondents took part in these 19 disputations.

402. Volder, Burchard de, d. 1709 (J). Disputationes philosophicae omnes contra Atheos. Medioburgi, Johannes Lateranus, 1685. 59 pp.

403. Die vornehmsten Europaeischen Reisen . . . Welchen auch beygefüget/LVI. [i.e., LVII.] accurate Post- und Boten-Charten . . . Die VI. Ausfertigung. Hamburg, J. C. Kissner, 1724. 456, 528 pp.

404. Die wahre Erfullung des Spruchs/in Apoc. 12, 12 . . . in Oliger Pauli . . . [N.p., n.d.] 64 pp. Cf. 311.

405. Walch, Johann Georg, d. 1775 (L), ed. Historische und theologische Einleitung in die Religions-Streitigkeiten. [1. Th.]. [Jena, Meyer, 1730]. 1024 pp. T.-p. and 2nd leaf of dedication mutilated. Imprint and vol. no. from University of Chicago copy.

406. Walch, Johann Georg, d. 1775 (L), ed. Historische und theologische Einleitung in die Religions-Streitigkeiten. [1. Th.]. 3. ed. Jena, Johann Meyer, 1733. 743 pp. Vol. no. from University of Chicago copy.

407. Walch, Johann Georg, d. 1775 (L), ed. Historische und theologische Einleitung in die Religions-Streitigkeiten. [2. Th.]. [Jena, Meyer, 1734]. 1148 pp. T.-p. mutilated; imprint and vol. no. from University of Chicago copy.

408. Walch, Johann Georg, d. 1775 (L), ed. Historische und theologische Einleitung in die Religions-Streitigkeiten. 3. Th. Jena, Johann Mayer, 1734. 1126 pp.

409. [Walch, Johann Georg], d. 1775 (L), ed. [Historische und theologische Einleitung in die Religions-Streitigkeiten]. [5. und letzter Th.]. [Jena, Meyer, 1739]. 1374 pp. T.-p. missing; imprint from University of Chicago catalogue card for the book.

410. [Wandal, Hans], d. 1710 (D). [ὑποτύπωσις sanorum verborum seu brevis expositio theologiae in thesi et antithesi]. [1703]. 373 pp. T.-p. missing; see MS. note on the recto of the first blank leaf; title verified in G and H.

411. Warhafftiger/glaubwirdiger und gründlicher Bericht von den vier Büchern vom Wahren Christenthumb Herrn Johannis Arndten. Lüneburg, Johan und Heinrich Stern, 1625. 136 pp.

412. Wedderkop, Magnus von, d. 1721 (AdB). Bibliotheca Wedderkoppiana, sive catalogus selectissimorum librorum . . . quos . . . collegit . . . Dn. Magnus à Wedderkop. Hamburgi, J. N. Gennagel, 1722. 734 pp.

413. Weickhmann, Joachim, d. 1736 (J). Theologischer und ausführlicher Unterricht von der Pestilentz. 2. ed. Zerbst, Samuel Tietz(e), 1711. 526 pp.

414. Weisbach, Christian, d. 1715 (J). Warhaffte und gründliche Cur aller dem menschlichen Leibe zustoffenden Kranckheiten. 4. ed. Strassburg, Johann Reinhold Dulssecker, 1722. 82, 569 pp.

415. Weise, Christian, d. 1708 (AdB). Neu-erleuterter politischer Redner. Leipzig, Sabina Gerdesin, 1684. 720 pp.

416. Weller, Jakob, d. 1664 (L). Fasciculus viventium Brunsvicensis, Braunschweigisches Bündlein der Lebendigen. Braunschweig, Müller und Duncker, 1649. 856 pp.

417. Werenfels, Samuel, d. 1740 (AdB). Predigten über einige Haupt-Lehren der Christlichen Religion. Basel, J. L. Brandmüller, 1717. 432 pp. Tr. from the French.

418. Wichmann, Peter. Kurtze und deutliche Erklärung des 9ten Capitels der Epistel S. Pauli an die Römer. Hamburg, J. C. Kissner, 1723. 280 pp.

419. Wilcke, Christopher. Der mürdige Communicant. Berlin auffm Friedrichswerder, Gotthart Schlechtiger, 1705. 222 pp.

420. Winckler, Johann, d. 1705 (AdB). Das christliche Wohlverhalten der Gläubigen in göttlicher Schickung. Hamburg, Gottfried Liebernickel, [1699?] 166 pp.

421. Winckler, Johann, d. 1705 (AdB). Eine kurtze Erklärung der schwersten Versiculn des ix. Capitels der Epistel St. Pauli an die Römer. Hamburg, Gottfried Liebernickel, 1702. 127 pp.

422. Winckler, Johann, d. 1705 (AdB). Gründliche Anweisung auss dem Evangelio Matth. xxi. v.1-9. Hamburg, Gottfried Liebernickel, 1695. 144 pp.

423. Winckler, Johann, d. 1705 (AdB). Heilsame Bewegungs-Gründe/ Sich von den Lüsten dieser Welt. Hamburg, Gottfried Liebernickel, 1702. 208 pp.

424. Winckler, Johann, d. 1705 (AdB). Neu-Jahrs Segen. Hamburg, Gottfried Liebernickel, 1705. 72 pp.

425. Winckler, Johann, d. 1705 (AdB). Vertheidigung seines gründlichen Beweises der Kinder-Tauffe. Hamburg, Gottfried Liebernickel, 1696. 480 pp.

426. Winckler, Johann Friedrich, d. 1738 (AdB). Kurtzer Begriff seiner im Jahr 1733. geführten Lehr-Art von dem Sieg der Glaubigen über die Hindernisse des Christenthums. Hamburg, J. M. Saalikath. Unpaged.

427. Winckler [Johann Joseph], d. 1722 (AdB; H-B). Arcanum regium, das ist ein königlich Beheimniss. [2. ed.]. Franckfurt a.M., 1703. [12] pp. The work originated with Johann Welmer, d. 1704.

428. Wohlgegründete und offt probirte Vortheile zur lateinischen Sprache. Hrsg. von dem Verfasser des zweyten Bandes der Acerra Philologica. Halle, Rengerischen Buchhandlung, 1722. 295 pp. For possible author identifications, see H-B under "Acer(r)a."

429. Wolf, Johann Christoph, d. 1739 (AdB). Absurdahallensia, oder Die irrigen und ungereimten Meynungen. [Flensburg?], 1707. 190 plus pp. Incomplete.

430. [Zeltner, Gustav Georg], d. 1738 (J). [Salome Christo afine: hoc est Synopsis logomachiarum vel pietisticarum] . . . Accessere ad calcem Christophori Forstneri . . . De dissidiis theologorum epistolae. Francofurti et Lipsiae, Tauber, 1726. 412, 38 plus pp. T.-p. mutilated; all after p. 38 of Forstner's work missing; data supplied by G. Published under the pseudonym George August Pachomius; for author identification, see H-B (pseu).

431. Zeumer, Johann Caspar. Exemplarischer teutscher Schulmeister. Jena, Johann Bielcke, 1701. 107 pp. J has the hanging reference: Zürner (Caspar), see Zeuner.

432. Zorn, Peter, d. 1746 (J). Opuscula sacra. T. 1. Francofurti ad Moenum & Lipsiae, Autor, 1723. 822 pp. Cf. 202, 203.

433. Zuverlässige Nachrichten von dem gegenwärtigen Zustande, Veränderung und Wachsthum der Wissenschafften. 13. [-16.] Th. Leipzig, J. F. Gleditsch, 1741. 306 pp. T.-p.'s missing for vols. 13 and 16; pp. 1-2 of vol. 13 missing.

434. Zuverlässige Nachrichten von dem gegenwärtigen Zustande, Veränderung und Wachsthum der Wissenschafften. 37. [-48.] Th. Leipzig, J. F. Gleditsch, 1743. 889 pp. T.-p. and pp. 1-4 of vol. 37 missing.

Appendix D

The Superiority of
American Common Law Illustrated

The following series of questions incorporates the safeguards of the American common law for the defendant who pleads guilty; it reflects the state of the law on December 1, 1975, the date at which the recently approved changes in the Federal Rules of Criminal Procedure officially took effect. Judge Hoffman presented this material at the American Law Institute-American Bar Association course on Federal Criminal Procedure at St. Thomas, Virgin Islands, on December 3-4, 1975, at which the author was present; it has been reprinted from the ALI-ABA Study Materials for that course. A better illustration could scarcely be provided to show the extent of sensitivity and concern for the accused in the American legal system.

PLEAS OF GUILTY

SUGGESTED QUESTIONS TO BE PROPOUNDED BY THE COURT TO A DEFENDANT WHO ENTERS A PLEA OF GUILTY OR NOLO CONTENDERE.

by

Walter E. Hoffman
Senior Judge
United States District Court
Norfolk, Virginia

General Statement:
(By Court)

Before accepting your plea of guilty (nolo contendere) I must ask you certain questions. If you do not understand any particular question, please tell me as it is important that you thoroughly understand each question.

Questions to Defendant:

1. Have you discussed with your attorney the nature of the charge(s) to which you have entered a plea of guilty (nolo contendere) and do you realize what the (each) charge is?

Note: If the defendant has waived or refused counsel, the court should read (or have read) to the defendant the indictment (information) and the court should attempt to explain in lay terms the precise nature of the charge(s).

2. The maximum possible penalty provided by law for this offense is imprisonment for a period not exceeding _____ (years or months) and a fine not exceeding $_____, either or both. (If the law provides for a mandatory minimum penalty, the court must *also* provide this information.) Do you understand the seriousness of the penalty provided by law?

Note: If the law requires the imposition of a mandatory special parole term (as required by the Comprehensive Drug Abuse and Control Act of 1970, 21 U.S.C. § 841 (b) (A) and (c), the court should (and in at least three circuits must) warn the defendant that the special parole term must be added as a part of the sentence. *Roberts* v. *United States,* 491 F.2d 1236 (3 Cir. 1974); *United States* v. *Richardson,* 483 F.2d 516 (8 Cir. 1973); *Bell* v. *United States,* ___F. 2d ___ (4 Cir. Aug. 11, 1975). ... If the age of the defendant is 18, but less than 22, explain the maximum possible punishment under YCA unless the offense calls for a maximum of six years or more. If the age at the time of the alleged commission of the offense is less than 18 years, the Juvenile Delinquency Act would apply and the maximum possible punishment provisions of that Act should be explained to the defendant.

3(a). You already have an attorney (if applicable); have you had full opportunity to discuss your case with your attorney, including the plea of guilty which you have entered?

3(b). I note that you are not represented by an attorney (if applicable) and that you have waived your right to an attorney. Do you understand that you have a right to be represented by an attorney at every stage of the proceedings and, even at this time, if you desire an attorney and qualify for the appointment of an attorney, one will be appointed to represent you without charge and further proceedings will be delayed? ...

4. Do you understand that you have a right to plead not guilty or, if you have previously entered a plea of not guilty, that you have a right to persist in that plea?

5. Do you realize that, if you plead not guilty, you have a right to a trial by jury and, at that trial, you have a right to the assistance of counsel, including the right to confront and cross-examine witnesses and that you cannot be required to testify against yourself?

6. If the Court accepts your plea of guilty (nolo contendere),

there will be no further trial of any kind. In other words, do you understand that your entry of a plea of guilty (nolo contendere) is a waiver of your right to a jury trial?

7. If you persist in your plea of guilty (nolo contendere), the Court may ask you questions about the offense and, if you answer these questions under oath in the presence of your counsel, your answers may later be used against you in a prosecution for perjury or false statement. Do you understand that the Court may question you along these lines?

8. Are you entering this plea of guilty (nolo contendere) freely and voluntarily on your part?

9. Is your plea the result of any force or threat on the part of anyone?

10(a). (If the Court has been advised that a plea agreement has been entered into.)

(1) I understand that you and your attorney have had some discussion with the attorney for the Government with a view toward reaching an agreement as to the recommendation (or disposition) of this case. I now ask your attorney to detail the agreed recommendation (or disposition).

(Defense Attorney responds.)

(2) I would like for the Government attorney to state whether this is the entire agreement and, if he does not concur, I want him to state his understanding of the agreement.

(Attorney for Government responds.)

(3) (To defendant) You have heard the attorneys state the details of the plea agreement. Is it absolutely correct? (Wait for answer.) Has anyone, wholly apart from the plea agreement, made any promise to you which induced you to enter this plea of guilty (nolo contendere)?

(4) (To defendant, if plea agreement involves only a recommendation or an agreement not to oppose defendant's request for a particular sentence) You understand, of course, that any recommendation by the prosecution, or any agreement not to oppose your attorney's request, is not binding upon the Court and, in the event the Court sees fit not to grant your attorney's request (not to accept the Government's recommendation), and if you then still persist in your plea of guilty (nolo contendere), you could receive a sentence which is less favorable to you than what was set forth in the plea agreement?

(5) (To defendant, if plea agreement involves the dismissal of one or more charges and/or an agreement that a specific sentence is the appropriate disposition of the case) You understand, of course, that the Court is not required to act favorably on the agreement; that is, the Court may see fit to reject the agreement. If the Court decides to reject the agreement, you will be so notified in open court at which time you will have an opportunity to withdraw your plea of guilty (nolo contendere)

and you may then enter a plea of not guilty. However, if the agreement is rejected by the Court and you still persist in your plea of guilty (nolo contendere), you are told that the disposition of this case may be less favorable to you than what was contained in the plea agreement. Do you understand?

10(b) (If the Court has received no information as to the existence of a plea agreement or any discussion of same.)

(1) I am required to ask you whether your willingness to plead guilty (nolo contendere) results from any prior discussions between you (and your attorney, if represented by counsel) on the one hand, and the attorney for the Government on the other hand. Do you know of any such discussions? (If answer is in the affirmative, follow procedure and questions set forth in 10(a) (2), (3), (4), (5).)

(2) (If answer is in the negative, ask the following.) Your attorney, of course, has a right to make recommendations to you as to your plea, but he cannot make any promises to you which are in any manner binding upon the Court. Has anyone made any promise to you which persuaded or induced you to enter this plea of guilty (nolo contendere)?

10(c) (If the Court is not prepared to accept or reject the plea agreement, or generally follows the practice of referring all plea agreements to a probation officer for recommendation as to acceptance or rejection) It is the Court's view that this plea agreement should be referred to a probation officer for a recommendation. With your written consent you may be (again) interviewed and thereafter the Court may inspect the presentence report for the purpose of determining whether the plea agreement will be accepted or rejected. (See Rule 11 (e) (4) as to procedure in event of rejection of plea agreement.) Are you willing to execute the written consent form to be (again) interviewed by the probation officer? (If answer is in the affirmative, have defendant execute consent form. While not required to be executed in open court, it is more convenient. If answer is in the negative, Court may then reject the plea agreement.)

11. (If counsel agree, or the Government is prepared to present the factual basis for the plea of guilty, it may be presented at this time or, at the option of the Court, this presentation may be deferred until the time of sentencing and/or the acceptance or rejection of a plea agreement. No factual basis is required as to a plea of nolo contendere.)

(a) The Court will hear the factual basis for the plea at this time.

(b) The Court will defer the factual basis for the plea until the date to be fixed for further proceedings.

12. This case is continued until _____ for sentencing or such other action as may be required. (To defendant if not in custody) You understand, of course, that you must be present on that date?

Additional questions *may* be asked defendant upon the circumstances of the case as well as the age of the defendant, his apparent lack of intelligence, his physical or mental condition and other factors, all as applicable to the existing situation.

A. Your correct name is _____? (as stated in the indictment or information)

Note: If name as stated in the indictment or information is incorrect, information may be amended by attorney for the Government. If name on indictment is incorrect, merely obtain correct name for the record without attempting interlineation.

B. What is your present age?

Note: If under 18 at time defendant allegedly *committed the offense,* he must ordinarily be tried under the Juvenile Delinquency Act if he consents to this procedure.

If 18 but less than 22, defendant *must* be considered for sentencing under the Youth Corrections Act. If Court finds that defendant is not suitable for treatment under YCA, Court must make such finding on the record but need not give reasons for same.

If 22 but less than 26, defendant *may* be considered for sentencing as a Young Adult Offender and *may* be sentenced pursuant to YCA.

C. What is the extent of your education and schooling?

D. Are you now, or have you recently been, under the care of a doctor or psychiatrist, or otherwise hospitalized for narcotic addiction or any physical or mental illness?

E. Have you had anything to drink of an alcoholic nature within the past 12 hours?

F. Are you in fact guilty of the crime (or crimes) to which you have entered a guilty plea?

Note: This question should not be asked of a defendant who enters a plea of *nolo contendere* as it destroys the effect of that plea. Likewise, no factual basis for a plea of nolo contendere is required. See Rule 11(6)(f). However, if a plea of nolo contendere is entered, the Court may wish to advise the defendant that a finding of guilty will be entered.

G. The Court need not accept your plea of guilty unless the Court is satisfied that you are guilty and that you fully understand your rights. Do you understand your rights?

Note: Delete first portion of this statement if defendant pleads nolo contendere.

H. Are you able to read, write, speak and understand the English language?

Note: This question is of increasing importance with a defendant who speaks only "broken English". Con; ·ess is now considering the Bilingual Courts Act bill which, if e.acted, will be a major development in the field of constitutional rights involving the right to the services of an attorney, confrontation of witnesses, etc. See *Negron* v. *United States,* 434 F.2d 386 (2 Cir. 1970). If there is doubt as to defendant's answer to this inquiry, it is the better course of action to appoint an interpreter for pretrial and trial proceedings.

Other questions may be required or optional where defendant is under the Juvenile Delinquency Act or eligible for sentencing under the Youth Corrections Act. Substantially, however, the same required questions must be asked of a defendant under the Juvenile Delinquency Act or the Youth Corrections Act. Under the optional questions, it is at least appropriate to secure information as to the defendant's age and education.

Bibliography

Andrews, Charles M. *The Colonial Background of the American Revolution*. Rev. ed. New Haven: Yale University Press, 1931.

Aron, Raymond. *Les désillusions du progrès. Essai sur la dialectique de la modernité*. Paris: Calmann-Lévy, 1969.

Asbury, Herbert. *Up from Methodism*. New York: Knopf, 1926.

Ashe, Geoffrey; Heyerdahl, Thor; *et al. The Quest for America*. New York: Praeger, 1971.

Auden, W. H. *The Age of Anxiety*. London: Faber, 1948.

———. *Thank You, Fog: Last Poems*. New York: Random House, 1974.

Babcock, W. H. *Legendary Islands of the Atlantic*. (Research Series, No. 8) New York: American Geographical Society, 1922.

Bailey, Thomas A. (ed.). *The American Spirit: United States History As Seen by Contemporaries*. 3d ed. Lexington, Mass.: D.C. Heath, 1973. 2 vols.

Bainton, Roland H. *Christian Unity and Religion in New England*. (Collected Papers in Church History, Series 3.) London: Hodder & Stoughton, 1965.

Baringer, William E. (ed.). *The Philosophy of Abraham Lincoln*. Indian Hills, Colo.: Falcon's Wing Press, 1959.

Barker, Lucius J.; and Barker, Twiley W., Jr. *Freedoms, Courts, Politics: Studies in Civil Liberties*. Englewood Cliffs, N.J.: Prentice-Hall, 1965.

Barzini, Luigi. *The Italians*. New York: Atheneum, 1964.

Bauer, Walter E., *et al. God and Caesar: A Christian Approach to Social Ethics*. Ed. Warren A. Quanbeck. Minneapolis: Augsburg Publishing House, 1959.

Becker, Carl L. *The Declaration of Independence: A Study in the History of Political Ideas*. New York: Vintage Books, 1958.

———. *The Heavenly City of the 18th-Century Philosophers*. New Haven: Yale University Press, 1932.

Bedford, Sybille. *The Faces of Justice: A Traveller's Report.* New York: Simon and Schuster, 1961.

Bellah, Robert N. "Civil Religion in America." In: *The Religious Situation: 1968,* ed. Donald R. Cutler. Boston: Beacon Press, 1968. Pp. 331-93.

Bellamy, H. S. *The Atlantis Myth.* London: Faber & Faber, 1948.

Billington, Ray Allen. *The Westward Movement in the United States.* Princeton, N.J.: Van Nostrand Anvil Books, 1959.

Boorstin, Daniel J. *America and the Image of Europe: Reflections on American Thought.* New York: Meridian Books, 1960.

———. *The Americans: The Colonial Experience.* New York: Random House, 1958.

———. *The Genius of American Politics.* Chicago: University of Chicago Press, 1953.

———(ed.). *American Civilization: A Portrait from the 20th Century.* New York: McGraw-Hill, 1972.

Boyd, Julian P., *et al. Fundamental Testaments of the American Revolution.* Washington, D.C.: Library of Congress, 1973. (Includes essays on Paine's *Common Sense,* the Declaration of Independence, the Articles of Confederation, and the Treaty of Paris of 1783.)

———. *The Spirit of Christmas at Monticello.* New York: Oxford University Press, 1964.

Brainerd, David. *Life and Diary.* Ed. Jonathan Edwards. Rev. ed. Philip E. Howard, Jr. (Wycliffe Series of Christian Classics.) Chicago: Moody Press, 1949.

Brauer, Jerald C. (ed.) *Reinterpretation in American Church History.* (Essays in Divinity, Vol. 5.) Chicago: University of Chicago Press, 1968.

Bridenbaugh, Carl. *Mitre and Sceptre.* New York: Oxford University Press, 1967.

Briggs, Asa (ed.). *The 19th Century: The Contradictions of Progress.* New York: McGraw-Hill, 1970.

Brooks, Van Wyck. *The Flowering of New England, 1815-1865.* New York: Modern Library, 1941.

Brown, Harold O. J. "The Passivity of American Christians." *Christianity Today,* January 16, 1976, pp. 7-10.

Bruckberger, R. L. *Image of America.* Trans. C. G. Paulding and V. Peterson. New York: Viking, 1959. (Bruckberger's theological conservativism is taken to task in the recent work by "New Shape" Catholic Hourdin, *q.v.*)

Burdick, Eugene; and Lederer, William J. *The Ugly American.* New York: Norton, 1958.

[Burton, Robert.] *The Anatomy of Melancholy.* By Democritus Junior. 6th ed. London: Crips & Lloyd, 1652.

Bury, J. B. *The Idea of Progress: An Inquiry into Its Origin and Growth.* Intro. Charles A. Beard. London: Macmillan, 1932.

Bushman, Richard L. (ed.). *The Great Awakening: Documents on the Revival of Religion, 1740-1745.* New York: Atheneum; Williamsburg, Va.: Institute of Early American History and Culture, 1970.

Butterfield, Herbert. *George III and the Historians.* Rev. ed. New York: Macmillan, 1959.

Carter, Alice Clare. *The English Reformed Church in Amsterdam in the 17th Century.* Amsterdam: Scheltema & Holkema, 1964.

Cassirer, Ernst. *The Philosophy of the Enlightenment.* Trans. Koelln and Pettegrove. Princeton: Princeton University Press, 1951.

Ceremony Held in Paris to Commemorate the Bi-Centenary of the Birth of Benjamin Franklin. Paris: Imprimerie Universelle, 1906.

Clark H. B. (ed.). *Biblical Law.* 2d ed. Portland, Oregon: Binfords & Mort, 1944.

Clouse, Robert G.; Linder, Robert D.; and Pierard, Richard V. *Protest and Politics: Christianity and Contemporary Affairs.* Greenwood, S. C.: Attic Press, 1968.

Collins, Gary R. (ed.). *Our Society in Turmoil.* Carol Stream, Ill.: Creation House, 1970. (Contains, *inter alia,* "Evangelical Social Responsibility in Theological Perspective," by John Warwick Montgomery.)

Columbus, Christopher. *The Columbus Letter of March 14th, 1493.* Chicago: Newberry Library, 1953.

———. *The Journal of Christopher Columbus.* Trans. Cecil Jane. New York: Bramhall House, 1960.

———. *Select Letters of Christopher Columbus.* Ed. and trans. R. H. Major. 2d ed. London, 1870.

Cornforth, Maurice. *The Open Philosophy and the Open Society: A Reply to Dr. Karl Popper's Refutations of Marxism.* New York: International Publishers, 1968.

Corwin, Edward S. "The 'Higher Law' Background of American Constitutional Law." *Harvard Law Review,* XLII (1928-1929), 149-85, 365-409.

Crèvecoeur, M. G. J. de. *Letters from an American Farmer.* Reprint ed. Gloucester, Mass.: Peter Smith, 1968.

Curti, Merle E. *The Growth of American Thought.* 3d ed. New York: Harper & Row, 1964.

Daiches, David. *Some Late Victorian Attitudes.* London: André Deutsch, 1969.

[Daley, Richard.] *Quotations from Mayor Daley.* Compiled by Peter Yessne. New York: Pocket Books, 1969.

Demaris, Ovid. *Captive City: Chicago in Chains.* New York: Lyle Stuart, 1969.

Després, Sylvain. . . . *Et devant les hommes.* Paris: La Pensée Universelle, 1973.

Dillon, John F. *The Laws and Jurisprudence of England and America: Being a Series of Lectures Delivered before Yale University.* Boston: Little, Brown, 1895.

Disch, Robert (ed.). *The Future of Literacy.* Englewood Cliffs, N. J.: Prentice-Hall Spectrum Books, 1973.

"The Disease of the Century." *Time,* October 20, 1975, pp. 67-68.

Dolbeare, Kenneth M.; and Hammond, Phillip E. *The School Prayer Decisions: From Court Policy to Local Practice.* Chicago: University of Chicago Press, 1971.

Donnelly, Ignatius. *Atlantis: The Antediluvian World.* Rev. ed. Ed. Egerton Sykes. New York: Gramercy, 1949.

Douglas, William O. *The Bible and the Schools.* Boston: Little, Brown, 1966.

Dutourd, Jean, *The Taxis of the Marne.* Trans. Harold King. New York: Simon and Schuster, 1957.

Earle, Alice Morse. *The Sabbath in Puritan New England.* Reprint ed. Williamstown, Mass.: Corner House, 1969.

Edwards, E. E. *References on the Significance of the Frontier in American History.* (Bibliographical Contributions, No. 25.) Washington, D. C.: U.S. Department of Agriculture, 1935.

Elert, Werner. *The Christian Ethos.* Trans. Carl J. Schindler. Philadelphia: Muhlenberg Press, 1957.

Elias, C. E., Jr., *et al. Metropolis: Values in Conflict.* Belmont, Ca.: Wadsworth, 1964.

Ellis, Edward S., *et al. The 19th Century: Its History, Progress, and Marvelous Achievements; the Wonderful Story of the World for 100 Years.* Philadelphia: American Book and Bible House, 1900.

Emerson, Ralph Waldo. *The Portable Emerson.* Intro. Mark Van Doren. New York: Viking Press, 1946.

Epstein, Joseph. *Divorced in America: An Anatomy of Loneliness.* New York: Dutton, 1974.

Erikson, Erik H. (ed.). *Youth: Change and Challenge.* New York: Basic Books, 1963.

Falconi, Carlo. *The Silence of Pius XII.* Trans. Bernard Wall. Boston: Little, Brown, 1970.

Farrell, J. G. *The Siege of Krishnapur: A Novel.* New York: Harcourt, Brace, Jovanovich, 1974.

Fehrenbacher, Don E. *Prelude to Greatness: Lincoln in the 1850's.* Stanford, Ca.: Stanford University Press, 1962.

Ferron, H. de. *Théorie du progrès.* Paris & Rennes: A. Leroy, 1867. 2 vols.

Fletcher, Joseph, and Montgomery, John Warwick. *Situation Ethics—True or False: A Dialogue.* Minneapolis: Bethany, 1972.

Franklin, Benjamin. *Autobiography.* Postscript by Richard B. Morris. New York: Pocket Books, 1955.

Froom, LeRoy Edwin. *The Prophetic Faith of Our Fathers: The Historical Development of Prophetic Interpretation.* Washington, D.C.: Review and Herald, 1946-1954. 4 vols.

Frothingham, O. B. *Transcendentalism in New England: A History.* Intro. Sydney E. Ahlstrom. Reprint ed. Gloucester, Mass.: Peter Smith, 1965.

Fussell, Paul. *The Great War and Modern Memory.* New York: Oxford University Press, 1975.

Fyfe, Hamilton. *The Illusion of National Character.* London: Watts, 1940.

Gay, Peter. *Deism: An Anthology.* Princeton, N.J.: Van Nostrand, 1968.

———. *The Enlightenment: A Comprehensive Anthology.* New York: Simon and Schuster, 1973.

———. *The Enlightenment: An Interpretation; The Rise of Modern Paganism.* New York: Knopf, 1966.

Gesell, Arnold, *et al. Youth: The Years from Ten to Sixteen.* New York: Harper, 1956.

Getzels, J. W. "The Child in the Changing Society." In: *New Directions in Public Library Development,* ed. Lester Asheim. Chicago: University of Chicago Graduate Library School, 1957. Pp. 45-56.

Gibson, Charles. *Spain in America.* New York: Harper Torchbooks, 1967.

Gigon, Fernand. *The Bomb.* Trans. Constantine Fitz Gibbon. New York: Pyramid Books, 1960. (Original title: *Formula for Death.*)

Gilmer, Lula Jane. "Some Aspects of the Ethical and Religious Thought of Thomas Jefferson." Unpublished M.A. thesis, Duke University, 1937.

Gilmore, Myron P. *The World of Humanism, 1453-1517.* New York: Harper, 1952.

Golden, Harry. *Only in America.* Foreword by Carl Sandburg. New York: World Publishing Co., 1958.

Gough, J. W. *John Locke's Political Philosophy.* Rev. ed. Oxford: Clarendon Press, 1956.

Graham, Billy. *World Aflame.* Garden City, N.Y.: Doubleday, 1965.

Grandgent, Charles Hall. "The Dark Ages." Reprinted in his: *Old and New: Sundry Papers.* Cambridge: Harvard University Press, 1920.

Grant, George P. *Philosophy in the Mass Age.* Vancouver, B.C., Canada: Copp Clark, 1959.

Grounds, Vernon C. *Revolution and the Christian Faith.* Intro. Sen. Mark O. Hatfield. (Evangelical Perspectives, ed. John Warwick Montgomery.) Philadelphia: Lippincott, 1971.

Guiterman, Arthur. *Gaily the Troubadour*. New York: Dutton, 1936.

Hakluyt, Richard. *The Principal Navigations, Voyages, Traffiques & Discoveries of the English Nation*. Intro. John Masefield. London: J. M. Dent, 1927. 8 vols.

Hall, Christopher. *The Christian Teacher and the Law: Rights and Opportunities*. Oak Park, Ill.: Christian Legal Society, 1975.

Hall, James Parker. *Constitutional Law*. Rev. ed. (American Law and Procedure, Vol. 12.) Chicago: LaSalle Extension University, 1955.

Haller, William. *The Rise of Puritanism; or, The Way to the New Jerusalem As Set Forth in Pulpit and Press from Thomas Cartwright to John Lilburne and John Milton*. New York: Columbia University Press, 1938.

Handlin, Oscar, and Burchard, John (eds.). *The Historian and the City*. Cambridge, Mass.: M.I.T. Press, 1966.

Harvard Guide to American History. Ed. Frank Freidel and R. K. Showman. Rev. ed. Cambridge: Harvard University Press, 1974. 2 vols.

Havighurst, Robert J. *Developmental Tasks and Education*. 2d ed. New York: Longmans, Green, 1952.

———. *Human Development and Education*. New York: Longmans, Green, 1953.

———. and Taba, Hilda. *Adolescent Character and Personality*. New York: John Wiley, 1949.

Hay, Denys (ed.). *The Age of the Renaissance*. New York: McGraw-Hill, 1967.

Hazen, Charles Downer. *Contemporary American Opinion of the French Revolution*. Baltimore, Md.: Johns Hopkins Press, 1897.

Hearn, Lafcadio. *Japan: An Interpretation*. New York: Grosset & Dunlap, 1904.

Heath, Dwight B. (ed.). *A Journal of the Pilgrims at Plymouth: Mourt's Relation*. New York: Corinth Books, 1963.

Hertzberg, Arthur. *The French Enlightenment and the Jews*. New York: Columbia University Press, 1968.

Hochhuth, Rolf. *The Deputy*. Trans. Richard and Clara Winston. Preface by Albert Schweitzer. New York: Grove Press, 1964.

[Hochhuth.] *The Storm over The Deputy*. ed. Eric Bentley. New York: Grove Press, 1964.

Hofstadter, Richard. *Social Darwinism in American Thought*. Rev. ed. Boston: Beacon Press, 1955.

———. "Turner and the Frontier Myth." *American Scholar*, XVIII (1949), 433.

Hourdin, Georges. *Les jardiniers de Dieu. Réponse au Père Bruckberger*. Paris: Calmann-Lévy, 1975. (Cf. Bruckberger's *Image of America*.)

Human Life Review. Ed. J. P. McFadden and Harold O. J. Brown. Vol. I, No. 1 (Winter, 1975) to date.

Hunt, Peter (ed.). *Eating and Drinking: An Anthology for Epicures.* Intro. André L. Simon. London: Ebury Press, 1961.

"I Knew Him Upwards of Thirty Years" [Whitefield and Franklin]. HIS [Inter-Varsity Christian Fellowship], XVI/6 (March, 1956), 1-4, 12.

Jackson, Robert H. *The Supreme Court in the American System of Government.* Cambridge: Harvard University Press, 1955.

James, Henry (the elder). *Christianity the Logic of Creation.* London, 1857.

Jefferson, Thomas. *The Life and Morals of Jesus of Nazareth: Jefferson's "Bible."* Intro. Cyrus Adler. Washington, D.C.: Government Printing Office, 1904.

————. *Papers.* Ed. Julian P. Boyd, *et al.* Princeton: Princeton University Press, 1950-1952. 5 vols.

————. *Works.* Ed. Paul L. Ford. New York: Putnam, 1892-1899. 10 vols.

Johnson, Clifton. *Old-Time Schools and School-Books.* Reprint ed. New York: Dover, 1963.

Johnson, William J. *Abraham Lincoln the Christian.* New York: Abingdon, 1913.

Jungk, Robert. *Tomorrow Is Already Here.* Trans. Marguerite Waldman. New York: Simon and Schuster, 1954.

Kakuzo, Okakura. *The Book of Tea.* 7th ed. New York: Duffield, 1926.

Kamm, S. Richey. "The American Revolution: Revolutionary or Liberative?" *Christianity Today,* VIII/20 (July 3, 1964), 905-7.

Kennedy, Gail (ed.). *Pragmatism and American Culture.* (Problems in American Civilization.) Boston: D. C. Heath, 1950.

Kirk, Russell. *The Roots of American Order.* LaSalle, Ill.: Open Court, 1974.

Knapp, Martin Wells. *Christ Crowned Within.* Cincinnati, Ohio: M. W. Knapp Revivalist Office, 1898.

Kranzberg, Melvin (ed.). *1848—A Turning Point?* (Problems in European Civilization.) Boston: D. C. Heath, 1959.

Latourette, Kenneth Scott. *A History of the Expansion of Christianity.* New York: Harper, 1937-1945. 7 vols.

Laver, James. *The Age of Optimism.* London: Weidenfeld and Nicolson, 1966.

Lawrence, D. H. *Studies in Classic American Literature.* New York: Viking, 1964.

Lerner, Max. *America As a Civilization.* New York: Simon and Schuster, 1957.

Lewin, Kurt. "Field Theory and Experiment in Social Psychology." *American Journal of Sociology,* XLIV (1939), 868-97.

Lewis, C. S. The Abolition of Man. New York: Macmillan, 1961.
——. The Discarded Image. Cambridge: Cambridge University Press. 1964.
Lewis, R. W. B. The American Adam: Innocence, Tragedy and Tradition in the 19th Century. Chicago: University of Chicago Press, 1955.
Life. Special Mid-Century Issue: American Life and Times 1900-1950. January 2, 1950.
Lincoln, Abraham. Speeches and Writings. Ed. Roy P. Basler. Preface by Carl Sandburg. Cleveland: World Publishing Co., 1946.
Lineberry, William P. (ed.). Priorities for Survival. (The Reference Shelf, Vol. 44/6.) New York: H. W. Wilson, 1973.
Locke, John; Hume, David; Rousseau, J.-J. Social Contract. Intro. Ernest Barker. New York: Oxford University Press Galaxy Edition, 1948.
——. The Reasonableness of Christianity, with A Discourse of Miracles, and part of A Third Letter Concerning Toleration. Ed. and abridged by I. T. Ramsey. (A Library of Modern Religious Thought.) Stanford, Ca.: Stanford University Press, 1958.
Loomis, Albertine. Grapes of Canaan: Hawaii 1820. Intro. A. Grove Day, Senior Professor of English, University of Hawaii. Testimonial by the Rev. Abraham K. Akaka. Honolulu: Hawaiian Mission Children's Society, 1966. (Original Dodd, Mead edition published in 1951.)
Lotze, Rudolf Hermann. Microcosmus. Trans. E. Hamilton and E. E. C. Jones. Edinburgh: T. & T. Clark, 1885. 2 vols.
Lynd, Staughton. Intellectual Origins of American Radicalism. New York: Random House Pantheon Books, 1968.
Macdonald, Dwight. Against the American Grain: Essays on the Effects of Mass Culture. New York: Random House, 1962.
McGiffert, A. C. Protestant Thought before Kant. Intro. Jaroslav Pelikan. New York: Harper Torchbooks, 1962.
Madariaga, Salvador de. Englishmen, Frenchmen, Spaniards. 2d ed. New York: Hill and Wang, 1969.
Manuel, F. E. and F. P. (eds.). French Utopias: An Anthology of Ideal Societies. New York: Free Press, 1966.
Marcuse, Herbert. "Repressive Tolerance." In: A Critique of Pure Tolerance, by Robert Paul Wolff et al. Boston: Beacon Press, 1965.
Maré, Eric de. London, 1851: The Year of the Great Exhibition. London: The Folio Society, 1972.
Mather, Cotton. On Witchcraft: Being the Wonders of the Invisible World. Reprint ed. Mount Vernon, N.Y.: Peter Pauper Press, n.d.
Marty, Martin E. Second Chance for American Protestants. New York: Harper, 1963.

Mathews, Tom, and Baker, James N. "The First 100 Years." *Newsweek,* May 26, 1975, pp. 38-39.

Mayo, Bernard. *Myths and Men: Patrick Henry, George Washington, Thomas Jefferson.* New York: Harper Torchbooks, 1963.

Mencken, H. L. *On Politics: A Carnival of Buncombe.* Ed. Malcolm Moos. New York: Vintage Books, 1960.

Miller, Perry. *Orthodoxy in Massachusetts.* Cambridge: Harvard University Press, 1933.

————. *Roger Williams: His Contribution to the American Tradition.* New York: Bobbs-Merrill, 1953.

————(ed.). *The Transcendentalist: An Anthology.* Cambridge: Harvard University Press, 1950.

Montgomery, John Warwick. "The Christian View of the Fetus." In: *Birth Control and the Christian: A Prostestant Symposium on the Control of Human Reproduction,* ed. W. O. Spitzer and C. L. Saylor. Wheaton, Ill.: Tyndale House, 1969. Pp. 67-89. (A summary of the argument of this essay appears in the author's invitational contribution to the *Journal of the American Medical Association,* CCXIV/10 [December 7, 1970], 1893-94.)

————. "Commentary and Response." *The Jurist,* XXXV/1 (1975), 4-5, 81ff.

————. *Cross and Crucible: J. V. Andreae (1586-1654), Phoenix of the Theologians.* (Archives Internationales d' Histoire des Idées, No. 55) The Hague, Netherlands: Martinus Nijhoff, 1973. 2 vols.

————. *The Law above the Law.* Minneapolis: Bethany Fellowship, Inc., 1975.

————. "The Libraries of France at the Ascendancy of Mazarin." Unpublished Ph.D. dissertation, University of Chicago, 1962.

————. *Principalities and Powers: The World of the Occult.* Rev. ed. New York: Pyramid Books; Minneapolis: Bethany Fellowship, Inc., 1975.

————. *The Shape of the Past.* 2d rev. ed. Minneapolis: Bethany Fellowship, Inc., 1975.

————. *The Suicide of Christian Theology.* Minneapolis: Bethany Fellowship, Inc., 1971.

————. "Transcendental Gastronomy." *Christianity Today,* November 22, 1974, pp. 69-70.

————. *Where Is History Going? Essays in Support of the Historical Truth of the Christian Revelation.* Reprint ed. Minneapolis: Bethany Fellowship, Inc., 1972.

————(ed.). *God's Inerrant Word: An International Symposium on the Trustworthiness of Scripture.* Minneapolis: Bethany Fellowship, Inc., 1974.

————(ed.). *Jurisprudence: A Book of Readings.* Strasbourg, France: International Scholarly Publishers; Washington, D. C.: Lerner Law Books, 1974.

———(ed.). *Myth, Allegory and Gospel.* Minneapolis: Bethany Fellowship, Inc., 1974.

———(ed. and trans.). *Chytraeus on Sacrifice: A Reformation Treatise in Biblical Theology.* St Louis, Mo.: Concordia, 1962.

Moran, Michael. "New England Transcendentalism." *Encyclopedia of Philosophy,* ed. Paul Edwards, V (New York: Macmillan & Free Press, 1967), 479-80.

Morgan, Edmund S. *The Birth of the Republic, 1763-89.* Chicago: University of Chicago Press, 1956.

———. *The Puritan Dilemma: The Story of John Winthrop.* Boston: Little, Brown, 1958.

Morison, Samuel Eliot. *Admiral of the Ocean Sea: A Life of Christopher Columbus.* Boston: Little, Brown, 1942. 2 vols.

———. *Christopher Columbus, Mariner.* New York: New American Library Mentor Books, 1956.

Morris, Richard B., *et al. The Development of a Revolutionary Mentality.* Washington, D.C.: Library of Congress, 1972. (Contains essays by Morris, Henry Steele Commager, J. H. Plumb, Edmund S. Morgan, Mary Beth Norton, and others.)

———(ed). *Encyclopedia of American History.* New York: Harper, 1953.

Muggeridge, Malcolm. *Jesus Rediscovered.* Garden City, N.J.: Doubleday, 1969.

———. *Jesus: The Man Who Lives.* London: Collins, 1975.

Mumford, Lewis. *The City in History: Its Origins, Its Transformations, and Its Prospects.* New York: Harcourt, Brace & World, 1961.

———. *The Myth of the Machine.* Vol. I: *Technics and Human Development*; Vol. II: *The Pentagon of Power.* New York: Harcourt, Brace, Jovanovich, 1967-1970. 2 vols.

[Munch.] *Edvard Munch, 1863-1944. Musée des Arts Décoratifs, Mars-Avril, 1969.* Strasbourg, France: Cabinet des Estampes, 1969. (Exhibition catalog, with essays treating Munch's work.)

Münsterberg, Hugo. *The Americans.* Trans. Edwin B. Holt. Garden City, N.Y.: Doubleday, Page, 1914.

Nakamura, Hajime. *Ways of Thinking of Eastern Peoples: India—China—Tibet—Japan.* Rev. ed. Ed. Philip P. Wiener. Honolulu: East-West Center, 1964.

Nakamura, Julia V. *The Japanese Tea Ceremony.* Mount Vernon, N.Y.: Peter Pauper Press, 1965.

Naravane, V. S. *Modern Indian Thought.* (Indian Council for Cultural Relations.) London: Asia Publishing House, 1964.

Nash, Roderick. *Wilderness and the American Mind.* New Haven: Yale University Press, 1967.

Nee, Watchman. *Spiritual Knowledge.* New York: Christian Fellowship Publishers, 1973.

Neuhaus, Richard John. *Time toward Home: The American Experiment as Revelation.* New York: Seabury, 1975.

Newman, Edwin. *Strictly Speaking: Will America Be the Death of English?* New York: Warner Books, 1975.

Nichols, Thomas Low. *Forty Years of American Life.* Intro. Scott Donaldson. New York: Johnson Reprint Corp., 1969. 2 vols.

Niebuhr, Reinhold. *The Irony of American History.* New York: Scribner, 1952.

Noonan, John T., Jr. *Persons and Masks of the Law.* New York: Farrar, Straus & Giroux, 1975.

Norton, Mary Beth. *The British-Americans: The Loyalist Exiles in England, 1774-1789.* Boston: Little, Brown, 1972.

Orr, J. Edwin. *The Second Evangelical Awakening in America.* London: Marshall, Morgan & Scott, 1952.

Padover, Saul K. *The Living U.S. Constitution.* Rev. ed. New York: New American Library Mentor Books, 1968.

Paine, Thomas. *Life and Works.* Ed. William M. Van der Weyde. New Rochelle, N.Y.: Thomas Paine National Historical Association, 1925. 10 vols.

Parrington, Vernon L. *Main Currents in American Thought.* New York: Harcourt, Brace, 1927-1930. 3 vols.

Payne, Robert. *Hubris: A Study of Pride.* Foreword by Sir Herbert Read. New York: Harper Torchbooks, 1960. (Rev. ed. of *The Wanton Nymph: A Study of Pride.*)

Picard, Max. *Hitler in Our Selves.* Trans. Heinrich Hauser. Hinsdale, Ill..: Henry Regnery, 1947.

Pierard, Richard V. *The Unequal Yoke: Evangelical Christianity and Political Conservatism.* (Evangelical Perspectives, ed. John Warwick Montgomery.) Philadelphia: Lippincott, 1970.

Pierce, Edith Lovejoy. "American Prayer." *Christian Century,* June 29, 1955, p. 752.

Popper, Karl R. *The Open Society and Its Enemies.* 4th rev. ed. London: Routledge & Kegan Paul, 1962.

Prescott, William H. *History of the Reign of Ferdinand and Isabella.* Ed. John Foster Kirk. Philadelphia: Lippincott, 1872. 3 vols.

Pringle, Henry F. *Theodore Roosevelt: A Biography.* Rev. ed. New York: Harcourt, Brace Harvest Books, 1956.

Reich, Charles A. *The Greening of America.* New York: Random House, 1970.

Reitan, E. A. (ed.). *George III: Tyrant or Constitutional Monarch?* (Problems in European Civilization.) Boston: D. C. Heath, 1964.

Riesman, David. *The Lonely Crowd.* New Haven: Yale University Press, 1950.

Robertson, Priscilla. *Revolutions of 1848: A Social History.* Princeton: Princeton University Press, 1952.

Rossiter, Clinton. *The Political Thought of the American Revolu-*

tion. New York: Harcourt, Brace & World Harvest Books, 1963. (A revision of Pt. III of the author's *Seedtime of the Republic.*)

Roszak, Theodore. *The Making of a Counter Culture: Reflections on the Technocratic Society and Its Youthful Opposition.* Garden City, N.Y.: Doubleday, 1969.

Rourke, Constance. *Trumpets of Jubilee.* Intro. Kenneth S. Lynn. New York: Harcourt, Brace & World, 1963. (A study of Henry Ward Beecher, Harriet Beecher Stowe, Lyman Beecher, Horace Greeley, and P. T. Barnum.)

Russell, Bertrand; Miller, Perry; *et al. The Impact of America on European Culture.* Boston: Beacon Press, 1951. (Essays originally presented on the BBC "Third Programme.")

Sabine, George H. *A History of Political Theory.* 3d ed. New York: Holt, Rinehart and Winston, 1961.

Sand, Peter H. "The Socialist Response: Environmental Protection Law in the German Democratic Republic." *Ecology Law Quarterly,* III/3 (Summer, 1973), 451-90.

Schell, Jonathan. *The Time of Illusion.* New York: Knopf, 1975.

Scott, John Anthony. *Trumpet of a Prophecy: Revolutionary America, 1763-1783.* New York: Knopf, 1969.

Seidman, Jerome M. (ed.). *The Adolescent.* New York: Dryden Press, 1953.

Sewall, Samuel. *Phaenomena quaedam Apocalyptica ad aspectum Novi Orbis configurata; or, Some few Lines towards a description of the New Heaven as it makes to those who stand upon the New Earth.* 2d ed. Boston: Eliot, Gerrish & Henchman, 1727.

Shaw, Mark R. "The Spirit of 1740." *Christianity Today,* January 2, 1976, pp. 7-8.

Sheehan, Bernard W. *Seeds of Extinction: Jeffersonian Philanthropy and the American Indian.* New York: W. W. Norton, 1974.

Singer, C. Gregg. *A Theological Interpretation of American History.* Philadelphia: Presbyterian and Reformed Publishing House, 1964.

Smith, Elwyn A. *Religious Liberty in the United States: The Development of Church-State Thought since the Revolutionary Era.* Philadelphia: Fortress Press, 1972.

Smith, H. Shelton; Handy, Robert T.; and Loetscher, Lefferts A. *American Christianity: An Historical Interpretation with Representative Documents.* New York: Scribner, 1960-1963. 2 vols.

Smith, Timothy L. *Revivalism and Social Reform in Mid-19th-Century America.* New York: Abingdon, 1957.

Smith, Wilbur M. *Before I Forget: Memoirs.* Chicago: Moody Press, 1971.

[Solzhenitsyn.] *Aleksandr Solzhenitsyn: Critical Essays and*

Documentary Materials, ed. John B. Dunlop, *et al.* Belmont, Mass.: Nordland Publishing Co., 1973.
———. *The Gulag Archipelago.* Trans. Thomas P. Whitney. New York: Harper & Row, 1974.
———. *The Gulag Archipelago Two.* Trans. Thomas P. Whitney. New York: Harper & Row, 1975.
———. *The Voice of Freedom: Two Addresses.* Washington, D.C.: AFL-CIO, 1975.
Stauffer Ethelbert. *Christ and the Caesars.* Trans. K. and R. Gregor Smith. London: S. C. M., 1955.
Stein, Peter; and Shand, John. *Legal Values in Western Society.* Edinburgh: Edinburgh University Press, 1974.
Sternsher, Bernard. *Consensus, Conflict, and American Historians.* Bloomington: Indiana University Press, 1975.
Stewart, Charles J. "Lincoln's Assassination and the Protestant Clergy of the North." *Journal of the Illinois State Historical Society*, LIV/3 (Autumn, 1961), 268-93.
Stromberg, Roland N. *Religious Liberalism in 18th-Century England.* London: Oxford University Press, 1954.
Sumner, Charles. *Prophetic Voices concerning America.* Boston: Lee and Shepard, 1874.
Sweet, William Warren. *Religion in Colonial America.* New York: Scribner, 1942.
———. *The Story of Religion in America.* Rev. ed. New York: Harper, 1950.
Symonds, John Addington. *Renaissance in Italy.* New York: Modern Library, n.d. 2 vols.
Sypher, Wylie. *Rococo to Cubism in Art and Literature.* New York: Random House, 1960.
Taylor, G. R. (ed.). *The Turner Thesis concerning the Role of the Frontier in American History.* (Problems in American Civilization.) Boston: D. C. Heath, 1949.
Theobald, Robert. *An Alternative Future for America II: Essays and Speeches.* 2d ed. Chicago: Swallow Press, 1971.
———. *Futures Conditional.* Indianapolis: Bobbs-Merrill, 1972.
Tocqueville, Alexis de. *Democracy in America.* Trans. Henry Reeve. Ed. Henry Steele Commager. New York: Oxford University Press, 1947.
———. *Journey to America.* Trans. George Lawrence. Ed. J. P. Mayer. New Haven: Yale University Press, 1960.
Toffler, Alvin. *Future Shock.* New York: Random House, 1970.
Toon, Peter. *The Pilgrims' Faith.* Linkinhorne, Cornwall, England: Gospel Communication [1970].
Turner, Frederick Jackson. *The Frontier in American History.* Foreword by Ray Allen Billington. New York: Holt, Rinehart and Winston, 1962. (A collection of Turner's essays, including "The Ohio Valley in American History.")
Updike, John. *A Month of Sundays.* New York: Knopf, 1975.
———. *Rabbit Run.* New York: Knopf, 1960.

————. *Rabbit Redux.* New York: Knopf, 1971.

————. *Verse.* Greenwich, Conn.: Fawcett Crest Books, 1965.

Van Doren, Carl. *Benjamin Franklin.* New York: Viking Press, 1938.

Voegelin, Eric. *The New Science of Politics.* Chicago: University of Chicago Press, 1952.

————. *Order and History.* Vol. I: *Israel and Revelation;* Vol. II: *The World of the Polis;* Vol. III: *Plato and Aristotle;* Vol. IV: *The Ecumenic Age.* Baton Rouge: Louisiana State University Press, 1956 to date. (For an excellent review of the just-published 4th volume of the series, which in some degree revises the plan of the total work, see: *American Journal of Jurisprudence,* XX [1975], 168-69.)

Wallace, Paul A. W. *The Muhlenbergs of Pennsylvania.* Philadelphia: University of Pennsylvania Press, 1950.

Waller, George M. (ed.). *Puritanism in Early America.* (Problems in American Civilization.) Boston: D. C. Heath, 1950.

Wechsberg, Joseph. *Blue Trout and Black Truffles: The Peregrinations of an Epicure.* New York: Knopf, 1953.

Weisberger, Bernard A. *They Gathered at the River: The Story of the Great Revivalists and Their Impact upon Religion in America.* Boston: Little, Brown, 1958.

Weiss, Benjamin. *God in American History: A Documentation of America's Religious Heritage.* Foreword by Dr. Walter H. Judd. Grand Rapids, Mich.: Zondervan, 1966.

Wertenbaker, Thomas Jefferson. *The Puritan Oligarchy.* New York: Scribner, 1947.

Whicher, George F. (ed.). *The Transcendentalist Revolt against Materialism.* (Problems in American Civilization.) Boston: D. C. Heath, 1949.

White, Frederic R. (ed.). *Famous Utopias of the Renaissance.* New York: Hendricks House; Farrar, Straus, 1946.

Whyte, William H., Jr. *The Organization Man.* New York: Simon and Schuster, 1956.

Williams, Charles. *The Image of the City and Other Essays.* Ed. Anne Ridler. London: Oxford University Press, 1958.

Williams, George H. *Wilderness and Paradise in Christian Thought.* New York: Harper, 1962. ("An expansion of Dr. Williams' presidential address to the American Society of Church History. It was delivered on the 50th anniversary of Frederick Jackson Turner's famous paper presented to the American Historical Association on the influence of the frontier on American history.")

Winslow, Ola Elizabeth. *Samuel Sewall of Boston.* New York: Macmillan, 1964.

Wu, John C. H. *Fountain of Justice.* London: Sheed and Ward, 1959.

Wyllie, Irvin G. *The Self-Made Man in America: The Myth of Rags to Riches.* New York: Free Press, 1966.

Young, Robert M., *et al. The Victorian Crisis of Faith*. Ed. Anthony Symondson. London: S.P.C.K., 1970.

Zuckman, Harvey L. "Recent Developments in American Divorce Legislation." *The Jurist*, XXXV/1 (1975), 6-16.